THE GREATEST
RAILWAY
BLUNDER

ADRIAN VAUGHAN

In Memoriam

Driver Don Kingdom (1925-2009)

Aberbeeg and Abergavenny Loco 1940-1946
Oxford Loco (1946-1990)

He epitomised the Commitment and Pride in the Job
of the
Public Service Railwayman

Acknowledgements

Professor Lord Bradshaw of Wallingford, ex-General Manager at Paddington, for his knowledge of railways and politics; Dr John Prideaux for the interview he granted me; Dr Terry Gourvish and Christian Wolmar for their knowledge and encouragement; David Collins for his knowledge of the modern railway signalling scene. Professor George Huxley for his assistance and encouragement; Keith Montague for two years of fortnightly packages of relevant newspaper and magazine cuttings; The late John Morris, Safety Production Manager, Railtrack; Stuart Mackay for his assistance with diesel multiple unit identification; Stuart of the Southern Electric Group, for information on the emu power car hauling freight; Brian Garrett, Brian Morrison and Steve Thompson, for their excellent photographs, Andrew McCarthy, Mike Christensen, Brian Druce and Peter Jordan.

Books consulted

The Re-shaping of British Railways, Dr Richard Beeching, HMSO, London, 1963; *British Rail after Beeching*, G. Freeman Allen, Ian Allan, London 1966; *British Railways Engineering*, ed Roland Bond, Mechanical Engineering Publications, 1981; *British Railway Privatisation*, Roger Freeman and Jon Shaw, McGraw Hill Company, Maidenhead, 2000; *Broken Rails*, Christian Wolmar, Aurum Press, London, 2001; *British Rail 1974-1997*, Dr Terry Gourvish, Oxford University Press, 2002; *Birmingham Footplateman*, Dennis Herbert, Oakwood Press, 2007. *Railwaymen, Politics & Money*, Adrian Vaughan, John Murray, London, 1997; *Dancing with Dogma*, Sir Ian Gilmour, Simon & Schuster, London,1992.

Other sources

Parliamentary debates and Parliamentary Committees' reports on privatisation in Hansard, Reports of Office of Rail Regulator;. Ministry of Transport statistics. Board of Trade Report on Llandulas viaduct at PRO MT6/238/13; Great Western Railway internal accident reports. *Rail* magazine editorials, Roger Ford on-line, reports in sensible newspapers. BBC documentary radio programmes on privatisation and also BBC news announcements. On line histories of companies and biographies of people. The sources of research are multitudinous.

First published 2009

ISBN 978 0 7110 3274 3

© Adrian Vaughan 2009

Published by Ian Allan Publishing

an imprint of Ian Allan Publishing Ltd, Hersham, Surrey KT12 4RG
Printed in England by Ian Allan Printing Ltd

Code: 0904/B2

Visit the Ian Allan Publishing website at www.ianallanpublishing.com

Contents

CHAPTER 1

The Problems of Railways

The privatisation of British Rail in 1994 returned the railway to its primitive early-19th-century roots. The economic fundamentalists who carried out this disorganisation of the railway attempted to justify their actions by invoking the name of their Prophet, the Professor of Economics and Philosophy, Adam Smith. Smith devised his theory of economics during the latter half of the 18th century and died in 1790. Smith's world was decidedly uncomplicated, compared to ours, yet his simple principles of 'market forces' and 'competition', were deemed to be suitable for the orderly arrangement of the modern world.

The first locomotive-hauled, public railway in the world, the Stockton & Darlington (S&DR), opened on 27 September 1825 with the motto 'At Private Risk for Public Service'. The Stockton & Darlington Railway Act permitted it to run trains but obliged it to allow anyone else to run a train on their rail-road in return for a toll. The railway was set up like a turnpike road or a canal – open access. In 1825 there was an excuse for this – no-one knew any better. In 1994 there was no excuse for returning to a thoroughly discredited system. Open access was the legal condition of every railway ever built in Britain. If you did not know that, it is because, within a handful of years, the practice lapsed – until 1994 – because it was found to be unworkable. On the S&DR track maintenance, the winding engines for the colliery inclines, the ropes around the drums of the winding engines, the water supply, the supply and maintenance of locomotives and the trains that ran on the track were all contractors' jobs. The contractor that maintained the winding engine sub-contracted the supply and maintenance of the haulage rope. Within a few weeks the contractors were arguing as to whose fault it was when a rope or a rail broke or a water pipe fractured, while the train operators were arguing about who was causing congestion on the tracks and delays in the loading of coal from wagons to ships.

But in those long ago and nostalgically pragmatic days, in 1833 in fact, the God-fearing and practical Quakers who ran the S&DR paid the train operators to cease trading and phased out the maintenance contractors who were there – of course – for their own profit rather than that of the company. The GWR used contractors to maintain its tracks – often these were the same contractors that had built that section of the line. On Brunel's advice track maintenance contractors were phased out over the years; Brotherhood of Chippenham was one of the last to lose his contract, in about 1855.

The Liverpool & Manchester Railway (L&MR) opened on 15 September 1830. By 1835 it too had bought out all the train operators and carrying companies like Pickfords so as to be 'master of its own house'. It never ceased, in law, to be an open access railway, but it was perfectly clear that unless the railway company could be in charge of all matters within its boundaries it could not provide an efficient public service or make a decent profit commensurate with the capital that had been invested.

The taking over of the entire operation of their routes by the railway companies, pushing out the private passenger and freight operators, was seen as the creation of a monopoly, and in 1839 a Parliamentary Select Committee was convened to investigate. Evidence was taken from railway officials and representatives of the 'carrying' trade, such as Pickfords and Chaplin & Horne. The outcome was that the Committee understood that railways had to have the monopoly of their whole operation in order to organise themselves efficiently for their work of carrying. The committee referred to a 'natural monopoly' (BPP, 1839, vol x) as being the nature of any railway. Railways were a monopoly nonetheless, and to control this it was considered only proper for the Government to run the railways as it ran the Post Office – a state monopoly for the public good.

Among the great Victorian statesmen – men who were the embodiment of those Victorian values so admired by Mrs Thatcher, and who believed that railways should be state-owned, were: the Tory 10th Earl of Dalhousie, who became Viceroy of India from 1848 to 1856, where he established state-owned railways; Samuel Laing, who became Finance Minister for India from 1855 to 1867, then Chairman of the London, Brighton & South Coast Railway; and W. E. Gladstone, Chancellor of the Exchequer 1852-55 and four times Prime Minister. Had the much-invoked prophet of private enterprise, Adam Smith, been alive in that time, it seems to me likely that he would have agreed with them.

An astonishing multiplicity of railway companies was formed after 1830, many of them of relatively short-distance: the Leeds & Bradford or the Rugby to Derby 'Midland

Counties Railway', then the North Midland and the York & North Midland to take the railway from Derby to Leeds and York. Or those incorporated to extend the original rail route of the Liverpool & Manchester, including the Grand Junction Railway and the Lancaster & Carlisle. On a map the line of a route was continuous, but in fact it was fragmented and the operating expensive because each company had to maintain separate facilities. This was 'healthy competition'. It was very wasteful but it generated a lot of bank loans.

The Victorian businessmen who ran the railways saw that this fragmentation of what ought to be a through route was a foolish thing. Thus the amalgamations of 1844, which formed the Midland Railway from York to Bristol and Derby to Rugby out of no fewer than seven companies, and in 1846 the amalgamation of at least as many to form the London & North Western Railway from Euston to Carlisle.

In the British system of railway promotion, parliamentary and land costs were severe. By British law, railways had to raise huge sums of capital just to get a piece of paper – their Act – from Parliament, then another vast sum to actually buy the land, then more large sums to compensate landowners for having been forced to sell, then to build the line. The result was that the companies had to raise fresh capital to complete a line, so were over-burdened with capital obligations by the time the route was opened.

The Eastern Counties Railway (ECR) – attempting to build a railway to Norwich and Yarmouth – paid £120,000 to get through the land of Lord Petre of Ingatestone Hall – this sum being one-tenth of the entire capital of the railway. And Lord Petre was just one of a dozen landowners to be pacified. Not surprisingly, the Eastern Counties Railway ran out of money at Colchester. An Ipswich barrister, Charles Austin, took fees from railway companies amounting to £95,833 during the 'Mania' years of 1844-48, which was almost double his total income for the previous 17 years. (Private diaries of Charles Austin, Suffolk Record Office, Ref 50.18.3)

The 'Railway Mania' bubble burst in September 1847 and Austin retired from legal work. He took his winnings and with them purchased the Brandestone Hall estate, near Framlingham, rebuilding the derelict, or run-down, farms, churches and cottages. So the money was put to good use, but it was not put to the use for which it had been subscribed by the ECR investors.

Samuel Smiles, author of that famous book in praise of individual initiative, *Self Help*, and *The Lives of the Engineers*, was also Company Secretary to the South Eastern Railway, which had suffered grievously because of fierce competition. Smiles wrote of the 1844-47 railway mania:

'The result of the labours of Parliament was a tissue of legislative bungling involving enormous loss to the Nation.'

If Smiles had been writing in 1994 he would not have changed a word of that.

The great railway engineer Robert Stephenson, MP for Whitby, strongly opposed what he called 'violent competition' and begged Parliament to legislate against it – but with so much money to be made out of abusing the system, rational sense was in vain. He used the occasion of his inauguration as President of the Institution of Civil Engineers in January 1856 to make a lengthy speech in which he laid out in detail the awful problems – and financial injuries – suffered by the railway companies as a result of a free-for-all dressed up as a legitimate 'market'. He said:

'Legislative sanction having been given to a line, it might be supposed that Parliament would grant it adequate protection [from competing lines] exacting from the railway company certain public advantages in return. But instead, Parliament had laid public obligations on the companies and far from protecting the interests of those to whom they have granted the right of making the line they have encouraged every description of competition.'

He described how it was vital to straighten the route from Euston to Crewe by constructing the Trent Valley Railway between Rugby and Stafford. This, he said, was a work of great national importance, yet Parliament allowed 18 other groups to come to Parliament, simultaneously, requesting permission to build it. The first attempt to get the Act was thrown out when it was discovered that a barn was shown on the plan in not quite the right spot. All legal fees were lost and the process had to start again in 1840. Then the Grand Junction Railway was permitted to make 450 objections, all of them based on the stipulations of Parliamentary Standing Orders. Arguments to prove whether these objections were contrary to Standing Orders lasted 22 days and employed a swarm of barristers representing the London & Birmingham and the Grand Junction Railways. Five of the objections were sustained – which should therefore have been the death of the Bill – but having put the companies to this expense, the Standing Orders Committee decided to let the Bill pass through to the debating chambers of both Houses. The Trent Valley route was supported by the Prime Minister, Sir Robert Peel, and a majority of the House, but still it had to be argued before Committee for 63 days – then Parliament was prorogued and the entire costs of the Bill were lost.

In his speech to the Institution of Civil Engineers, Stephenson said:

'Judged by such a case the policy of Parliament really would seem to be to put the public to expense to make costs for lawyers and fees for Officers [of Parliament]. Is it possible to conceive of anything more monstrous than to condemn 19 parties to this contentious litigation? Of the £286 millions expended on railways it is believed that nearly a quarter has been paid for land and conveyancing. The ingenuity of man could scarcely devise a system more costly than that of getting a railway bill.'

The Trent Valley Railway Bill became law on 21 July 1845. Having obtained the Trent Valley Act, Robert Stephenson stated that the cost of now building the line 'would not be much greater than the cost of obtaining the Act'.

Competition in the naturally monopolistic railway industry was effected by Parliament permitting competing routes to be built. Competition was supposed to provide the passengers with cheaper fares, increased speed and comfort – but only on routes where there was direct competition between companies. Where companies did reduce their fares, indulge in greater speed and more luxurious carriages, their profits were reduced, their dividends were less, and share values fell – even to below par. The much-lauded GWR refused to compete in the 19th century. From 1838 until 1892 it was undistinguished for its speed – with the exception of two show trains in its early days when the broad gauge had to be made to look like a superior technology. Costs never ceased to rise and had to be kept down. There was for decades resistance to investment in proper brakes and signalling worthy of the name. Some companies from 1876 invested in proper braking on their trains – the GWR, the Midland and the Great Eastern, for instance – but many did not. The Manchester Sheffield & Lincolnshire, a large concern, and, most notoriously, the gold-plated London & North Western retained an actually dangerous braking system until Parliament made a law forcing the installation of proper brakes in 1889.

The smaller companies were brought to the edge of – or were plunged into – insolvency by competition. Those in East Anglia were a prime example and for decades the South Eastern and the London Chatham & Dover bled each other white through competition.

Private enterprise built the railways but a free-for-all in building competing railways was profoundly damaging. Railway promotion was throughout the 19th century an opportunity for the banks and insurance companies of the day to lend money, for individuals to gamble in shares and for contractors to raise companies merely as a speculation to sell to whichever established company felt most threatened by the proposal. It built the national railways system but it was not sensible. European governments watching the British railway phenomenon of the 1830s-40s were aghast at the mad free-for-all, the bankruptcies, the social upheaval and the sheer expense of getting an Act of Parliament, but they recognised the benefit a railway network would bring to a nation. Hence the strict government control of railway building in Europe.

The advantage of having large railway organisations was that a large area of the United Kingdom's transport system would come under the control of a few strong-minded men who, growing up within the company, knew its business thoroughly and devoted their lives to its maintenance and improvement. The Board of Directors of the great companies, the GWR, LNWR, Midland and North Eastern, were sometimes aristocrats, sometimes Quakers, but they seriously devoted their working life to the care of the railway. There were no 'revolving doors' and no bonuses, large or small, merely for doing the job they were paid for until recently.

Reporting to them they had a General Manager, a Chief Engineer, a Chief Locomotive Engineer, a Goods Manager and so on. It was commonly the case that these top management people had begun their careers at the lowest level and worked their way up, so devoting their whole working life to the company. They knew the staff and they knew all the different jobs carried out by their staff. They had sole control in their field, subject to their plans being agreed by the Directors. Felix (later Sir Felix) Pole started on the GWR as a deliverer of telegrams and reached the rank of General Manager. His brother, Reginald Pole, rose to become Divisional Superintendent at Bristol in the 1930s and retired in 1950. His Assistant of seven years became DSO on Pole's retirement.

In 2000 my friend John Morris was filling the post of 'Safety Production Manager' for Railtrack at Carmarthen. Under British Railways he would have been the 'District

Joseph Loftus Wilkinson joined the GWR as a boy clerk in 1859. In 1876 he became Principal Assistant to the Chief Goods Manager. In 1886 he left to take up the post of General Manager of the Buenos Aires & Pacific Railway but was invited to return to the GWR two years later to become Chief Goods Manager. Eight years later he became General Manager of the GWR on the death of Henry Lambert. A new Chairman was in place, Lord Emlyn, and these men were at the heart of the GWR's 'Great Awakening' – several hundred miles of new main lines and faster trains. *GWR/Adrian Vaughan Collection*

Inspector', a title going back to 1835. John reported to me, one Friday evening, that he had spent the five days of that week giving a man a crash course, a quick run through the various safety rules books: Rule Book, Signalling Regulations and Local Instructions. This person had not worked on the railway before but had been appointed to the position once known as Divisional Superintendent. He was in charge of – supervising – the safe working of the railway and all the operating staff, from Newport to Fishguard and Milford Haven.

To return to the account of the arrangements of the real railway. The Divisions came together through a series of conferences to review the working timetable of the year drawing to a close and to see what changes needed to be made to next year's schedules. There were the one-off great events to be catered for – the Cup Final, the Ideal Homes Exhibition at Olympia, and the Motor Car Exhibition, as well as Christmas Parcels Post Specials, the Channel Islands potato specials and broccoli specials. Then there was the summer season timetable to draw up, covering about two months. There were also excursions, which were arranged 'off the cuff', so to speak, day trips or half days to the seaside, horsebox specials for race meetings. Newbury race meets were very special for the GWR/BR (WR) because the railway owned the course the specials when the crowds at a major station became too great. There were the 'Ocean' specials, which were run to connect with incoming transatlantic liners from Plymouth and Fishguard to Paddington. The Fishguard Atlantic liner service did not survive the Great War, but the Plymouth 'Ocean Specials' were run even in BR days. These trains could not be timetabled since no-one knew quite when a liner would arrive. Instead these trains had a 'point to point' timing printed in the timetable. A train leaving Plymouth at 11.00am would therefore be passing Newton Abbot in 45 minutes and so on up the line, and the signalmen, with a couple of hours' notice, cleared a path for them. They were probably the fastest trains on the route and it was a matter of honour for all concerned that they ran to time.

On the subject of Fishguard, from 1906 until 1914 the GWR ran day trips from Paddington to Killarney – 4½ hours to Fishguard with one stop at Cardiff to change engines.

On summer Saturdays, when Bristol Temple Meads became swamped with people wanting to get to the beach at Weston-super-Mare, the nearest engine and some carriages would be commandeered and a special would be run – just like that. Where traffic did not warrant a special train, cheap tickets were advertised for events – sheep fairs, cricket matches, market days.

Main express trains from Paddington to the West Country at Easter, Christmas and all summer would, if necessary, be run in two or three parts – that is to say the 'First Part' of the 10.30am Paddington would leave at 10.28, then the 10.30 itself, the 10.32 'Second Part' and the 10.35 'Third Part'. These 'paths' were printed in the working timetable so that a simple 'box to box' message all down the line would advise all concerned. It was simple.

This great concern, this tradition, for a great public institution serving the public, was how the GWR earned its living, and the nationalised GWR, as BR (WR), carried on as before. So, I am certain, did the Southern and the rest of them. Without service to the public how can a railway survive? It is therefore ridiculous to say, as the Professors of Economics who think they can run railways do say, with disparaging intent, 'They were production-led railways – what is needed is business-led railways.' What does it mean? The coal-fired railway certainly produced trains when they were needed and it was this concern for their passengers that men like Beeching condemned as 'unbusinesslike'. The production-led railway did not cancel trains at a moment's notice, did not substitute buses for trains and did not sail close to the wind where safety was concerned – at least, not after 1890.

During two World Wars British railways were, for all practical purposes, nationalised. Common use of freight and passenger vehicles was introduced, while the traditional, militarily-strong, hierarchy of the railway (much despised by the fragmentation lobby) and the hard labour of the railwaymen and women, enabled the system to carry at least double the traffic compared to peacetime while being one-third below their pre-war staffing level. It is a fact that, when the most serious national crises occurred – two vast wars – the Governments of those periods saw that the only way to run the country, not just the railway, was by a centrally directed, planned, amalgamated, system.

CHAPTER 2

Masters in their own house

The people who sold the railway in 1994-96 sometimes tried to justify their actions by referring back to 'the old companies', and in particular to the Great Western Railway. It was even once referred to in Parliament as 'God's Wonderful Railway'.[1] I am old enough to have seen the Great Western Railway at work at the last and most stressful period of its history – after six years of wartime carrying and lack of maintenance. In 1948 the GWR was nationalised, together with the rest of the railway system, as the Western Region of British Railways. I grew up in close and regular contact with that railway, as a welcome trespasser in a couple of signal boxes and on the footplates of locomotives. The officers and men, the locomotives and the equipment of BR (WR) were all ex-GWR – they did not become new men or their equipment new when the new title was brought into use by law on 1 January 1948. I knew those men well, they trained me, schoolboy trespasser though I was, and I know more about the history and spirit of that railway than any of those people who invoked its memory as they set out to sell the railway to their friends in 1992.

The Professors of Economics from their Schools of Management, the neo-conservative extremists in the Treasury, the politicians who saw a way of making a lucrative job for themselves, all justified their blind dogmatism by talking about the need to 'change the culture' of British Rail. They invoked the virtues of the former private companies in order to justify the destruction of the very 'culture' that had made those companies great – which was, first and foremost, their solidly integrated, centrally controlled, 'monolithic' organisation. This system of organisation was exactly what had enabled the railway companies to suffer the heavy maltreatment they had suffered in two World Wars and still do their job for the nation.

The epitome of the railway spirit: long service and lifetime learning proving a man's reliability and commitment and 'Pride in the Job'. Fred Ward, the Paddington Locomotive Foreman, makes sure everything is in order before the engine crew of *Fawley Court* take a South Wales express out of Paddington in1919. *W. L. Kenning/*

---

1. *A ridiculous expression never used by any railwayman, but invented in the 1970s for a television programme.*

Driver Wilkins and Fireman Ernie Williams in the cab of a 'Bulldog' at Radley in 1917. To the driver's left is the distinctive 'cut-off' indicator rod, which proves that this is an engine fitted with steam-operated reversing gear. The heads of two large nuts show the mid-gear position so the engine is in about 45% cut-off. The driver's 'long feeder' oilcan is lodged on top of the sight-feed lubricator control, and an earthenware jar containing – it is to be supposed – cylinder oil is keeping warm above the firehole. The picture was taken in winter. Just above the fireman's left shoulder is the steam pressure gauge for the carriage radiators; the needle is vertical – indicating 100psi in the carriage radiators – so the passengers are very cosy.
W. L. Kenning/ Adrian Vaughan Collection

They took risks with the safety culture of BR – which was exactly the same as that of the much praised Great Western – in order to increase profit.

While GWR trains and those coal-fired trains of BR were nothing like as fast as those that run over its track today, they had more comfortable carriages, additional carriages at times of peak demand could easily and within minutes be added to a train to reduce overcrowding, they were reasonably punctual, and certainly not liable to cancellation without notice, and they were not disabled by water falling on their roofs as was the case with the Virgin 'Voyagers' along the Dawlish Sea Wall. I travelled regularly behind steam engines on this stretch and in winter I hung out of the window and saw the waves actually enveloping the locomotive – which ploughed on imperturbably and so, of course, did the crew.

GWR and BR trains were rarely prevented from moving because of the weather – and if they were then it was pretty certain that the rest of the country's transport had already stopped.

This was the Great Western's fastest locomotive type in 1900, perhaps the fastest in Britain, and surely the most beautiful – dignity and speed. It is one of the 79 members of the 'Achilles' class, which was the mainstay of GWR express train services from 1892 until the single driving axle, carrying 7ft 8in diameter driving wheels, became insufficiently powerful for increasingly heavy trains. *Sultan* is standing on sidings near Westbourne Park, Paddington. *GWR/ Adrian Vaughan Collection*

The 10.35am Paddington to Falmouth train, precursor of the 'Cornish Riviera Express', passes Bathampton down the Avon valley towards Bath on 10 August 1899.
GWR/Adrian Vaughan Collection

The modern jargon phrase 'vertical integration' is best translated into proper English as 'master in their own house'. From the common sense of lifelong railway engineers and operators, we have been taken by these economic wizards into a Byzantine world where nothing can be done, not even a simple little thing – lengthening of a pair of platforms, erecting a bicycle shed on a platform – without extensive, expensive, time-consuming consultation with all the various parties who now have an interest in the site. Frequently the consultants are ex-BR people, well paid to depart from BR, then making small fortunes out of being 'consulted' about what they used to do for a normal salary. And this is cheaper than British Rail? Clearly the wizardry of economics is a rather narrow discipline – one might call it 'tunnel vision'.

The old companies' records are full of remarkable train running and feats of civil and mechanical engineering, and British Railways continued the engineering and safety tradition of the companies. Modern economists call this a 'production-led' railway and assert that what is really required is a 'business-led' railway, a railway concerned with establishing tie and sock kiosks at every major, and not so major, station – 'marketing opportunities'. As one

leading member of Railtrack said in 1997 on the BBC when asked why a supermarket was being built on railway land at Leeds, when Leeds signal box cabling needed replacing: 'Supermarkets are as important as signalling.' That's the 'business-led' railway.

During two great wars, what the railway companies did to support the war effort and keep the civilian population moving might seem today simply beyond belief. The success was due to the local organisation of the job. The operation was organised by Divisions and major centres within a Division had the equipment and men to deal with almost any emergency. The railwaymen on the spot were expected to get on with the job. They were masters in their own house. Although the expression 'the railway culture' was unheard of until 'management speak' arrived, this independence of thought and action directed towards keeping the trains running was the neo-cons have destroyed.

All this direct command, this vertical integration, this local control of daily events, was crushed by a mass of Byzantine systems in 1994, created by men and women who believed that they were so clever that they could run anything even when they had never done it before. They remind me of nothing as much as children who decide that the clock on the wall, ticking away and telling the time, would be improved if they cleaned its works. Having dismantled it they find they are unable to restore it. The outcome will be to take the bits to some skilful old man who has spent his life studying clocks and he will put it back together. Thousands of dedicated railwaymen hope that their industry will be put back together.

In 1871 the GWR Directors decided that it was time to convert the broad gauge line from Swindon to Milford Haven, via Gloucester, to the standard gauge. This involved 188 miles of double-track and 48 miles of single-track railway, making 424 miles of running line plus 76 miles of sidings. Also included in the gauge change were satellite railways: the Carmarthen & Cardigan, South Wales, Mineral, Llynvi & Ogmore and the Severn & Wye.

The first stage of the narrowing was the line from Milford Haven to Grange Court, 163 route miles. Except for 40 miles of cross-sleepered, chaired track, the tracks were laid to Brunel's plan, with a continuous, longitudinal sleeper supporting the rail, and the rail screwed down to this.

The distance between the two rails of each line was maintained by a cross-piece or 'transom' at 11-foot intervals. During April 1872 each transom was carefully measured and marked precisely so that 2ft 3½ inches could be cut off it so that the longitudinal could be levered inwards by a gang of men using iron bars. The ballast had to be shovelled out and a speed restriction imposed. Nuts were undone, bolt threads oiled and nuts replaced tightly. The rails nearest the outer edge of the track bed remained in place and the rails nearest the centre line of the trackbed were levered towards the outer rails. On curves this resulted in the levered rail being too long for its new position. E. T. McDermott, in his 'History of the Great Western Railway', commissioned by the GWR, states that 'short rails were provided at curves.' Apparently, rails of the correct length were calculated and cut for every curve on the line and placed in their correct position for use. This in itself seems to constitute a heroic feat of non-computerised mathematics. New pointwork was built and laid beside the points to be changed. The GWR carried out the work over four weeks without stopping the trains. They ran the Down line as a single track while they converted the Up line, then the Up line became a single track while the Down was converted. If you think about the implications of this you will begin to see the wonderfully clever and detailed planning that was undertaken to complete the entire route change in just four weeks.

On Sunday 17 August 1879 a cloudburst over the western hills of North Wales caused the little Afon Dulas to swell into a raging torrent of such power that it swept away the Llandulas Viaduct. This was a viaduct of stone arches 75 yards long and 40 feet high, 2½ miles west of Abergele & Pensarn station. The double-track Anglo-Irish Mail route was completely severed and for two days the swollen brook prevented any remedial work from taking place. However, during those two days the entire plan for rebuilding the viaduct had been completed. By the afternoon of the 17th the Chief Engineer, William Baker, had arrived on the scene from Crewe. He decided, no-one else was involved, and he gave the orders. These were:

starting from half a mile on each side of the viaduct, to cut a ramp into the approach embankments on a gradient of 1 in 23 wide enough to carry the Up main line as a single line of rails, then to drive piles for additional firmness of support and, when the brook had returned to its normal dimensions, to build a timber trestle bridge across. This work was carried out by District Engineer, Bangor. Baker then returned to Crewe where the LNWR had its superb factory including its own iron- and steel-making plant and metal rolling plant. There he set the steelworkers on the job of rolling the steel flat plate and angles to construct 42 lattice girders, each one 32 feet long. Within a week not only were the girders completed, but two signal boxes with properly interlocked levers to work points and signals had been erected to control the junctions to the single track. Five days after the brook subsided, the timber bridge was ready and trains began to run on the temporary single track down the side of the embankment and across the stream at Llandulas. Banking engines were provided for the steep grades and all went so well that the passengers were hardly aware that anything unusual was taking place.

The stone piers of the viaduct were rebuilt and it was waiting for the cement to set that caused the double line to remain closed for a full 28 days. The double-track line was re-opened over the new viaduct on 14 September.

The final abolition of the broad gauge on the GWR took place over the two days of 21-22 May 1892. Mixed gauge was already laid from Paddington to Exeter, but from there to Penzance all but 42 miles of the main line, and all of the branch lines and sidings, were purely 7-foot gauge. That was 171 route miles of single track, comprising 'bridge' rails laid on longitudinal sleepers in the manner designed by Isambard Kingdom Brunel in 1835. On the double track there were 36 miles laid using bullhead rail on chaired cross-sleepers in the practical manner designed by Joseph Locke in 1835. Mixed gauge had already been laid on this section.

The GWR had all the men – skilled men – to do the job and directed them without having to consult anyone beyond their own engineers. Land was purchased west of the Swindon factory and 15 miles of sidings were laid to accommodate the redundant broad-gauge locomotives, carriages and wagons. Other, smaller, disposal depots were established further west. Standard gauge locomotives were sent to Newton Abbot and Plymouth on broad gauge wagons. The broad gauge track was fully prepared for alteration.

The last goods trains into Cornwall left Exeter on the evening of 17 May and after that the only broad gauge goods trains coming east were trains of empty wagons. On Wednesday 18th a procession of special trains set out from Bristol, Chester, Crewe, Milford Haven, Paddington, Swindon, Tondu and Weymouth, all converging at Exeter St David's. They carried a total of 4,200 track workers to reinforce track gangs from Devon and Cornwall. They also carried with them their own food, while the GWR supplied the cooking facilities and living accommodation,

When a railway is unified and owns all its staff and resources, problems can be dealt with promptly and with the least inconvenience to passengers. When the seven 42-foot-high arched spans of the Llandulas Viaduct were washed away in a flash flood in August 1879, the railway's initial intention was to build wooden platforms to detrain passengers at each side of the gap and to cut a cart track ramp down each approach embankment and a wooden bridge suitable for horses and carts. Passengers would then walk half a mile, their luggage being transferred on the carts. On second thoughts, the company's officers were disgusted at such an idea and 'determined to make the works of such a character that trains might be taken across and the immense inconvenience to passengers and delay due to a break of journey would be avoided.' The viaduct went down at 4.00pm on 17 August. A new railway down the embankment side and over a wooden bridge at river level was opened for passenger trains at 4.17pm on the 25th. The temporary arrangements also called for two signal boxes and signals to be erected. This work design and construction was done from the Bangor Divisional Office, as was the rebuilding of the brick piers for the new, permanent, viaduct. The Girders for the permanent viaduct were made at Crewe Works from steel made and rolled there. The new viaduct was opened for traffic on 24 September 1879.

All National Archives (MT6 238/13)

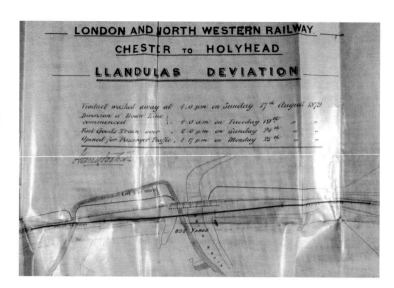

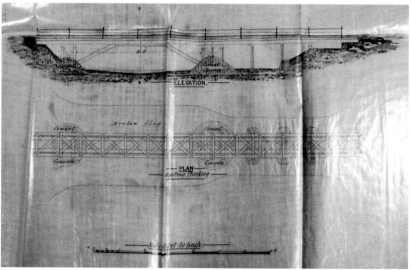

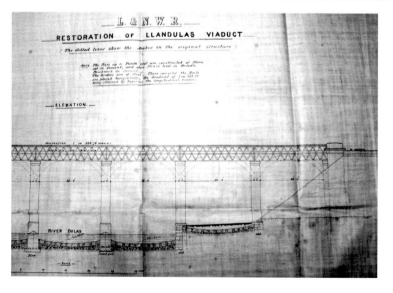

which included some sort of bedding in goods sheds, stables and in marquees in lineside fields. Without a doubt the men would have viewed the whole thing as an important event, even a bit of an adventure in which they were pleased to participate. Except for the Bristol train all the others were standard gauge, so all the men had to transfer into broad gauge trains waiting at Exeter. This in itself was a grand timetabling feat. Each gang of men was an identified group and from Exeter the trains took the men to their previously designated posts.

The last Down broad gauge train left Paddington at 5.00pm on Friday 19th. The last Up broad gauge train was the 9.45pm Penzance Mail. The men moved onto the track at dawn on the 20th. Each gang was allocated one mile of track. They worked so well that at 3.00pm that afternoon the first standard gauge locomotive ran from Exeter to Plymouth. By Sunday night or early Monday the line to Penzance was ready. The 9.00pm Paddington-Penzance Mail, which had proceeded from Exeter to Plymouth over the L&SWR route, left Plymouth for Penzance at 4.40am. And this event was on time – it had been timetabled at least a month in advance.

The Act of Parliament for the 31 miles of the high-speed 'South Wales Direct Railway' was obtained in 1896. This took 10 miles off the distance between Paddington and Newport, shortened slightly the distance from Paddington to Bristol, avoided steep gradients and shortened running times. Construction began in 1897. *GWR/Adrian Vaughan Collection*

Three years after this final abolition of the inconvenient, non-standard gauge, the GWR decided on a huge project to build new railways, long main lines and useful short curves to improve through connections. The Acts were gained, the land was purchased, civil engineering contractors were found, viaducts were designed, orders were placed at Reading signal works for dozens of new signal boxes and their locking frames, thousands of signals were constructed and the work commenced. The work was expedited because the GWR had to consult no-one but its own employees; furthermore, all GWR buildings and equipment were to standard designs and the job was designed, administered and carried out by engineers, technicians and craftsmen who were long-service GWR men or they were men who intended so to be.

Between 1900 and 1914 the GWR opened 477 miles of new railway, most of it heavily or very heavily engineered: fine stations, station masters' houses and wages-grade housing, a large harbour created out of virgin cliffs at Fishguard, great viaducts and long tunnels, including Chipping Sodbury, 2½ miles through the Cotswold escarpment, which pierced a water aquifer. The Gloucestershire Niagara was contained and the tunnel completed on time although from that day to this it has been liable to flooding. In the days of steam haulage this was not too great a problem as steam engines can traverse a couple of feet of water, but modern traction is another matter. All of this work was carried out to the highest specifications, on time, within budget and all as a matter

Right: In spite of the need to make a profit, GWR spent handsomely on fine stations with good operating facilities. The Duke of Beaufort lived close by Badminton station, at the summit of the line. His coat of arms was carved in stone, set into the station wall, and he had the right to stop any train he wanted at the station. *GWR/ Adrian Vaughan Collection*

Middle: New lines would bring increased traffic, so major stations became 'bottlenecks' to be opened out. The reconstruction of the approaches to Paddington and to the station started in 1900 and took several years. No trains were stopped while the works were in progress. The great locomotive depot of Old Oak Common was built and the old sheds at Westbourne Park demolished to provide space for more tracks and carriage lines into Paddington. Bishop's Road viaduct was strangling the 'station throat' and had to be removed in favour of a single-span bridge across all tracks. Here we see the construction of the bowstring girder bridge with the old arches beneath. The photographer's camera used 12x10-inch glass negatives, which he carried in the leather case that can be seen in the right foreground. *GWR/ Adrian Vaughan Collection*

Right: The very cramped 1871-75 Birmingham Snow Hill station was replaced between 1906 and 1912 by a new superbly designed one, architecturally and operationally. *GWR/ Adrian Vaughan Collection*

Above: Birmingham Snow Hill's layout was worked by electricity from 1912 to 1960. The GWR installed two signal boxes housing Siemens miniature levers. This is the view south from the North signal box in 1936. *GWR/Adrian Vaughan Collection*

Below: Exeter St David's station was rebuilt between 1911 and 1914. The last remnants of the 1844 overall roof can be seen at the far end of the rebuilt station. *GWR/Adrian Vaughan Collection*

of course, taken for granted. No management upsets at the top, no walking off with vast bonuses just for doing the job they were paid for. Just honest men, doing an honest job.

While the GWR was rapidly building high-speed railways and complex chords and connections with other lines, the LNWR commenced an even greater scheme between Euston and Watford. The four tracks into Euston were very heavily occupied with long-distance, semi-fast freight and suburban trains. So in 1907 the company obtained its Act for an additional double-track electric railway out to Watford, for the rebuilding of the tracks between Primrose Hill Tunnels and Camden, for a new branch line from Watford to Croxley Green, and for new stations between Euston and Watford. Even more remarkable, perhaps, to modern eyes was the co-operation between the LNWR and the Baker Street & Waterloo Company – better known as the 'Bakerloo' – which amicably joined the project by agreeing to construct an extension from Baker Street out to the new Watford line at Queen's Park, where the LNWR would welcome that company's Underground trains onto the new railway all the way to Watford. To that end the new LNWR line was to be laid with the 630-volt DC system, using separate positive and negative rails, fed with current from a power station built by the LNWR at Stonebridge Park.

In December 1908 the North London Railway (NLR), which had always been closely associated with the LNWR, was amalgamated into the latter, although it remained a separate operation with its own Board of Governors.

A month later work on the huge engineering project began. The new railway was planned to diverge from the Watford-Rickmansworth branch after Watford High Street station, which had to be rebuilt, widening the cutting. A new branch line was built to Croxley Green with a junction to the new electric line, making a triangular junction just before climbing up to a 17-arch, sharply curved viaduct at Bushey. Two extra platforms were added to Bushey station and new stations built at Kenton, Hatch End, Headstone Lane and North Wembley. A skew-angled underpass had to be dug beneath the quadruple-track West Coast Main Line to bring the new line to the Up side at Stonebridge Park. A new station was built at Harlesden and beside the existing Willesden Junction, with the new line cutting underneath the North London Line and making a junction with the latter for Watford-Broad Street trains. A double-track tunnel had to be bored alongside the existing tunnels at Kensal Green. In four years all the engineering work from Willesden northwards was complete and a steam-hauled service commenced running between Willesden (New) and Watford on 10 February 1913. On 10 May 1915 the Bakerloo trains started running to Willesden.

The greatest work of all was carried out between the Primrose Hill Tunnels and Camden. A new double-track

The steam railway was adorned with great engineering feats, one of the greatest being the Severn Tunnel, just over 4½ miles long, built between 1873 and 1886. During its construction an underground river was tapped, and to this day 20 million gallons of water a day have to be pumped away. This was done with steam-driven beam engines made at the Hayle Foundry, which were installed at Sudbrook, on the Welsh side of the river, in 1880. There were eight – two with a steam cylinder 50 inches in diameter, and six with a power cylinder 70 inches in diameter. Some electric pumps were installed, but three of the great beam engines remained at work until November 1961.
Adrian Vaughan Collection

Above: To ventilate the vast tunnel a very high-speed 'Guibal' fan of 40-foot diameter was installed and driven by a high-speed stationary engine. *Adrian Vaughan Collection*

Left: The Kemble pumping station sent water 13½ miles to Swindon engine shed and the railway works through a lineside pipeline. There were two 'compound' steam engines supplied by the Hydraulic Engineering Co of Chester. Two Lancashire boilers supplied steam at 100psi to the high-pressure cylinders of 18-inch bore, and the exhaust from them passed to the low-pressure 32-inch-bore cylinders. The pistons had a stroke of 24 inches. When pumping, the weight of water in the pipeline was 2,350 tons, to be lifted 200 feet from the well to the storage tank above the coaling stage at Swindon shed. Electrically-driven turbine pumps replaced the majestic steam engines in the later 1930s and the Lancashire boilers were scrapped, but the engines were retained as standby when the turbines were off for maintenance. The steam engines were then supplied by a tank engine's boiler. This picture, taken in 1963, shows Freddie Boots, the maintenance electrician from Swindon, who kept the engines polished when he had done his job on the turbines. *Adrian Vaughan*

tunnel was bored, 'tube style'. The hillside on the Down side of the existing four tracks was cut away and seven extra tracks were laid: two in a walled cutting, four on the surface and one in a tunnel below the latter. At one point there are 17 tracks above and below ground. The entire vast work was carried out without suspending the train service and, indeed, it did not at once stop because war came in August 1914. The lines from Broad Street to Willesden (High Level and New) and Richmond were electrified in 1916 and the following year the new line north to Watford Junction. Work was suspended in 1917 but recommenced in 1918 and the entire work was completed, with electric trains running from Euston to Watford, on 10 July 1922.

During the Great War all the railways carried a greatly increased traffic for a fixed rent. This was a double tragedy for their finances because the investment they had made did not produce a return. The Great Central Railway opened Immingham Docks in July 1912 – the largest deep-water docks in Britain – only to have them commandeered by the Royal Navy two years later. Birmingham Small Arms Company's investment in new equipment was highly productive of profit between 1914 and 1918 – but not the investments of the railway

companies, which were either commandeered by the Government or, because of the war, were unable to give their proper return. The companies were obliged to take all this abuse in their stride and they soldiered faithfully on, solid and reliable, with their tradition of honest service to Britain.

From 1914 to 1918 there was a continuous flow, day and night, of trains loaded with Welsh coal to Thurso for Scapa Flow, the base of the British Home Fleet – and the empties back again. They never ceased, they never failed, they took precedence over passenger trains, and the men were always available, as were the locomotives and the wagons. These were the 'Jellicoe Specials'. They wore out the single-track Highland Railway and brought that company to the brink of bankruptcy after the war. The company never flinched from what it had to do, but government compensation was miserly.

There were thrice-weekly trains of gelignite from Lando, near Carmarthen, to Queensborough in Kent. They ran throughout the war, right through Kensington and Clapham Junction, and no-one ever knew they were moving. Not a hot axle-box, not a derailment. For most of its communications at this time the railway used the 'single needle' telegraph instrument. Letters of the alphabet were indicated by a visual code of deflections of the needle on the face of the instrument. Commonly used sentences on a host of subjects were condensed to a code word, and a code book was issued, common to the entire United Kingdom. The code word for a gelignite train was gallows humour – IGNITE.

The railways, prior to applying 'management techniques' to their operations, solved every domestic emergency speedily because the men were allowed –

Various main-line railways saw the need to electrify between 1890 and 1900, but the great difficulty of raising capital prevented most projects from being realised. The London Brighton & South Coast managed to raise funds to electrify from London Bridge to Victoria via Wandsworth. The German system of overhead wire carrying current at 6,700 volts was chosen. Installation work commenced in 1905 and the system was brought into use in 1909. The system was replaced by the Southern Railway's 'third rail' system in 1929. Here is a train at Wandsworth Road around 1914. *LB&SCR/Adrian Vaughan Collection*

A GWR waiter and his silver cruets. One cannot help wondering, if we had such things today, whether there would be anything left on the table by the time it got to Bristol.
GWR/Adrian Vaughan Collection

The main-line companies tried to restore pre-war grandeur in the post-Great War period. This is the interior of a Great Western Railway dining car around 1923 – none of your mega-matchstick tea stirrers here, only silver service under an elegant, plaster-moulded ceiling. *GWR/Adrian Vaughan Collection*

trusted – to do their job intelligently. Their actions were not necessarily dictated by the Area Control, much less by higher management. The latter had laid down the Rule Book and Signalling Regulations – pre-ordained contingency plans for every possible situation that might arise – and expected their men to follow those instructions. The Rule Book and the Signalling Regulations were like sacred texts to the men. The civil police never dreamed of becoming involved, and no fantastic 'safety' department of the Government had been invented.

On 22 April 1941 a German parachute mine landed and exploded in a field 125 yards south of the east end of Wivelscombe (Shillingham) Tunnel on the GWR Cornish main line between Wearde and St Germans. The railway was not affected but it is possible that this mighty explosion disrupted underground water courses, which could explain the landslip that took place on 8 December late at night in the bank of the cutting leading to the east end of Shillingham Tunnel. At 11.00pm on 8 December 1942 a farmer's wife, walking along a farm track that ran parallel with the top of the cutting, came across a deep, long, subsidence in the path. She intelligently realised that

the cutting side over the fence must have collapsed onto the line, hurried home, and raised the alarm by calling the GWR at Plymouth.

The Divisional Civil Engineer arrived at the scene on a 'light' engine around 1.00am. The slip was unstable but was not fouling the Up line, so goods trains could be worked past, using the Up as a single track between Wearde and St Germans signal boxes, which were 4 miles apart. Railwaymen, to act as handsignalmen and Pilotman, were woken from their slumbers by the local police, a field telephone was installed at the slip site communicating with the two signal boxes and Plymouth, and at 3.15am the first goods train passed by at walking pace. The driver of each train was instructed by the Pilotman to be alert for 'Danger' handsignals approaching the slip.

The complete clearance of the slip was expected to take two months and it was unthinkable for the GWR to operate the railway with such a heavy delay as a 4-mile section of single track would create. The GWR Superintendent of the Line, Mr Gilbert Matthews, was master in his own house, and had at his command all necessary resources. On the morning of the 9th he decided

During the six years of the Second World War, with one-third of staff in the armed forces, the railway companies managed to keep a civilian traffic running while also providing special trains for the military and civilian authorities. Aerial bombardments of great magnitude became a daily occurrence on all the railways, in cities, towns and in the countryside. The companies restored their services in double-quick time thanks to their unified organisation and engineering-rich competence. Children were evacuated 'out of harm's way' from London and other great cities to the countryside. This is a scene at Paddington in early 1940. The railways had the coaching stock to do it. *GWR/ Adrian Vaughan Collection*

that two signal boxes would be required, fully equipped, one three-eighths of a mile east of the tunnel, the other one-eighth of a mile to the west. This would make the single line about three-quarters of a mile long. He called together Mr Quartermaine, the Chief Civil Engineer, and Mr Page, the Chief Signal & Telegraph Engineer, told them what was required and they took the most rapid steps to supply it.

Reading signal works was told on the 10th to supply two fully equipped signal boxes and have them loaded into rail wagons in the works sidings by the 12th. Each was to be a proper, glazed, roofed wooden building with a floor 15 feet by 8 feet to take an eight-lever frame, properly interlocked, instrument shelves, electric train token instruments, double-track signalling instruments, signal arm repeaters, batteries, battery cupboards, facing point locks, point rodding, automatic train control ramps, signal posts, ground disc signals, lamps – all the paraphernalia of electric circuitry indoors and out to the signals. Each signal box required a stove, a clock, lockers for the signalmen's food, a booking desk, Tilley lamps – all that domestic stuff. At that time the works was engaged on routine renewal work, new signal boxes and locking frames at a dozen locations, and rebuilding signalling systems that had been destroyed by bombing – not only at large places like the Paddington area or Birmingham, Bristol or Plymouth, but also at Castle Cary and Newbury, the former the victim of a 'tip and run' raid, the latter a near miss. The works was also engaged in the signalling of new goods loops and providing new signal boxes on parts of the Swindon Town-Andover line and the entire resignalling of the Didcot-Newbury-Winchester line, which was being converted to double track.

The kit of parts was loaded by late on the 12th and forwarded by the 12.50am Reading-Plymouth goods. It must also be noted that these were the shortest days of the year, and working time was restricted because no strong lights could be used after dark owing to the war. During the two days that Reading was assembling the signalling kit, the Plymouth S&T Department was preparing sites for the boxes, digging holes for signal posts, and running out wires ready to be connected between the signal boxes and the lineside equipment. A Messing Coach was provided for the installation gang to sleep and eat in. The kit had to be unloaded from a train standing on the single line, interrupting the train service for a couple of hours or so. There was more delay while the facing crossovers were laid into the track and their ancillary equipment connected. To avoid some delays to trains the signal posts were erected without the use of a crane – which would have fouled the single line. The circuitry was connected, the signals connected to the levers and the two boxes – Shillingham East and West – were brought into use at 2.45pm on 18 December. Reading Works had taken two days to prepare the kit and the local S&T men and permanent way workers had taken five days to install them, the men living on short rations, working from dawn to dusk, say 8.00am to 5.00pm.

The speed at which this work was carried out was due to magnificent 'housekeeping' on behalf of the GWR departmental chiefs, who counted 'costs' in broader terms than would a Professor of Economics. The other vital factor was the beautiful mechanical signalling system employed. Had the GWR been working with 'track circuit block' and a central control panel at Plymouth, the work could not have been done in five days, taking perhaps five weeks.

At 4.00pm on 23 October 1942 a pilotless target-pulling plane – a 'Queen Bee' – took off from the Doniford artillery range in very strong winds. It was unable to gain height, and its fixed undercarriage caught and broke the telegraph wires near Watchet's Down Distant signal. This entirely arrested its progress and brought it nose first onto the track. The breaking of the telegraph wires prevented the Watchet or the Williton signalmen from obtaining an Electric Key Token for the single line, so the obstruction was automatically protected. The local Signal & Telegraph Department gang were called and also the artillery range. The GWR men re-strung the wires, the Army's No 67 Maintenance Unit removed the plane, and the line was clear for traffic at 8.33pm.

On 16 September 1946 the 4.50pm Penzance-Crewe service, with 13 carriages, was running well, east of Exeter, behind a pair of 'Hall' class locomotives. As the train passed through Stoke Canon the rearmost axle of the 11th vehicle – an LMS eight-wheeled passenger carriage – broke. One wheel dropped inside the rail, became wedged, and was dragged over the sleepers, while the other fell away and was alternately passed over and dragged along by the other three vehicles. This wheel and its stump of axle bowled over and over until it came to rest outside Stoke Canon Crossing signal box. The damaged train passed Stroke Canon Crossing at 10.30pm. Signalman Coles

heard the bumping, heard the ballast hammering against his box and was galvanized into action, sending 'Stop & Examine' (7 bells) to Hele & Bradninch and 'Obstruction Danger' (6 bells) to Cowley Bridge Junction.

The errant wheel had broken the brake pipe on the last vehicle and the train came to a stand with the rearmost vehicle a few yards in advance of Stoke Canon Crossing's Up Starting signal. Signalman Coles telephoned Hele and Cowley Bridge Junction signalmen to tell them why he had sent the emergency signals, then walked up the line to speak to the two guards of the train. These three men assessed the situation and decided what had to be done. Their train was derailed but the Down line was not obstructed and single-line working could be instituted. Coles walked back to his box to call Control and set rescue proceedings in motion. One guard went to speak to the engine crew and the other went to attend to the passengers

On 25-27 April 1942 Bath was bombed and strafed during air raids, and one or more bombs penetrated the stonewalled railway embankment to the west of the station. The Up Main line was blown away but the Down line was less seriously damaged. The GWR soon filled that side of the crater and erected two signal boxes with all necessary signalling and instruments to allow single-line working to commence while the Up side was repaired. On 15 May No 6001 *King Edward VII*, with the Divisional Engineer's Saloon, is testing the strength of the repairs while the engineers assess their next move. *GWR/Adrian Vaughan Collection*

3/211861

On 3 September 1942 Castle Cary station was bombed and strafed. One bomb went through the roof of the signal box just as a Down train was passing. The explosion killed the signalman, threw the heavy lever frame high into the air, lifted the 45-ton loco off its wheels and spun it across the tracks. In spite of the Government confiscating its entire store of rails and sleepers in 1939, the GWR had the damage repaired – with some help from the Royal Pioneer Corps – in quick time. No contractors!
GWR/Adrian Vaughan Collection

– and to prevent sailors from jumping out of the train. The fireman on the leading engine had already been sent forward three-quarters of a mile by his driver with a red light and with three detonators to place on the rail of the Down line. A red light was placed on the leading engine and the white headlight removed.

Control called out the Exeter GWR breakdown equipment vans at 10.47pm. When the vans left St David's they carried the usual team of experienced locomotive fitters from the shed, trained mechanics every one, under their Foreman, and travelling with them was the Exeter Permanent Way Inspector, Arthur Wilson. At 11.25pm the civil police were requested to call out the signalmen for Thorverton, Cadeleigh and Tiverton on the Exe Valley branch so that Up trains could be routed over that line and re-join the main line at Tiverton Junction. This was the sole contribution required from the police. Opening the Exe Valley line would considerably assist the working of Down trains through the temporary single line. The Southern Railway volunteered the Exmouth Junction 45-ton crane, and this was ordered out by Control at 11.30pm. At 12.55am the Southern crane passed through

Exeter St David's station and was stabled on the Up Main at Cowley Bridge Junction, in advance of the Barnstaple line junction. As soon as the track had been sufficiently repaired by the local gang, it could proceed to the site.

At 11.30pm Ganger Sydney Scorse arrived at Stoke Canon Crossing box. He went off to examine the tracks and came back very sad, since he had recently been awarded the prize for the best-kept 'length'. But the Down line was in perfect order. By now the guards had decided that the best way forward for them was to transfer the passengers in the last three coaches into the rest of the train, uncouple the damaged carriage and get on their way. This they duly did, departing at 12.05am, running at reduced speed to Taunton. There, Carriage & Wagon Department examiners

The GWR Control Office for the Exeter District is seen on 26 August 1943. A train service was being operated, the like of which has never since been carried out. These were the people, behind the scenes in such rooms up and down the land, who managed the complexity of operating with a telephone and a bit of paper, receiving information from signalmen, engine sheds, marshalling yards, stations and docks on an orderly plan and sending out instructions as required. *GWR/Adrian Vaughan Collection*

gave the vehicles a thorough checking and found nothing. They left Taunton two hours late.

At 12.45am Signalman Coles left his box to wake up Signalman Cornish, the Stoke Canon Junction signalman, to ask him to go and switch into circuit his signal box so that the Exe Valley line could become a diversionary route, and so that the single-line working could be conducted over the shortest length of line. Points that would become facing at Silverton were clamped and padlocked by the permanent way gang.

Arthur Wilson and Ganger Scorse walked the track and made a detailed list of exactly how many sleepers, chairs, rails and points parts were required to reinstate the track. Half a mile of track had been damaged, 361 chaired sleepers had been destroyed together with a barrow crossing, two point stretcher bars, and nine special cast-iron chairs. In addition 150 sleepers had been gouged or had cracked chairs. Point rodding was bent, the rollers on which they ran were smashed and a detonator placer smashed. By 3.00am three members of the Stoke Canon gang were working on Wilson's first priority – the repair of damaged blades of the points leading from the Up Relief line into the Up Main at the Crossing box. Ganger Scorse used his great knowledge to straighten those blades with the tools he had to hand, so that they worked perfectly. At 6.45am the steam crane drew the coach and vans back onto the Relief and pushed them up into the siding and sand drag at the end of the said Relief line.

The 18-man Exeter mobile relaying gang came on duty at 7.15am. They set off with a special train and collected 400 sleepers lying alongside the track between Cowley Bridge and Stoke Canon. The Exeter men were reinforced by the Taunton No 2 relaying gang. All these experienced men were at the company's service, constantly employed in a rolling programme of routine re-laying, but always available for these emergencies. Ganger Scorse arrived at 11.30pm on the 16th and did not leave the scene until the Up Main was again fit for traffic – with a speed restriction – at 6.00pm on the 17th. Scorse was 62 years old. How can a price be put on such a man? Or any of these dedicated railwaymen? To a Professor of Economics they would have looked like hobnailed sons of toil, a drain on the wage bill, something to be automated. What is the cost of cost-cutting?

The Exeter Divisional Engineer recommended that Ganger Scorse be given a guinea in addition to his pay, and Sir James Milne, General Manager, was sufficiently moved by the loyalty of Scorse and all the men to agree.

Railwaymen took responsibility up on themselves. They just 'got on with the job'. When a wooden footbridge over the line near Little Bedwyn caught fire at 7.45pm, due to a hot cinder from the chimney of the hard-working 6.00pm Paddington-Weymouth train, the village Postmaster, Mr Mills, phoned the Station Master. The Station Master advised the signalmen to stop and caution trains in both directions, then called the Ganger. With the aid of a stirrup pump, and a human chain of villagers to supply buckets of water, they had the flames out at 8.00pm. A watch was kept

and at 9.00pm the fire broke out again. The stirrup pump was brought into action and the fire was finally extinguished at 10.00pm. A watchman was kept there all night and in the morning the Ganger and his men replaced a burnt timber upright post and two footboards.

At 3.13pm on 30 March 1949, at Drayton, near Norwich, the signalman received a report from the permanent way Ganger, Fred Bridges, that he had found a bomb in a ditch on the Up side of the line near the Dolphin bridge. The signalman reported this to the Norwich Station Master at 3.15pm, and he called the police to attend at Drayton. The Ganger appeared in the station yard with the bomb in his wheelbarrow at 4.15pm. The police took the bomb away and the line was pronounced safe at 4.30pm.

On 5 August 1947 the driver of the 6.42pm Portishead to Bristol train saw a man hanging by his neck by a rope around the branch of a tree. He stopped his train where the passengers could not see the awful sight, walked back, collecting the guard as he passed, and together they cut the man down and laid him on the grass. From the appearance of the body he had been hanging there for several days. They then rejoined their train and went on to Clifton Bridge station, where they reported the matter to the police.

On 15 July 1950 the 10.35am (SO) Paddington-Penzance train, comprising No 6027 *King Richard I* and 14 coaches, was running at 75mph, 12 minutes late. The train was 1½ miles west of Edington & Bratton station, approaching a farm track crossing the line, when a tractor towing an elevator began to cross. The engine driver braked hard but the front of the engine collided with the elevator, wrapping it around the front of the locomotive. The vacuum brake pipe was, luckily, undamaged, and the tractor and the two men on it were unharmed. The engine and train stopped 750 yards further down the line. While the footplatemen were waiting for their train to stop the driver got out the detonators and a red flag, and, once stopped, his fireman ran forward to protect the Up Main because the elevator, tangled up with the front of the locomotive, was projecting across that line. The fireman got far enough in advance of his train to put down detonators in front of the 9.45am Churston-Paddington express, which came to a stand a few feet from the obstructing elevator. The driver of the 10.35 Paddington was already working on the bent wreckage with a coal pick and a fire-iron, and was now joined by the men off the Churston service, similarly equipped. Just then the farm-hands off the tractor came running up and also helped with the prising away of the elevator. The wreckage was thrown on the lineside grass, and within 17 minutes of stopping No 6027 was away with its train. (NA. Ref:AN125/1.)

No police, no 'managers', just railwaymen doing their job. This was the freedom people once had to use their initiative and solve problems promptly and with minimum fuss and expense. But that was only possible in a unified railway. With the railway operation broken into separate 'profit centres', there can be no co-operation between them – each is responsible only for its own little fiefdom.

Above: As the post-First World War decades progressed the railway companies became more hard pressed financially. They managed to build some new locomotives and carriages, while the Southern pushed on rapidly with electrification and some widespread power signalling schemes. Unaided by government, the companies gave good value in spite of declining income, and were able to do so by virtue of their strong basic structure. Very old and very new locomotives and carriages worked side by side.

No 237, an ex-North Staffordshire Railway 0-6-0 stands at Ashbourne Old Station waiting to leave with a train of pedigree draught horses on 29 September 1929.

Below: Here at Reading Southern, with the GWR station in the background, a brand-new 'U' class 2-6-0 awaits the 'Right away' on 5 June 1930. *Dr Jack Hollick/Adrian Vaughan Collection*

Above: 'Badminton' class No 4116 *Shrewsbury*, built in November 1898, waits to go onto Oxford shed on 9 June 1930. After 28 years' service, the GWR decided that its nameplate was confusing passengers into thinking that the train's destination was Shrewsbury and the plates were removed. The entire engine was cut up for scrap in March 1931.
Dr Jack Hollick/Adrian Vaughan Collection

Below: An antique Midland Railway tank engine on station pilot duties at Derby station on 5 July 1930.
Dr Jack Hollick/Adrian Vaughan Collection

Above: No 1095 was one of a class of 195 'compound' express engines built from 1925 by the LMS to a design closely similar to that drawn up by Mr Deeley of the Midland Railway in 1910. It is seen here at Derby in the capable hands of Driver Holmes and Fireman Hamm on 5 July 1930.
Dr Jack Hollick/Adrian Vaughan Collection

Below: An ex-Great Northern Railway 'Atlantic', known as a 'Klondike' because the design dated from the Klondike gold rush, looks less than golden in the poisonous, soot-and-sulphur-laden atmosphere of King's Cross station on 25 April 1931. These engines were legendary for taking loads of double the weight they were designed for at express speeds, sometimes standing in for the new and glamorous 'Pacific' locos of the LNER.
Dr Jack Hollick/Adrian Vaughan Collection

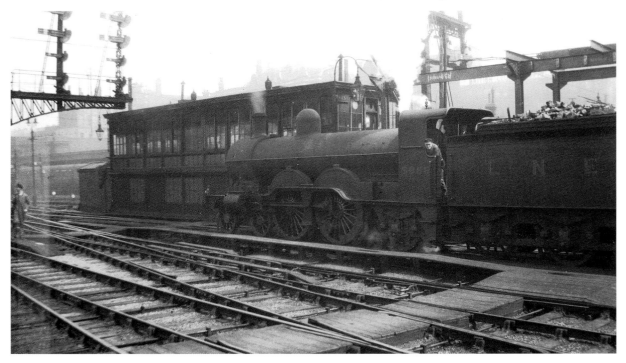

Above: The steam railway was the greatest free show in the world. The young lad watches and learns about railway work in the fumes beside No 4804 at King's Cross on 25 April 1931. *Dr Jack Hollick/Adrian Vaughan Collection*

Below: A view over Weymouth station on 10 September 1931. In the centre is GWR 'Bulldog' No 3324 *Glastonbury*, built in 1899; on the right is ex-London & South Western 'T9' class 4-4-0 No 730; and on the left is a GWR steam rail motor of a 1903 design. It had a steam boiler inside the carriage body, feeding steam to two cylinders mounted on one of the two four-wheel bogies that supported the coach body. In the days before efficient petrol or diesel engines were available this was the only way to construct railcars. *GWR/Adrian Vaughan Collection*

Above: The Up 'Flying Scotsman' is seen at York behind 'A3' 'Pacific' No 2744 *Grand Parade* on 15 July 1932. It is not carrying the famous headboard but the photographer's caption states that it is the 'Scotsman'.
Dr Jack Hollick/ Adrian Vaughan Collection

Middle: North Eastern Railway 'V1' class 'Atlantic' No 710 is at York on the same day. These engines were designed in 1903 but were such magnificent steam-raisers and 'flyers' that they remained in service, alongside the 'A3' 'Pacifics', up until the Second World War.
Dr Jack Hollick/ Adrian Vaughan Collection

Left: Working conditions at most busy engine sheds looked like this, even in 1932. It seems that even in a period of high unemployment labourers to keep the place clean were hard to find. Here an unidentifiable 'Brighton Atlantic', smothered in grime, stands amid grime on New Cross shed on 14 September 1932. In the background there is a crane with a large bucket, which is filled by hand, then lifted and swung over the locomotive's tender ready for someone to heave over to tip the coal out.
Dr Jack Hollick/ Adrian Vaughan Collection

In 1927 the GWR recommenced the station rebuilding programme that had been going on since 1900, interrupted by the Great War. This was brave and professional at a time of increasing financial difficulties for the railways and for the country generally. The first station to be dealt with in the post-war period was Newton Abbot, followed by Taunton, Bristol Temple Meads, Newport, Cardiff and Leamington, while some of Paddington's platforms were extended. Oxford, Banbury and Plymouth were also intended for rebuilding, but by the time the company was ready, another great war stopped progress. The picture shows one of the new platforms at Bristol Temple Meads on 21 September 1934. *GWR/*

Middle: Small stations were also not forgotten, among them Parson Street, Bourton-on-the-Water and Stoke Canon. The wooden station at Challow, on whose platform Brunel had stood in 1841, was rebuilt and the tracks to Wantage Road quadrupled

Bottom: This is a classic Great Northern/LNER scene – not a superior 'Pacific' on an express but a hard-working, cram-packed commuter train. An 'N2' tank, the LNER development of a GNR design, is hauling two sets of four 'quad arts', close-coupled articulated carriages with two carriage ends sharing one bogie, enabling 630 commuters to be seated in a train 350 feet long. This was required for the short platforms of inner-London suburban stations, built when fewer people had to travel. The carriages were designed by Nigel Gresley in 1903 who improved on the original over the years, in particular the riding quality of the bogies. Ninety-eight sets of four were built between 1905 and 1929, the last being withdrawn from service in 1966. Only one set of these carriages remains in the world – on the North Norfolk Railway. The view is near Potters Bar, on 29 April 1933. *Dr Jack Hollick/ Adrian Vaughan Collection*

Above: In May 1931 the GWR fitted No 2935 *Caynham Court* with new cylinders and inlet and exhaust valves of the 'mushroom'-headed 'poppet' variety, which were opened and closed by cams on a rotating shaft, thereby increasing the weight of the engine by 7 tons. The hope was that a greater amount of steam could be got into the cylinders at every opening of the valve, and exhausted with equal facility. The inlet side did as hoped, but the exhaust side could not let the steam out fast enough; there was 'back pressure' and no advantage was found. The engine is seen at Oxford on secondary duties, working a Wolverhampton to Weymouth train on 27 February 1932.
Dr Jack Hollick/Adrian Vaughan Collection

Below: The Southern Railway was the most modernising in Britain. Created in 1921 from several older companies, its management and engineers developed superbly comfortable and handsome electric trains as well as high-quality steam engines – and this in spite of serious loss of income from road competition. Here is one of its superb electric trains, a 2HAL built in 1939 in British Railways ownership, near Bickley on 27 July 1955.
Brian Morrison

Above: Maunsell's three-cylinder 'U1' class engines first entered traffic in 1928. Like all his engines they were modern, efficient and carefully thought out in every detail – and very successful. No 1901 entered service in 1931 and is seen here at New Cross shed on 14 September 1932. In all 21 were built and all were still at work in 1960.
Dr Jack Hollick/
Adrian Vaughan Collection

Right: Another very successful engine, powerful far beyond its modest dimensions, was the Great Northern Railway large 'Atlantic' type, introduced in 1910. They were the finest engines on the East Coast Main Line until the introduction of the Gresley 'Pacifics' – and even after that they gave a good account of themselves. When *Mallard* created its speed record in 1938 – and wrecked its inside big-end – it was an old GNR 'Atlantic' that towed the crippled engine and its train to King's Cross. This is No 3287 at Oxford in 1932; GN 'Atlantics' worked daily through Oxford to Swindon. *Dr Jack Hollick/*
Adrian Vaughan Collection

Above: Maunsell's greatest phenomenon and gift to the passengers of the Southern Railway was the 'Schools' class. These engines were intended to raise levels of speed over the difficult routes of Kent where the power of a 'King Arthur' was needed but where a 'King Arthur' could not go. The 'Schools' was a three-cylinder, four-coupled 'Lord Nelson' with the power of the six-coupled 'Nelson' or 'Arthur'. Luckily for all the financially struggling railway companies, they were blessed with great engineers. 'Schools' No 914 *Eastbourne* passes Waterloo East on a Charing Cross-Hastings excursion on 2 September 1934. *Dr Jack Hollick/Adrian Vaughan Collection*

Below: On the LNER Gresley provided a modernised fleet of locomotives to cover duties from suburban commuter trains to 100mph expresses and the haulage of vast trains of coal. This is No 2394, one of the two experimental Class P1s. This engine is an 'A1/A3' 'Pacific' but with eight 5ft 2in driving wheels, the trailing axle under the cab driven as a booster engine. The 'P1s' were used to pull 1,600-ton coal trains from Peterborough to London, and on the 5 miles at 1 in 200 from Three Counties to Stevenage the booster was needed. No 2394 is stopped near Potters Bar on 17 June 1933. *Dr Jack Hollick/Adrian Vaughan Collection*

CHAPTER 3

Nationalisation

During World War 2 the four railway companies were effectively nationalised. Some 109,000 railway staff left for the armed forces, railway workshops went over to producing military equipment and weapons, Sir William Stanier, Chief Mechanical Engineer of the LMS, went to the Ministry of Production in 1939, and one of his most brilliant assistants, R. A. Riddles, Mechanical & Electrical Engineer for the LMS in Scotland, was appointed Director – or Chief Engineer – for War Transport. The Government agreed to pay – between the four – a fixed rent of £43 million. Any money earned by the railways above the value of the fixed rent went to the Government – which had never given the railways one penny in their entire existence – and railway fares and freight charges were fixed for the duration, no matter what happened to inflation. By 1945 the total civilian 'passenger miles' of the railways were 68% greater than in 1938, and civilian freight tonnages increased by 50%. In addition, the railways ran 538,559 trains for military purposes. Track renewal programmes were reduced by 30% annually from 1940. The railways received their rent and the 'surplus' income went to the Government. (Derek Aldcroft, *British Railways in Transition*, p.98) It would be interesting to know if the Birmingham Small Arms Company, or Hawker or Supermarine, worked for a fixed rent during the war. From 1940 to 1945 the Government received from the railway companies a total of £195 million at 1945 prices. (Government Control of Railways: Financial Returns, 1940-46, Command Paper. *Railwaymen, Politics & Money*, p.336. Railway Clearing House, Tables of Statistical Returns Relating to the Railways of Great Britain. Derek Aldcroft, *British Railways in Transition*, p.98)

According to the *Journal of the Royal Statistical Society* (Series A, Vol 118, No 2), the total dis-investment of the four railway companies between 1937 and 1953 amounted to £440 million at 1948 prices. The companies – pre-war – were not able to raise capital from share issues, for the electrifications, carriage building, station renewals and all the other renewals that they well knew were essential. Had they been allowed to retain their earnings, like any other business they would have been in a far better position to

repair the track, locomotives and carriages After the war, totally worn-out carriages had to be scrapped because they could not be mended. There were 5,100 fewer carriages in 1946 than 1938.

A poor-quality photograph, but of great interest: a Southern Railway 6-PUL electric multiple unit power car, No 3002, is hauling a goods train from Norwood to Three Bridges, somewhere in south London. At the far end is a 'C2X' class steam engine, to give assistance should the electric require it. It is likely that this is an episode during the Southern Railway's early experiments to produce an electric locomotive. The picture was taken on 8 November 1936 by a member of the Southern Railway Electrical & Mechanical Engineers Department, and is part of the author's collection.

Above: In 1941 O. V. S. Bulleid introduced CC1, a powerful electric locomotive, to greatly reduce building and operating costs. The railway was unable to proceed to fleet production because of wartime shortages, and the second engine, CC2, seen here as BR No 20002, was not built until 1945. *Adrian Vaughan Collection*

Below: Bulleid was allowed to have the materials to build steam engines during the war, and the streamlined 'Merchant Navy' and 'West Country' 'Pacifics' were the result. He also designed the 'Q1' class – or 'Charlies' – a design that sums up wartime austerity shortages perfectly. *Adrian Vaughan Collection*

In 1945 the LMS became the first railway in Britain to plan main-line diesel locomotives for express-train working. In 1946 H. G. Ivatt recruited English Electric and Crompton Parkinson to design a 1,600hp diesel-electric. The railway running gear was made at Derby and the engines and electrical equipment at English Electric. The first locomotive, No 10000, came out of Derby Works in December 1947 and went into service in July 1948. Meanwhile, on the Southern, Bulleid was working with English Electric to design a 1,750hp diesel-electric. A pair were built, and the first of them, No 10201, went into service in 1950. The LMS and SR machines ran long daily mileages when they were in good order, but because they were prototypes they suffered lengthy periods in the works. Here the second Southern prototype, No 10202, is seen running into Watford Junction station with a Down express in 1954. *Les Reason/Adrian Vaughan Collection*

In August 1947, on the GWR, the best maintained of the railways, 53 steam locomotives or diesel railcars were reported as having failed on trains. In the case of steam engines this was usually due to being short of steam, but occasionally from a breakage of part of the mechanism. In September 1947, 87 locomotives failed 'short of steam', but two had overheated axle bearings and one had a broken valve rod. In November, 62 steam locomotives had to be replaced en route. No 6015 *King Richard III* suffered the loss of its left-hand coupling rods at speed passing Athelney, and a few days later, at Curry Rivel, No 6018 *King Henry VI* lost its left-hand inside connecting rod when a lack of lubrication caused the big end to overheat and disintegrate. The locations are significant – at the end of a long period of sustained fast running – although there was a 60mph speed limit over the whole railway at the time. (GWR Internal Reports in author's collection)

At the end of the war in Europe, on 7 May 1945, Britain was close to bankruptcy. In July a Labour Government under Clement Attlee was voted into power by 47.8% of voters. In September President Truman, disapproving of the new government, suspended US aid to Britain – food, petrol, tools, and weapons – which had been coming in since March 1941 to the value of $43 billion up to the time it was terminated. Britain's dire financial straits were made worse by the US demand that the aid that had been given free to Britain – as part of the defence of America – had now to be paid for. The aid was valued at $4.3 billion, to be repaid at 2% interest. Britain then had to borrow money from the Americans and the Canadians to pay the annual 2% instalments – and sometimes had to default – but finally paid off the debt in 2006. I only mention this to show how desperate was Britain's plight in 1945 and, indeed, for many years after that.

Britain was a victorious nation but in such an economic mess that it had the appearance of a defeated one. Electricity black-outs and coal shortages caused deaths from cold in 1947. In February 1947 the Atlee Government informed the Americans that Britain, beset as it was with revolting populations throughout the Empire, could not afford to fight Communist partisans in Greece. Britain was a bankrupt, ex-world power. However, it occurred to this Labour Government that possession of nuclear weapons might be a substitute for the possession of an Empire – and quite as luxuriously expensive. Ernest Bevin, Foreign Secretary, famously announced that Britain was going to have an atom bomb 'with a Union Jack on top of it'.

The US Government looked with dismay at the shattered state of Europe and the inroads being made by Communism, and in April 1948 President Truman signed into US law the European Recovery Program, otherwise known as the 'Marshall Plan', to lend billions of dollars to all Western European nations and Japan to help those nations develop their economies and thus fend off Communism.

Europe was physically and economically devastated more comprehensively than Britain, and cold and hunger killed even more people, yet the European nations were far more efficient at reorganising themselves. The same applies to Japan. Britain was the largest beneficiary of the US loans, taking $1.3 billion in 1948-49 and, by the time the scheme finished at the end of 1951, a total of $12.7 billion.

The Labour Party had, since its inauguration in 1893, declared itself to be Socialist and had always promised the nationalisation of railways. Throughout the country there were people in positions of authority, from mayors of cities to the Cabinet, who had begun their careers in public life in the late 19th century and had been inspired to advocate some form of Socialism as a result of their experiences of poverty and unfairness brought about by an unregulated capitalist system. Some better or fairer way of organising

society was also in keeping with the mood of the time – even some leading Conservatives felt that changes had to be made. In a society such as had developed during the war, the generality of people came to believe in unity, in 'all pulling together' – an idealism about 'the common good'. And indeed, co-operation, 'common user' – integration – had been proved to be a much stronger and more efficient method of running a railway than competition. Of course this idealism required a practical realisation, and that depended on having the money and really high-quality, imaginative administrators, devoted to the service of the railway, before it could be realised.

The four railway companies had been making plans for post-war reconstruction from 1942, and they had the great men to do it – but would they, left to themselves, have had the money? If the railways had remained in the hands of the shareholders, would they have received any dividends while the huge expense of rebuilding went forward? Many, many shareholders had not been in receipt of dividends before 1939, and it was certain that their number would have increased after six years of war damage. Who would have bought shares in such a severely run-down railway when there were much more promising prospects in other newer, better paying industries.

It is a moot point whether, if they had won the 1945 election, the Tories would have nationalised the railways, not only on the evidence given above but also on a statement made by the leading Conservative politician R. A. B Butler. Butler was President of the Board of

In 1946 Mr Hawksworth, CME of the GWR, persuaded his Directors to pay for the construction of two experimental gas turbine locomotives. No 18000 was built in Switzerland by Brown-Boveri, the company that had pioneered the machine, and No 18100 by Metropolitan Vickers. Both locomotives ran on two three-axle bogies, but No 18000 had only the outermost axle of each bogie under power, making it a 2,500hp machine – and one would think, rather poor on adhesion – while No 18100 had all its wheels driven, making it a 3,000hp machine – and probably less prone to wheelslip when the power was turned on. No 18000 was delivered in 1949 and, after trials, made its first revenue-earning run in May 1950. Both engines suffered from weakness in the turbine blades and were withdrawn in 1958.
Adrian Vaughan Collection

Education, 1941-45, and Minister of Labour at the time of the 1945 General Election. In the Conservatives' 'Industrial Charter', published in 1947, he wrote that 'in the interests of efficiency, full employment and social security, modern Conservatism would maintain a strong, central guidance over the operation of the economy.' (R. A. B. Butler, *The Art of the Possible*, p.126) This was also the desire of the Labour Party.

It seems very likely that if the LMS and LNER had been left in private ownership they would have been insolvent by 1950. On 10 May 1950, in the House of Commons, Richard Crossman (Labour) said, 'Mr Churchill remarked the other day that we nationalised at the wrong time, by which he meant that if we had waited two years at least two of the main railways would have been in the hands of the Receiver and we should have got them cheaper.'

The LNER Directors, owners of the most run-down railway in the country, offered to sell the infrastructure of the LNER to the Government and become the Government's tenant, paying a rent to run their trains – which they would renovate with the proceeds of the sale – on the state system. That was rejected, probably because it required the Government to hand out money. Straightforward nationalisation had the advantage for the Government of removing the very expensive necessity to pay any compensation to the companies for the damage inflicted during the war. But the nationalised railway had to pay compensation to the ex-shareholders. The Government did, however, graciously allow the nationalised railway to keep the renewals funds of the four, late, companies.

Although in Britain there was a government that called itself 'Socialist', that government was afflicted with delusions of imperial grandeur just like a Tory government. Britain's defence expenditure for 1950-1 diverted 7.7% of the gross national product (GNP) into weaponry, and mostly on the development of British nuclear weapons. This was money that would otherwise have been spent on the post-war reconstruction – which would include the rebuilding of the railways.

Mainland European nations were not encumbered with any *folie de grandeur* and, indeed, the countries that modernised fastest were those that were forbidden to have anything more than small internal defence forces.

Starting in 1948, Britain received $2.7 billion in American aid under the Marshall Plan. France got about the same and Germany $1.7 billion. The Germans had begun in 1946 to rebuild their national infrastructure. By 1958 they had spent Deutschmarks to the equivalent of £2.225 billion on creating a brand new railway. The Belgians began in 1947 and by 1957 had rebuilt, with one-third of the routes electrified. The Dutch railway hardly existed in 1945, but by 1953 all its trunk lines were rebuilt and electrified, and by 1958 its secondary lines were new and dieselised. The whole Dutch network rivalled the Swiss for its efficiency.

Britain's railways became fully state-owned under the control of the BTC from 1 January 1948. The BTC was charged by the Transport Act of 1947 with the task of running 'an efficient, adequate, economical and properly integrated system of public inland transport and port facilities within Great Britain for passengers and goods with due regard to safety of operation.' (Transport Act 1947 Sect 3) Road haulage businesses operating more than 25 miles from their depots were also nationalised by purchase and came under the BTC with the purpose of co-ordinating all forms of transport throughout the country. The railways would continue to carry the bulk of national freight tonnage and road lorries would act as feeders to rail-heads. While doing this the railway was obliged by the Act of Nationalisation to rebuild itself and 'pay its way taking one year with another'. There was no well-thought-out plan as to how this would be managed and no money available to enable the railway to reliably carry out its task. The railway was expected to 'soldier on' as best it could. After all, that is what it had always done.

In 1949 the Atlee Government passed the 'Special Roads Act' to enable the unrestricted building of motorways. The first of these, opened in 1954, was the 8¼ mile Preston bypass – later to be part of the M6. This cut through the Preston-Longridge railway line; a bridge was constructed to carry the railway over the intruding road, and the British Transport Commission (BTC) had to pay for the bridge and its subsequent upkeep!

The first Chairman of the BTC was Lord Hurcomb, a career civil servant and avid birdwatcher; he became Chairman of the RSPB in 1960. He had no understanding at all of engineering or running a railway and did not trust the opinions of the great railwaymen engineers and managers who were his executives. His right-hand man was Miles Beevor, a lawyer, who was Acting General Manager of the LNER at nationalisation. Beevor became Managing Director of Brush Electric at Rugby from 1954 to 1958 and supplied diesels to BR.

There were five 'Executives' under the Commission. The Railway Executive, usually referred to as British Railways (BR), was divided into six Regions under the control of the Railway Executive. The men running BR in 1948 were some of the most senior men of the old companies. Among them were Sir Eustace Missenden, ex-General Manager of the Southern Railway, and David Blee, ex-Chief Goods Manager of the GWR, while Robert Riddles became Chief Mechanical Engineer. The BTC was able to undertake short-term borrowing against its revenue, up to £25 million on overdraft, and could borrow up to £250 million for capital projects with the approval of the Minister. The BTC was entirely at the mercy of the Minister of Transport whenever any large decision had to be taken. It could not even carry out its statutory duty of integrated road/rail services in a small area of the country without first obtaining ministerial approval.

Railway passenger fares in 1952 were 90% higher than in 1939, but the retail price index was 160% above 1939. (BTC Annual Report 1952, para 19) BR fares were controlled by the Government, which had political reasons for not allowing fares to rise – not even in line with inflation. Keeping down fares, for example, in London commuter areas helped to ward off pay claims by commuting civil servants. As ever, the railway was used by government to subsidise other activities. But of course, any railway fare rises that were made were greeted with loud protests of 'BR inefficiency' in the newspapers, and so the reputation of BR was steadily slandered and reduced in the mind of the public.

BR had to pay the ex-shareholders of the four old railway and canal companies 3% of a valuation based on the average price of railway shares in 1946, the best post-war year for railway shares before the full, dreadful, realisation dawned of the worn-out state of the assets. The news of 3% was especially joyful to holders of certain LNER and LMS stocks, who had not received such a high dividend – or indeed any dividend – for years before the war. (Holders of shares in the Midland & Great Northern Railways Joint Committee, which had been absorbed into the LNER in 1936, received no dividend for decades *until* nationalisation.) All holders of Preference shares in any of the four companies would have lost something by this arrangement, always supposing that, had the companies stayed private, they would have been able to continue to pay 5% or 6% Preference share interest. Holders of ordinary shares in the GWR and the Southern gained 0.5% in this deal. The BR 3% dividend was 0.5% higher than what the Government paid to holders of its Bonds, and these payments took £31 million out of BR's revenue in 1949.

The BTC had been forced by the 1947 Act to purchase the entire fleet of 540,000 private owner wagons. All these were of low capacity and of a design unchanged since the 19th century, which prevented them from travelling safely at more than 20mph. These old wooden tubs had been

The newly nationalised British Railways, run entirely by former officers and engineers of the old companies, set out on a steam-engine building project; because much of the motive power fleet needed heavy repairs due to wartime neglect, a fleet of new, highly standardised locomotives would be cheaper than patching up, while the diesels were still prototypes and unreliable. American manufacturers such as General Motors had very reliable diesels for sale, but Britain did not have the dollars to buy them. The 'Britannia' class, designed at Derby and built at Crewe, first entered service in 1951 and was then the largest of the new standard designs. No 70004 *William Shakespeare* is being prepared on Stewart's Lane shed for the 1.00pm Victoria-Dover service, the 'Golden Arrow'. *John Ashman*

The tough men who ran Stewart's Lane shed. From left to right: Chief Running Foreman Fred Pankhurst, on duty seven days a week, together with the Shed Master, Mr R. H. N. Hardy, who was in charge of this large London depot from 18 August 1952 until 2 January 1955. In his time the steel faces of the buffers of No 70004 would have been brightly burnished.
R. H. N. Hardy/
Adrian Vaughan Collection

condemned by two Royal Commissions in the 1920s. The GWR, and probably the LMS and LNER too, had offered to lease modern, 20-ton wagons to colliery companies, but the latter were not willing to invest in facilities at their collieries to enable the more economical wagons to be used. So the railways continued to carry the extra expense – higher repair bills, more breakdowns, slower trains – and difficulties of handling antiquated trucks carrying small amounts of coal. The purchase of these antiquated wagons (rather than spending that money on building 20-ton-capacity, steel, vacuum-braked coal wagons), and the payment of the 3% dividend to tens – hundreds – of thousands of railway and canal shareholders made a total charge on BTC revenue of £1.65 billion a year, at 1947 values. (D. H. Aldcroft, *British Railways in Transition*, p.110)

How was it possible, with such financial burdens, for the BTC to run an 'adequate and efficient' railway and restore the infrastructure to pre-war standards? The Labour Government's attitude towards the railway was dismissive. The railways were not only denied the capital they needed, but were even denied the full amount of steel they needed to re-lay track and build modern carriages and wagons – steel had to go to the car industry to be made into exports, and the railway was expected to haul the exports to the ports as best it could. It was quite astonishing how badly the Labour Government treated its own railway. This was demonstrated by the recommendation of a 1949 parliamentary committee on national capital investment, which recommended that supplies of materials for railway track renewal should be 'reduced to current needs –

without overtaking arrears'. (*British Railways Engineering*, ed. Roland Bond FEng FICE, p.48)

A Conservative government replaced Labour in October 1951. BR re-started two electrification schemes begun before the war by the LNER: between Liverpool Street and Shenfield and between Manchester, Sheffield and Wath (MSW). The Shenfield electrification was inaugurated on 26 September 1949, while high on the Pennines for the MSW a new double-track tunnel was required at Woodhead, 3 miles through solid rock and taking three years to complete. The MSW was opened for electric traction from Wath up to Penistone on 2 February 1952 and to Manchester, through the new Woodhead Tunnel, on 20 September 1954.

The management of British Railways produced a 'Development Programme' in April 1953. This had to be based on what money they could lay their hands on, and was to cost £500 million spread gently over 10 to 20 years. £160 million was allocated to the electrification of King's Cross-Newcastle; Euston-Birmingham/Manchester/ Liverpool/ Glasgow; St Pancras-Manchester; and Paddington-Bristol/ South Wales. This would, incidentally, have displaced enough steam engines to make 14 million tons of coal available for export. Diesel railcars were to be built for suburban and branch lines. Diesel locomotives were to have been introduced cautiously, after proper trials, for the remaining routes, as the standard steam engines came to the end of their booked life. There was to be no hasty destruction of perfectly useful steam engines. £40 million was allocated to the construction of *helicopter* terminals and services.

Above: The BR standard engines were designed and built at the ex-railway company works at Brighton, Crewe, Derby, Doncaster, Horwich and Swindon. The 75xxx series had parts designed at Brighton, Derby, Doncaster and Swindon, but the engines, from No 75000 to No 75079, were all built at Swindon. This is No 75073 being erected at Swindon in 1956. *Adrian Vaughan Collection*

Left: A total of 251 of the 92xxx class BR Standard 2-10-0s were built, 53 of them at Swindon, the rest at Crewe. They were introduced to traffic in 1954 and turned out to be the most successful of all the standard designs. Designed for the heaviest freight trains, they were capable of 90mph when called upon to deputise for 'Deltics' on express trains. The last of them, No 92220 *Evening Star*, came out new from Swindon Works in 1960 – the last steam engine to be built for British Railways. Five years later it was redundant, its work taken over by the diesels. *Adrian Vaughan*

By May 1953 five main-line diesels were on trial, the magnetic form of the Automatic Warning System (AWS) had been installed as an experiment between King's Cross and Grantham, and the London-Kent electrification was in planning. In 1952 £300 million of government money was invested in roads and £50 million in railways.

In May 1953 a new Railways Act was passed. Winston Churchill was Prime Minister and, in spite of his fulsome praise for railwaymen's wartime efforts, he was no friend of railways. During the drafting and cabinet discussions of this Bill, Alan Lennox Boyd, Minister of Transport and Civil Aviation, wrote a memo to Churchill that read: 'The main principle is that road-hauled should be allowed to expand to the extent of demand and British Railways should effect economies to off-set its losses.' (MT62/138)

The 1953 Act was a cynical piece of work, reflecting the Government's contempt for railways. Road haulage was denationalised as fast as the BTC could sell off the lorries. This proved to be difficult and chaotic, even increasing BTC's costs. Its Act allowed the BTC 'to vary charges so as to improve the ability of railways to compete with other transport. Within prescribed limits the BTC will be free to raise or lower charges subject to the approval of the Minister.' Some freedom. R. A. B. Butler, Chancellor of the Exchequer, said, 'There will be competition for both passengers and goods between railways and roads.' Clearly this was not the case. While the BTC was lobbying the Minister for a reduction in its charges to compete for this or that traffic, the private road haulier, subjected to no restrictions, had already quoted for and was carrying the traffic. The Act abolished the all-powerful Railway Executive, and the six 'Regions' became relatively self-governing fiefdoms under the BTC. Each Region then had to produce its own set of annual accounts, a costly and time-wasting procedure. Having separate Regions was supposed to benefit the railway by 'introducing a healthy rivalry'. The railway did not need rivalry but re-investment. There was no proper principle, no idea of benefiting the population through integrated and co-operative transport, just a spurious competition. The railways, a great national asset, were to be neglected and held down so as to ever increase the monopoly of the oil companies in the provision of transport. Several Cabinet Ministers were urging more and more road building and even suggesting that as yet non-existent internal airlines would take from the railways what did not go to the roads.

The 1953 reorganisation suspended the BR Development Plan and in January 1955 the BTC published its Modernisation Plan for BR. The cost of the plan was estimated at £1.24 billion, over 15 years – £82.66 million a year. Of that sum, BR would find £400 million from its annual revenues and the rest would be borrowed from banks. All the Government did towards this was to guarantee to the banks the interest on the loans. Not all of this money was for modern equipment: £210 million of the money raised would be required to replace worn-out track, which should have been replaced years earlier. In 1955 road investment was £575 million against £75 million for rail, and in 1960 roads cost the country £950 million while rail enjoyed an investment of £175 million. (BTC 1962 Accounts, quoted in Bagwell's *The Railwaymen*, Vol 2, p.11)

The thoughtfulness of the Government people in charge of transport is summed up by the statement of Harold Watkinson (later Viscount Watkinson) Minister of Transport 1955-59, who thought that this little sum of money would be enough to create a new railway. He said in Parliament, while recommending the plan to the House, 'The railway industry has it within its power to get out of debt [government policies put it into debt] by its own efforts. We want the nationalised industry to pay its own way without outside help.' (Hansard, Vol 536, col 1327, 3.2.55)

This tiny amount of money could not modernise and reduce costs on British Railways because there was too much of British Railways. A few of the most rambling railways in Britain were closed to passenger traffic by the BTC in 1952, but there was still plenty left – and the BTC was ordering lots of diesel railcars to run them on in their delightfully Victorian branch lines. The DMU and railbus could bring down costs on East Anglian branch lines by removing steam engines, but the branches also required their signalling to be transformed and all the level crossings automated. Given the state of Britain's finances – and the fact that the railways were considered to be a total waste of space by the narrow-minded, car-and-competition-obsessed Tories, it was impossible to obtain the money needed to modernise BR as it stood in 1955-60.

Mr R. A. Riddles's original plan of holding the railway fort with new, standard-pattern steam locomotives until all trunk-line electrification was complete was not going to work. Costs of steam operation rose and there was difficulty in finding men to take on the work – not just on the footplate but, more importantly, all the dirty jobs on shed. The decision was taken in the Modernisation Plan to replace steam with diesel haulage as soon as possible and to slow down the drive for electrification. A main-line diesel could work for 22 hours a day against half that for a steam engine. But then the wholesale dumping of steam locomotives, some of them only five years old, must have been a waste of money. Having so many different types of diesel locomotive, brought into use so precipitately without proper trials, was also a waste of money. Some of these diesels were design failures, all adding to BR's costs.

BR had to fund its purchases from borrowing and from its fares and freight charges to the public and industry at a time when roads were being hugely improved, the railway's share of traffic was diminishing while the said fares and charges were consistently below the rate of inflation owing to Government orders to 'contain price increases'. The modernisation of the railway placed BR at the mercy of contractors to a very great extent. The equipment purchased from the contractors was subject to no government price restriction and these prices rose with, and perhaps even beyond, the rate of inflation. So BR bought other industries' outputs, giving industry a subsidy, as was the Government's intention, paying the full price to industry for the equipment it needed. As ever, BR was the 'Cinderella'.

The Glasgow suburban trains were ripe for modernisation and BR took up the challenge with all good energy. The new services began on 7 November 1960. The bodies of the new trains were supplied by Pressed Steel of Paisley and the electrical equipment by AEI. Together with these handsome trains came a colour-light signalling system power-operated from two electrically-operated, push-button control centres. The trains ran at up to 75mph at frequent intervals and had a strong identity – the Glasgow 'Blue Trains'. They were widely regarded as the best-designed multiple units ever built in Great Britain, both from an aesthetic and operational standpoint. At the end of the first week of operation the passengers carried totalled 400,000, compared with 170,000 in the same week in 1959.

By 18 December, 17 trains were disabled due to transformer explosions. The whole fleet had to be withdrawn and steam engines hauling carriages were substituted. This shows how dependence on contractors – third parties – introduces an expensive element of uncertainty into the operation of the railway. The problems were of course put right and the Glasgow 'Blue Trains' were as successful and popular as the High Speed Trains of 1974. A similar story can be told of the diesels purchased by the Western Region from the North British Locomotive Co. The power units of these locomotives were so defective that they all had to be replaced, but luckily they were still under guarantee; North British carried the cost.

In 1948 BR made a surplus of £23.8 million, but after interest payments to the ex-company shareholders and to the Government there was a loss of £8.1 million. When one remembers that the Government owed the railway millions in compensation for the unusual wear and tear of rolling stock and infrastructure inflicted while carrying government traffic during the war, some might think that the Government owed British Railways money.

By 1952, after all charges had been paid, there was a tiny surplus of £333,000. In 1953, the year that the Tories unleashed the road hauliers, BR made a working surplus of £34.6 million, but a net loss of £2.8 million. The following year the loss was £21.9 million. In 1955, the year of the Modernisation Plan, the loss was £38.3 million. In 1957 BR was borrowing money to modernise and borrowing to pay its interest charges to shareholders and government. This borrowing to pay interest on earlier debts was accounted for in a separate account. The ordinary account for BR in 1959 showed a total income of £457.4 million, working expenses of £499.4 million, an operating loss of £42 million and an overall loss of £84.8 million.

CHAPTER 4

'A railway, not a museum'

On 14 October 1959 Ernest (Ernie) Marples became Minister of Transport in Harold Macmillan's Government. Ernie Marples was a triumph of democracy, a very sharp operator from the ranks of the Labour Party. He was born in Manchester and had worked as a coal miner, postman and chef, before – very remarkably – qualifying as an accountant. He joined the Territorial Army and by the end of the war was a Captain and a Tory. In 1945 he stood for Parliament and bucked the national trend by holding the Wallasey seat for the Conservative Party, holding it until he retired in 1974 – clearly a very popular man in Wallasey. With his savings and a loan, after the war he set up a company dedicated to road-building – Marples, Ridgeway & Partners – but on becoming an MP he divested himself of his shares by putting them in his wife's name, which was sufficient to disarm any accusation of corruption.

Harold Macmillan's background as a Director of the Great Western Railway did not prevent him from thinking that the railway system was too large for its own good: it could not all be modernised, so some of it would have to go. On 11 March 1960 he said in the House of Commons that 'the railway system must be remodelled to meet current needs and the modernisation plan must be adapted to this new shape.' It therefore seems likely that he would have said the same had the GWR still been in existence and he still a Director of it. The Age of the Car, smart, glossy and fashionable, had arrived. Sharp men like Marples, and conventional Tory gentlemen like Macmillan, believed that roads, the car, buses and the lorry, would solve all problems of transport in an economy they hoped would expand.

The Ministry of Transport was made up largely of people concerned with advancing the interests of roads and the manufacturers of motorised road transport; this had been the case since its formation in 1919. People connected to road building and motor transport manufacturers moved into and out of positions within the Ministry, just as, now, Marples had done. The bias towards roads was blatant, as if railways were not a major, national system. Three Under-Secretaries – very high-ranking civil servants – controlled the road transport departments within the Ministry, and they had the power to initiate and pursue road-friendly policies. Only one Under-Secretary dealt with all railway and canal matters, which were mainly concerned with safety, and he had no policy-initiating function. By 1970 75% of the 15,500 people employed in the Ministry were dealing with road matters. The Ministry was there to be lobbied by the Road Haulage Association, the Society of Motor Manufacturers & Traders, the AA and the RAC, and to put into practice their demands.

Professor Bagwell, in Volume 2 of *The Railwaymen*, page 7, gives us a glimpse of the working of the Ministry. On 16 October 1978 a memorandum was sent to William Rodgers, Secretary of State for Transport, signed by the Under-Secretary of the Ministry's Freight Directorate, Mr J. Peeler. The memo concerned a proposal for an 'impartial inquiry' into whether or not the maximum axle weight for Lorries be raised from 32 to 38 or 40 tons. Peeler was concerned that the inquiry should not be impartial but should 'establish in the public mind a clear and overwhelming case for heavier lorry weight'. Then 52 County Councils could pay for bridges to be strengthened so the road hauliers could have a more profitable existence.

Not surprisingly, Marples's appointment as Minister of Transport ended the year on year, seven-year rise in railway investment, which then entered a decline that did not cease until he left the post in 1964.

Within days of becoming Minister of Transport, Marples and Macmillan established the Stedeford Advisory Group to find out what the shape of the new railway should be. Sir Ivan Stedeford was an exceptionally brilliant industrialist, banker – and motor car engineer. Sitting with Stedeford were Mr David Serpell and Dr Richard Beeching. Serpell was at that time a Permanent Secretary at the Ministry of Transport – so no redundancy for him. After recommending the closure of 84% of the railway network, and thus the redundancy of thousands, he received a knighthood. His Report was so extreme that it was not published until Dr Richard Beeching, an exceptionally brilliant, analytical thinker, was Technical Director of the giant chemical industry ICI. The Stedeford Group's Report laid about the BTC – and the Government – with a large stick. It was so severe in its condemnation of railways that it was kept a secret – even from Parliament – until 1991. It advocated complete commercial freedom for BR – but a BR with a network of about 3,000 miles. It also denigrated the BTC plan to electrify the Euston-Glasgow line and associated routes, saying that the costs would not be justified by the returns. So their arithmetic was wrong somewhere.

Marples was full of bright ideas but, as a builder of motorways, promoting railways was not one of them. His road-building company had built the Chiswick flyover, costing £1.3 million and opened in 1959, which was eventually incorporated into the M4. It also built sections of the southern section of the M1 known as the 'Hendon Urban Motorway', which he formally opened in May 1967. His company built parts of the M45, the M6 from Gravelly Hill ('Spaghetti Junction') to Bromford, the new Laira bridge dual-carriageway at Plymouth and other roads.

As Minister of Transport Marples decided what road or rail project was built and what was not built. When, in 1960, Liverpool County Council wanted to increase the capacity of the Mersey railway tunnel because at that time 75% of cross-Mersey journeys were done by rail, BR made a study and found that for £13 million the capacity could be increased by 25%. This entailed longer trains, longer platforms and 'flying' junctions at the Wirral and Liverpool ends of the tunnel. Marples vetoed this while authorising the construction of a second Mersey road tunnel at a cost far in excess of £13 million – Marples Ridgway constructed the pilot tunnel. This led to increased road congestion in Liverpool to which Marples answer would surely have been to build more roads. In 1960 the Manchester/North-east Cheshire Highway Plan intended to cater for 2.5 times the 1960 number of cars coming into the central area by 1982. The scheme included the provision of new roads and 47,000 car parking spaces, and would cost £500 million. The planners soon realised that even this level of town destruction to make way for the roads and car parks would not be sufficient to cope with increased car use. The answer had to be better use railways. (*Modern Railways*, January 1968. pp.44) Marples commissioned 264 miles of motorway while he was Minister of Transport, his (wife's) company building parts of it. Until 1970 motorways had no speed limit, and no central crash barrier. Perfect individualism, a Tory free-for-all, making money out of death instead of 'keeping death off the roads', which all the old railwaymen used to say was one of the functions of the railways.

Year	Accidents	Deaths	Serious injuries	Casualty rate per billion vehicle kilometres
1958	237,000	5,970	69,000	107
1960	272,000	6,970	84,000	124
1965	299,000	7,592	98,000	170
1970	270,000	7,499	93,000	205

(*Department for Transport statistics*)

There were 11 years between 1951 and 2002 when no passenger was killed while travelling on a train: 1954, 1956, 1966, 1976, 1977, 1980, 1982, 1985, 1990, 1993 and 1994. There were six years when only one passenger was killed: 1959, 1963, 1974, 1981, 1995 and 1996. No more detailed statistics are required. Given the extreme safety of rail travel and the extreme cost to the nation of road accidents, why not invest in more railways and less in roads?

The Macmillan government passed a Transport Act in 1962. This re-introduced competition for inland transport. It abolished the all-embracing British Transport Commission and instituted the British Railways Board, giving the railway regions as much commercial freedom as possible. The Act abolished BRB's £475 million debt to the Treasury, but left the interest bearing capital of the railway at £857 million, making the BRB liable to annual interest payments of £50 million. The common carrier obligation was abolished. BRB could carry or not carry as it chose and it could charge what it liked – unless the Minister intervened. The BR workshops were forbidden to compete outside engineering works for work. The BRB was ordered to arrive at a 'break even' situation by 1968, notwithstanding any difficulties in the general economic situation which might arise as a result of government policies elsewhere. The Act came into force on 1 January 1963. There is no Chairman of the Road Board who could be castigated and lampooned for incompetence and making a loss. If there were such a Roads Authority, charged with 'breaking even', the cost of motoring and freight haulage would be much higher than it is.

The 1962 Act established the legal framework for the easy closure of railway routes. It also gave the Minister of Transport, motorway magnate Ernest Marples, power to veto any railway expenditure over £250,000. The southern section of the M1 cost almost £23,000 a mile – £50 million for 72 miles. As Minister for Roads he could approve any road building scheme without limit. Those economic advisers who gathered around Conservative and Labour governments were generally of the opinion that money spent on railways was wasted – roads were going to solve all transport problems. The odd thing, I think, about economists is that while they must hope that the advice they give will lead to an expansion of business activity and therefore more cars and more lorries, they do not make allowance for the increased traffic – except to build more roads. Traffic jams where the dual-carriageway ended and the urban streets began did not – apparently – occur to them, although it was very obvious to me, even in 1963. So while BR's essential modernisation was repressed, money was poured out on self-defeating road-building.

In May 1963 Dr Beeching produced his 'Reshaping of British Railways' report, proposing the closure of 6,000 miles of the 18,000 miles of Britain's railway network. There was a need to reduce the size of the BR network, but we all loved our railways, especially the most under-used, and there was such a 'shock-horror' surrounding the Beeching Report that it became mythical. He is even cursed for closing lines that were closed years before he arrived on the scene. Map No 9 in his Report, showing proposed line closures, was not as severe as the myth that has grown up since. Several dozen small stations that were included in his closure proposals had been under threat of closure before he came along. The 'Reshaping' plan did not select for closure King's Lynn-Wisbech-March; King's Lynn-Hunstanton or King's Lynn-Dereham-Norwich – these were closed later by the Party of the railwaymen's trade unions. The Oxford-Cambridge line was not included in the closure proposals; this was a line intended to be developed into a fast east-west traffic artery, avoiding London, and money was spent on the Bletchley flyover to carry heavy-duty east-west traffic clear of the north-south West Coast Main Line.

Some stations closed under the 'Reshaping' plan were usefully acting as railheads for wide rural districts or for conurbations around provincial cities and could have been developed – especially as the national economy was bound to expand. In selecting lines for closure Beeching seems to have made a remarkable blunder for an economist. On page 56 of the Report he says that he has 'made no novel assumptions about the future distribution of population and industry. It has been assumed that the pattern will continue to be basically similar to that which exists at present.' So he thought the country would stagnate? But then, a few words further on he says that the increasing population in the south-east of the country would not be favourable to the future of the main-line network. Well no, of course not, but these burgeoning communities were going to need railway transport. What he might have suggested was the building of new main lines to by-pass commuter lines. But railways were for closure or to be left as they were. His tendency to denigrate the need for railways in commuter areas left new towns, like Haverhill in Suffolk, without a railway and, indeed, many major provincial cities were denuded of their feeder systems. The Beeching Plan seems to have been flawed at the very root – but not as flawed as the myth would have it.

Almost all of the closures that Dr Beeching did recommend were carried out under the authority of the Labour Government, thus confounding the railwaymen who had urged me to 'Vote for 'arold [Wilson] and he'll get rid of this **** Beeching'. One of the powerful organisations urging the Labour Government to go further than Beeching was the lorry drivers' union, the Transport & General Workers, led by ex-Communist Frank Cousins, who is said to have urged Barbara Castle, then Minister of Transport, to 'close the lot down.' The Paddington-Birmingham 100mph main line was downgraded to single-track branch-line status by railway managers – after it had served a vital purpose of acting as a diversionary route while the West Coast Main Line was electrified. In fact, so useful had it been in carrying Euston traffic that one would have thought that a reason for not singling it.

Diversionary routes, like additional carriages to cater for peaks of traffic, were frowned on: Carlisle-Hawick-Edinburgh, for instance. Passengers would have to suffer overcrowding, trains would be of set formation, and if a line was blocked they would just have to use buses. It was not the way railwaymen were used to treating their passengers – and yet, the people carrying out these cuts often accused railwaymen of not caring! The branch lines around large cities were closed, forcing more traffic jams and more hacking through residential areas with dual-carriageways. Challow station which served Wantage, Faringdon and the Vale of the White Horse was closed in 1964. Kidlington and Bicester served Oxford commuters, but were closed in 1968 (Bicester was re-opened in 1987). The short route to London from Yarmouth and Lowestoft, through Beccles, Halesworth and Saxmundham, all but closed, but survived and proves the folly of shutting down many other places. The North London Line, Richmond to Broad Street and Barking, with connections to every major trunk railway was – amazingly – listed for closure in the Beeching Report. It struggled on in a decaying state and was finally saved by Ken Livingstone and is again a vital, heavily used, artery. The Sheffield-Marylebone route was recommended for closure by Dr Beeching and closed by a Labour Government in 1966 – what traffic that route could now be carrying into Europe! The Didcot, Newbury & Southampton line was a truly strategic railway connecting the Midlands with the rapidly expanding Southampton area; it was condemned as a passenger line by Beeching but lingered on very usefully for heavy freight until 1967. The excellence of the route is demonstrated by the fact that much of the southern section went under the motorway-like A34. This was in conformity with a Conservative Party pamphlet of 1957 entitled 'What wonderful roads they will make'.

In 1994 the 10 miles of A34 around Newbury – cutting through three 'Sites of Special Scientific Interest' – cost £10 million a mile purely for their construction. This did nothing to prevent congestion. On the opposite side of the town lies Newbury Racecourse. There was then and there still is a Racecourse station to which, in the days of BR, when it 'did not care about passengers', lengthy special trains were run. By the time of the building of the Newbury bypass the new caring-for-the-customer railway had given up running lengthy trains for special occasions; only ordinary little railcars, entirely inadequate for the job, stopped there. So the racecourse's governing body supported the bypass, thinking that it would increase patronage on race days. Intending racegoers could drive around the bypass dual-carriageway at 70mph but then the vast flood of traffic would meet the stuff coming off the M4 and the whole lot would have to queue – and queue – to enter the racecourse car park. The reputation of the traffic jams spread and actually discouraged people from attending meetings. But there are still no special trains to the Racecourse station.

A great many of our major towns have been very badly vandalised and beautiful countryside and wildlife destroyed in order to make way for road traffic. Chemical pollution from road traffic is a known fact, but nothing stands in the way of road-building, cars and Lorries. The costs of building the roads, of strengthening road bridges over rivers and even culverts under roads, and the costs of road accidents are not a problem to the Treasury. Road accident fatalities rose steadily until they reached an all-time peak of 7,500 in 1970. Not until that year was a 70mph speed limit imposed on motorways.

One railway track can carry three times the tonnage of one lane of a motorway with far less consumption of fuel. Roads are wasteful of resources, but conspicuous consumption – or waste – is what makes profit. More roads mean more car sales, more insurance business, more tyres, more oil, and more petrol. The proprietors of tyre manufactories, car insurance companies, oil companies and indeed, a civil engineering business might well view the extension of the railway with alarm. Those who travel by train are not supporting them. Railways stand in the way of these great industries. That is the problem for railways.

The Crewe-Manchester electric trains had commenced running in September 1960 and in January 1962 the Euston-Birmingham-Crewe-Liverpool electrification had just started. With evident reluctance, Marples allowed the work to continue. Work on the M6 began in 1963 and by the end of that year there were 273 miles of motorway open. Marples Ridgway built the M6 from 'Spaghetti Junction' (exclusive) to Bromford. The electric train service from Euston to Birmingham commenced in April 1966, when 456 miles of motorway were open and double that was either under construction or planned. The Euston-Birmingham electrics commenced running in March 1967.

Electrification was a thundering success, carried out by a BRB short of money. In the first month passenger journeys from London to Manchester and from London to Liverpool increased by 60% and receipts increased by 54% and 46% respectively. (*British Railways Engineering*, p.236) The Birmingham service immediately increased passenger journeys by 25% and receipts by 10%. (*Modern Railways*, 1968, p.52) The following year results were even better. In spite of these figures – or perhaps because of them – the continuation of electric traction northwards from Liverpool/Manchester to Glasgow was held up for some years, reducing the value to the BRB of the scheme so far carried out.

The Euston-Birmingham-North electrification scheme, up to January 1968, had cost £160 million and had resulted in a 16.5% increase in revenue. (*Modern Railways*, 1968, p.52) I have not read any congratulations from the economics wizards, but I did read criticism of the BRB for carrying out electrification without first asking any of its profession for an opinion on the relative merits of diesel and electric traction.

Dr Beeching was in favour of British Railways carrying containerised freight at 75mph on hauls in excess of 100 miles. For this the BRB would copy the American practice of containerisation to transfer loads from road to rail and vice versa. This was the 'liner' train carrying 12½ ton containers. Five trunk routes were selected to carry liner trains and road hauliers were canvassed to put their loads on rail. The container lorries of private enterprise would deliver to the nationalised railhead and collect from the nationalised railhead. The plan was somewhat similar to the 1948 nationalisation plan, where road hauliers would be the feeders of loads to the railway – but not even the nationalised British Road Services wanted to be the first to try the liner train system, and the National Union of Railwaymen was opposed to private road hauliers coming into railway yards. The NUR saw the redundancy of its railway lorry drivers in the scheme when they had recently had to acquiesce in the redundancies of thousands of workshop staff – and Marples had just refused to allow nationalised BR workshops to construct containers for the privately-owned lorries.

Beeching returned to ICI in May 1965. By that time dieselisation, electrification and the automation of signalling were under way and the total deficit for the year was £132.4 million, of which £60.9 million was interest paid to the Government.

Mr Marples ceased to be Minister of Transport when Labour won the 1964 election, but remained as Member for Wallasey until 1974, when he was created a life peer. It was after his questionable business practises that he decamped to a chateau in France, and the Treasury froze what assets he had in Britain until he paid a fine of £7,000. This he did, but he never returned to England. He died in France in 1978.

Dr Beeching was replaced as Chairman of British Railways in 1965 by a hard man, Mr Stanley Raymond. Raymond had started work on the railway in 1956. He became Chairman of the Western Region of British Railways in 1962 on the retirement from that position of Mr Reginald (Reggie) Hanks. The two men, so completely different, sum up for me the divide between two eras.

Reggie Hanks is remembered as a devoted railwayman by the dwindling band of staff who knew him. His life story is uniquely peculiar in railway history since his greatest successes were in the manufacturing of motor vehicles. He joined the GWR in 1911 as an engineering apprentice at Swindon Locomotive Works and, on completing his time in 1915, he volunteered for the Great War and went to France, dealing with railways. He returned briefly to Swindon in 1919 but did not like the post-war atmosphere in the works. Like Mr Churchward, he thought the unions had too much say in how things were done and, also like Churchward, he felt obliged to leave. He took a job as Assistant Engineering Inspector for the Crown Colonies Department, stationed in Glasgow, and in 1922 joined Morris Motors at Oxford. He had a very distinguished career with Lord Nuffield's organisation, becoming Vice-Chairman of Nuffield Exports in 1947. He retired from the Nuffield Organisation and from the Board of the British Motor Corporation in 1955 and was at once appointed Chairman of the Board of the Western Region. At the same time he was Vice-President of the Society of Motor Manufacturers & Traders! Yet Hanks was a steam engine man to the core. On his appointment to Chairman of what was almost the Great Western Railway, he said, 'Now I can ride on steam engines whenever I like.' And he took full advantage.

He used regularly to fire the 'Castle' class locomotive that hauled his morning train from Oxford to Paddington. Hanks reintroduced cream and brown carriages and the 'titled trains' with their handsome headboards. He caused No 7005 *Lamphey Castle* to be renamed *Sir Edward Elgar*, and ensured that it was always based at Worcester for working the 'Cathedrals Express'. At weekends he entertained Oxford locomotivemen on the engines he personally built for his garden railway. Now that is leadership. The railway staff would go to any lengths for such a man.

Hanks was responsible for replacing his much-loved steam engines with diesels, a job he regarded as essential while he detested doing it. As an internal combustion engine expert, he judged that the German Maybach engine with hydraulic transmission was the best way forward. In Germany they worked superbly well, but it was to be a different story on the Western Region of British Railways.

In September 1963, when he was presenting long-service awards to Oxford engine drivers, he said:

'It is a sad thing to see steamers rusting all over the system. We shall never feel the same affection for these new-fangled devices as we did for the old steam engines. But the departure of steam engines has brought an end to the heavy, dirty work which human beings ought not to be asked to do.'

Of Raymond, *Modern Railways* magazine wrote, 'He has left sharp marks in his rise up the ladder.' Raymond was a ruthless hatchet-man. Gerald Fiennes, one-time General Manager of the Western Region, said of him, 'Before you call a man a bastard, make sure he isn't.' When Raymond took over from Hanks in 1962 the Western Region was still very much the 'Gentleman's Railway'. Raymond set out to destroy the old ways, passed on through generations of railwaymen. He ordered the complete clearance of all the wall-encrusting relics from the corridors of Paddington, the name and number plates and the photographs. His words on this occasion were sent down the railway, from Paddington to Bristol, in minutes. He said, 'I am running a railway, not a museum.'

The encrusted traditions of 100 years, the nameplates, number plates, photographs – the fertile soil in which pride in the job and loyalty to the resultant service grow – were removed. The resultant barrenness of hundreds of yards of the cream-painted walls of the Paddington corridors were enlivened – just here and there – with posters carrying a picture of steel-capped boots and urging railwaymen to wear such things at work. It was a beautiful comment on the new regime. Marples and Raymond had no warmth, no feeling for style and quality – they might have been economists. And unfortunately, they were in charge. They destroyed the natural order and then had to invent 'customer care' where 'operatives' speak to a script. When the Labour Party, under Harold Wilson, took over from the Tories in October 1964, the national economic situation was difficult. British gold reserves were low, there had been a run on the pound, the International Monetary Fund was shoring it up, and the Bank Rate stood at 7%. Working peoples' wages were being blamed for all this, and a 'pay pause' was in place. It was these national conditions, which the Labour Party was unable to improve, that the national railway had to pay millions in interest to the government and still 'break even'.

The automation of signalling went ahead slowly as BRB could afford it and the Government released loans. My experience of the re-signalling on Western Region, under Raymond, was that great risks were taken with safety. This was due to modern signalling and motive power married to old-fashioned vehicles.

There were 40 derailments on BR in 1965, most of them on the Western Region. Powerful diesel locomotives were hauling old-fashioned wagons, with oil-and-pad-lubricated white metal bearings, too fast and for too long. Long periods of relatively fast running created overheated axle bearings, running on tracks unsupervised by signalmen. There was a real risk of derailment due to the collapse of the axle or the instability of the wagons at speed. There was a particular problem with a certain type of newly designed BR box van, which was very prone to derailment at speed. These derailments sometimes took place when another train was passing. Signalmen could not carry out the safety measures laid down in the Regulations because – with automated signalling at that time – they lacked the equipment with which to do it. Several 'near-miss' situations and actual derailments occurred. (See my *Signalman's Nightmare*, Chapter 4) The travelling public got away unharmed, but they were put at risk by WR and BRB management.

'We would never compromise safety!' Raymond resigned in December 1967 at the request of Barbara Castle, Minister of Transport. In his resignation letter he said that he was concerned for morale on the railway! He departed from railways to sell his versatile talents to the Horse Race Betting Levy Board.

Between 1950 and 1970 the railways had been very largely reconstructed. The network had been reduced from 20,000 to 11,000 miles, and staff had been reduced from 640,000 to 296,000. The accident rate measured in passengers killed per million train miles was declining. Power-operated signalling controlled long distances and was being extended. Diesel and electric locomotives and multiple units were running much faster – for instance, 100mph running was permitted on half the total mileage of electrified line on the LMR, and on the ER and the WR there was considerable 100mph running. Freight wagon numbers were reduced from 1,165,000 to 430,000. The abolition of the traditional goods train wagon reduced very considerably the risk mentioned of death to passengers. The last traditional daily goods train, with oil-lubricated white-metalled axle bearings and a guard's van at the rear to run on Western Region was, so we were told at the time, the 11.00am train from Reading to Exeter via Westbury. It was abolished at the end of 1975. The Beeching concept of the 'liner' train was well established and earning

The wreck of the 9.2 p.m Acton-Cardiff, 'C' headcode vacuum goods, a mile west of Uffington. An overheated axle bearing destroyed the axle and the wagon came down onto the track just after midnight on 7 January 1966. Single line working was put into force quickly and the wreckage was put down the bank by the cranes, the debris cleared, damaged track re-laid and opened with a speed restriction all within 24 hours.

The wreckage at he foot of the embankment could be removed on a Sunday within some other engineering occupation.
Author

money. Comparing 1973 with 1953, in round figures BR had 8,000 fewer miles of route, 10% less passenger miles, and 7% of the travel market against 15% in the relatively car-free days of 1953. Staff employed by BR in 1953 numbered 594,000; in 1973 there were 223,000. BR's gross income, at constant prices for 1993, was £6.4 billion in 1953 and £4.9 billion in 1973. (Gourvish, *British Rail 1974-97*, Table 1.1, p.5) Against this one could chart the increase in car and lorry use and the construction of great roads on which to run them. The revenue of the railway helped to keep down the amount of subsidy required from the taxpayer, but the roads and the road user were subsidised to a far greater extent.

As fast as BR improved its performance and reduced its costs, and came closer to meeting 'the bottom line', the economic and political situation in Britain – and in the Middle East, upon which territory we are totally dependent – deteriorated constantly, changing the economic situation and moving 'the bottom line' further away. It was very much like chasing a rainbow. The great economic theorists could do nothing about the Arab-Israeli War of 1973 or the resultant cessation of oil shipments from Arab countries, which raised the price of diesel sky-high, but everyone could castigate BR for 'not paying'.

But was BR 'not paying'? In the 1970s BR was 'breaking even taking one year with the next' before the money owed in interest to government was taken into account. How does the road system repay interest on the money spent on it? There is no organisational body for the roads from which cash can be demanded and which can be sniped at, ridiculed and pilloried by the media. Between 1971 and 1979 the total operating surplus before interest payments to government was £141 million. (*Gourvish, British Rail 1974-97*, p.22) In 1978 the Freightliner business returned 9.2% on the estimated capital employed, and the railway as a whole 6.1%. (*British Rail 1974-97*, p.42)

While the clever laymen were criticising the BRB, the latter was doing a great deal to improve the railway on its shoestring budget. Far higher quality was built for far less in the days of the integrated railway. In 1964 the superb 65ft 4 ¼ in Mk 2 coaches started to roll out of BR workshops on a new type of bogie. They had large windows with the seating coinciding with the windows – now there's a clever idea. They had decent-sized tables at the centre of each window, leg room and high ceilings. In four years 322 were built and all the while BR engineers were thinking how they could improve on them. In 1968 the air-conditioned Mk 2B design was ready and BRB asked permission from the Ministry of Transport to build 600. The Ministry was then under the control of Barbara Castle, the great shutter-down of railways. She was responsible for the refusal to sanction the expenditure as well as for the order that 600 Mk 1s should be refurbished to Mk 2B standard. BR engineers had to go to the expense of proving the obvious – that it would be cheaper to build the Mk 2Bs than rebuild stock dating back to 1951. But permission was still refused – there was, by implication, money for the more expensive rebuilding but not for the cheaper new stock. In February 1969 the new Minister of Transport, Richard Marsh, visited the BR Research Establishment in Derby, and was buttonholed by the engineers who had designed the new carriage. He agreed to release the money. (*British Railways Engineering*, ed. Roland Bond, p.285)

Marsh became Chairman of the BRB in 1971. In May 1972 yet another good thing was done by the BRB – Bristol Parkway station was opened, situated conveniently at the convergence of several motorways. Marsh asked the Ministry of Transport to put directions to the new station on all the motorway signs locally. The Ministry refused. There was a hiatus, then the Ministry complied and sent the bill to the BRB!

CHAPTER 5

Thatcherism and Sectorisation

The railway, solidly unified and under the management of railway professionals, was steadily improving its performance and maintaining the track in good order in spite of all the 'downward pressure' on the budget. Roger Ford, who started writing for *Modern Railways* magazine in 1976, stated in the August 2003 edition: 'I spent the first 17 years on this magazine writing about a railway going forward and improving. There was always some new project to write about.'

In May 1978, the then Secretary of State for Transport, William Rogers, asked the BRB to investigate the likely profit of the high-voltage electrification of the major routes of British Rail. This was part of a 'value for money' road and rail transport policy, announced in a White Paper of the previous year. To assist the members of the BRB a very senior civil servant from the Department of Transport, John Palmer, was appointed co-Chairman of the Board. Palmer was an ardent defender of taxpayers' money and was there to ensure that the BRB did not exaggerate the benefits of railway electrification. It has been reported to me by an unimpeachable source in the House of Lords (who unfortunately still does not wish to be named) that John Palmer was sent to the BRB to 'oversee the orderly run down of the railways'. Palmer commenced a study that carefully and in great detail over a period of 17 months came to the conclusion that if 52% of the existing routes were electrified the cost would be £500 million and operating savings would be £12 million a year at 1978 prices – £3 billion in today's money. It is always possible that the other 48% of routes that Palmer did not consider as suitable candidates for electrification would have been closed.

John Palmer's report stated that the annual rate of return on the investment would be 11%. Revenue was sure to increase with faster, more frequent electric trains. Electricity is generated using fuel in a more efficient way than by the

Railway work, being at all times a public service, requires a strong commitment to 'The Job'. That commitment was tested more rigorously in the days of the manual railway, when much of the work was a daily 'outward-bound course' for the men. This picture shows locomotives outside the 1871-built, nine-road, engine shed at Swindon in 1963. The building was considered unsafe and locomotives were not allowed inside.
Adrian Vaughan

Right: Inside Swindon shed engines have passed over the 'table and are 'heads to the wall' to throw some light on the front ends to assist fitters in their work of changing the rings on the piston valves.
Adrian Vaughan

Left: Chucking out the ashes from No 22 *Brading* at Ryde St John's shed in 1965.
Adrian Vaughan

millions of little engines burning fuel in road vehicles. Electric trains can also generate electricity using the 'regenerative braking' system. There would also be the saving to the national exchequer of the cost of 120 million gallons of oil, and that saving would be even more worthwhile should there be renewed crises in the price of oil, as happened in 1973. A great deal of British electricity at that time was produced with the UK's own coal, employing a UK workforce, and preventing, by providing, a great deal of our present social problems. Increased railway efficiency would save the taxpayers' money by taking more

car and lorry journeys off the road. This would reduce road accidents and thus ease the cost burden on emergency services and the NHS. The case for BR electrification was overwhelming – even the Man from the Ministry said so.

The economic conditions of Britain had continued to decline through successive Conservative and Labour governments. In 1977-78 severe cuts in public spending on Health and Education, by James Callaghan's Labour government led to the infamous 'Winter of Discontent' with strikes by coal miners, grave diggers and rubbish collectors, the upshot of which was, in the General Election of 1979, to bring in a Conservative government under Margaret Thatcher. 'Out of the frying pan and into the fire.'

In May 1979 a General Election during a time of ridiculously unruly trade union upheavals in Britain brought Margaret Thatcher to power as Prime Minister. Hers would be a ferociously one-sided government. Her declared aim was to 'roll back the boundaries of the state', and permit what she called 'market forces' to rule the life of the country. She succeeded in restoring to late-20th-century Britain the economics of Adam Smith, the 18th-century Scottish philosopher and economist who died before the Industrial Revolution began. He originated the idea that true freedom and wealth could only come

The railway was always able to deal quickly with any sort of upset because it had plenty of engineering staff and the correct tools for the job. They were not encumbered with fussy regulations or police crime scenes, but could freely get on with the job to the full extent of their skill. On Saturday, 14 November 1925, near Hayward's Heath station, the engine hauling the 9.40am Worthing-Victoria train had its trailing driving wheel axle shear off, dropping the wheel flat on the ground. The Brighton breakdown gang – a proper team of locomotive fitters, just like a fire brigade – set out within 30 minutes of being called. Meanwhile the carriages were drawn back into the station, 'Gladstone' class 0-4-2 tank No 299 New Cross was attached, and the passengers were soon London-bound.
W. L. Kenning/Adrian Vaughan Collection

In September 1963 the driver of No 6800 *Arlington Grange* on the 9.02pm Acton to Newport (Monmouthshire) fully fitted vacuum goods, running on the 3-mile-long Down Goods Loop from Didcot to Steventon, saw the green lights on the Down Main, took them for his own and put on steam. He ran out of track at the end of the loop at just on midnight. The cranes were called out, Single Line Working was instituted, delays were minimal, and no passengers were taken out of their sleeping berths or carriage seats. The engine was lifted back on the rails and ran 'light' to Swindon for examination and the line was cleared by noon that day. *H. O. Vaughan*

through a system of trade without taxation on goods, home-made or imported – and a freedom for everyone to follow their own self-interest in business. The 18th-century economics system introduced an 18th-century effect into 20th-century industrial society – huge extremes of wealth and poverty.

Mrs Thatcher loathed all nationalised industries on principle. They were 'socialist'. Railways in particular incurred her extreme dislike. Railways are naturally socialistic – they work best as top-down, centralised organisations – even in the days of the old companies. People wishing to travel by train must congregate in one place at a pre-arranged time. Trains are communal. She believed in 'individual choice'. It was a narrow choice, championing the individualism of the motor car: choose your own décor, choose who you travel with, and when you would travel. Choose your own traffic jam.

She believed in 'them and us'. When her Chancellor of the Exchequer, Geoffrey Howe, in his intended 1980 budget, saw the need to increase by 20% the taxable value of a company car, she overruled him. 'It is wrong to treat *our own* people so harshly.' In 1987 the Tory manifesto revealed the Community Charge or 'Poll Tax'. This was to let her sort of person off the hook of local rates. Local services would be funded by a fixed tax to be paid irrespective of the taxed person's income. So, in effect, the poor paid more than the rich. And there was no choice. Howe objected in Cabinet and was screamed at by

Thatcher. John Biffen, a Tory right-winger and Leader of the House of Commons, defended Howe, and he too was screamed at. 'I will not be screamed at by that woman,' he said a little later. (Lord Biffen's obituary, *Guardian*, 15.8.07)

In May 1969, when she was Shadow Transport Minister, Mrs Thatcher was invited to visit the Railway Staff College at Woking while a course was taking place. The Chairman of the BRB, Henry (later Sir Henry) Johnson, was present, together with James Urquhart, Assistant General Manager of the Eastern Region, and Leslie Lloyd, General Manager of the Western Region. Some agenda questions had been chalked on a blackboard in the hope that the railwaymen and Mrs Thatcher might have a discussion. Apparently Mrs Thatcher took one look at the blackboard, turned on them in her strident, hectoring voice and said, 'You people can't think on your feet. You can't work out what you want.' She was so bad-tempered that she later had to apologise.

In October 1977 she told Sir Peter Parker, then Chairman of the BRB, that 'to be nationalised was an admission of failure.' (See Gourvish, *British Rail 1974-97*, p101 and enlightening notes on p.547) Her policy of '*de-regulating*' the money lending market has led to the said market asking for public assistance which is, by her definition, an admission of the failure of her policies.

Mrs Thatcher's deep dislike of anything that looked to her like 'socialism' was instinctively lower-middle-class shopkeeper. But it was reinforced by Alfred, later Sir Alfred, Sherman. Sherman had been born into an East End of London family in 1919. The squalid poverty of his upbringing propelled him to membership of the British Communist Party, where he studied and eagerly accepted the economic theories of Karl Marx. He was of a brave, or even fanatical, disposition. He risked his life for his ideals and fought for the Republican government of Spain against the fascist rebellion of General Franco. During World War 2 he was sent by the British Government to the Balkans to assist the Serbian/Yugoslav partisans against the Nazis. The Serbs were such devotedly brave fighters that Sherman developed a lifelong admiration for them and their leader, Marshal Tito. In 1948 Sherman was expelled from the Communist Party for expressing sympathy with the defiance of Stalin by Marshal Tito, then Prime Minister of Yugoslavia, completely disillusioned with the Communist denial of free speech and freedom of thought. One would have thought that Sherman would have noticed this trait years earlier. He then abandoned the economic theories of Karl Marx and went to the London School of Economics to study and earn a degree in the free market, non-interventionist, and economic theories of the time.

In 1974 Sherman founded the Centre for Policy Studies (CPS) with his kindred spirit Sir Keith Joseph. Sherman was Thatcher's mentor at that time and groomed her for the office of Prime Minister. He was her personal adviser and wrote many of her speeches. He seriously advocated turning all railways into roads.

In 1980 Alfred Sherman wrote a pamphlet in which he demanded a 'Minister for Denationalisation'. This Minister would 'dismantle the vast, parasitic, apparatus of nationalised corporations whose exactions can destroy all hope of recovery and the freedom and rights which depend on its early achievements.' At a press launch of the pamphlet Sherman is reported as saying, 'British Rail is sucking the nation's economic blood. Denationalisation would see the end of most rail traffic in Britain. The demise of BR is a natural, evolutionary, development because railways are an anachronism today.'

In 1979 railway investment was 0.63% of Gross National Product – hardly parasitic. A severe antipathy towards railways was not the exclusive preserve of the right-wing. Professor Frank Blackaby, a leading protagonist for unilateral nuclear disarmament, wrote a book – *British Economic Policy 1960-1974* – in which he referred to British Rail contemptuously – and inaccurately – as 'part of the soft morass of subsidised incompetence'.

Sherman's free-market fanaticism became an embarrassment even to Thatcher. He was sacked from the CPS in 1984. But nevertheless he had encouraged Margaret

The 1850 station at Oxford was rebuilt during 1972. The first stage was to raise a footbridge to replace the closed subway. The crane did the job in about 20 minutes, starting at 3.00am. No trains about, so no delay.
Adrian Vaughan

Thatcher to take the course she was now set upon, and she gave her fanatical friend a consolation knighthood in 1983. In 1984 Sherman gave an interview to *Pravda* in which he was quoted as saying: 'As for the lumpen, the coloured people and the Irish, let's face it, the only way to hold them in check is to have enough well-armed and properly trained police.' During the uproar that followed, Sherman merely complained that the quotation missed the word 'proletariat' after 'lumpen', and denied using the phrase 'well-armed'. Sherman was still well enough liked by Margaret Thatcher for her to attend the launch of his memoirs in 2005 – for which Lord Tebbit had written a Foreword. It seems unlikely that she had read the book. It contains the sentence, 'Lady Thatcher is great theatre as long as someone else is writing her lines; she hasn't got a clue.' (Sherman's obituary, *Daily Telegraph*, 28.8.06)

With this rabid, anti-public-services attitude, the Thatcher Government spelled bad news for the BRB. Between 1979 and 1990 government expenditure on transport fell 5.8% (Annual Register 1990) and even in the only boom years of the Thatcher Government – 1986-89 – transport spending was reduced. This was because tax reductions were part of Thatcher's dogma and more important to her than improving public services. To adapt a phrase, 'Why do they not drive cars?' Traffic on Britain's roads increased by one-third between 1980 and 1990, and rail freight declined.

The BRB was in receipt of an annual 'Public Service Obligation' (PSO) grant instituted in 1974 by a Labour Government. This was paid on unremunerative – but desirable – passenger services. The total PSO grant received in 1975 by the BRB from central and local government was £324.1 million. This constituted 43% of the BRB's total passenger income. By 1979 the purchasing power of money had been so reduced that the equivalent purchasing power of £324 million was £543.8 million. In 1979 the BRB's PSO grant was £522.5 million, which represented 40% of income. Inflation was more severe in the 1980s. To equal the purchasing power of the 1979 PSO in 1990 required £1.119 billion. In 1989-90 the PSO actually received by the BRB was the £586 million, which was only 25% of the BRB's income. (These figures are from BRB accounts given in Mike Anson's Appendices to Gourvish, Vol 2.)

Sir Peter Parker said in December 1980, 'If investment in railways is to be confined to existing levels, then by 1990 3,000 miles out of the 11,000 will be unusable. And more will be in a bad state and the worse the track gets the greater the cost of repairing it.' The 1979 Annual Report of the Chief Inspecting Officer of Railways, Lt Col McNaughton (*Modern Railways*, February 1981) had also drawn attention to the threat to safety by deferring the renewal of track. The Treasury's response was, as ever, to

Relaying track took place somewhere every weekend. With a gang of maybe 30 men and the assistance of a crane, half a mile could be lifted and re-laid between 10.00pm on Saturday and 4.00 or 5.00pm on Sunday, while trains continued to run on the temporary single track. Before the crane was used, workmen liaised with the signalmen. This photograph was taken at Uffington, Berkshire, in 1961. *Adrian Vaughan*

expect the railways to save money and the PSO was ordered to be reduced by 25% over the four years to 1986.

The only way for BR to save itself for the nation was to control maintenance and operating costs more rigorously, to lay off more staff and to earn greater revenue when the national economy improved. In 1981 the BRB closed the, by then, freight-only electrified line between Manchester and Sheffield through the Woodhead Tunnel. The tunnel route was expensive to maintain, although it was very useful as a diversionary route when the Hope Valley line between the two cities was blocked. The BRB's Estate Department sold as much land and buildings as possible to raise money. The original Brunellian terminus at Bristol might have been demolished if a member of the Estate Office staff had not 'leaked' the intention to Tony Benn, then MP for Bristol South-east. During the 1980s all the BRB's subsidiary businesses – from Advertising, to Ferries, to Hotels, to Horwich Works and the Vale of Rheidol Railway – were privatised and the proceeds of these sales helped to keep the actual railway business running. The gross receipts from these never-to-be-repeated sales were £1,390.5 million. Consultants' fees, sales commissions and legal fees – never forget the private enterprise of such as Coopers & Lybrand –- took £310.5 million, leaving £1,080 million for the BRB. Competition is apparently unnecessary in the world of financial consultants and

A gang of men is less likely to break down than a machine, and with men doing the work the job stands a better chance of being finished on time. Here a gang of men armed with nothing more mechanical than crowbars – and working in unison – make short work of levering into place an entire junction that has been assembled at the lineside during the week. The entire re-laying could be done during a Sunday. This picture was taken at Slough in the 1930s. *GWR/Adrian Vaughan Collection*

accountants. Coopers & Lybrand was formed in 1957 from the amalgamation of one Canadian and three British accountancy companies. In 1998 Price Waterhouse joined to produce a monolithic financial consultancy and IT company, with the only other major players being KPMG, Ernst & Young, Deloitte and Arthur Andersen, accountancy companies became practically immune from competition. These great companies saw the advantages of 'economy of scale' which was exactly the opposite of what was being done to the railway.

A new system of management of the railways was considered necessary if income was not to be swallowed by expenditure. From December 1977 the idea of Sectorisation was contemplated – to reorganise BR along 'business-led' principles. The British Rail Board took the advice of such accountancy/consulting companies as Coopers & Lybrand and Price Waterhouse in the matter. At Coopers & Lybrand was the economist Sir Christopher

Left: When the new track was in place the ballast train was brought in. Sometimes the rearmost vehicle was a 'plough van', a guard's brake specially adapted for working ballast trains. The wagons dumped the stones and the guard in the van lowered the plough and levelled the pile to some extent. This photograph was taken at Bruton on 24 April 1975. *Adrian Vaughan*

Below: The permanent way men finish off the levelling at Bruton. *Adrian Vaughan*

Foster. He was a leading figure in the Royal Automobile Club and had given all governments since 1965 advice on how to run railways. He had also approved of Margaret Thatcher's very peculiar and unfair Community Charge, otherwise known as the 'Poll Tax'. Mrs Thatcher refused to acknowledge the existence of 'Society' but the word 'Community' has a cosy ring to it – so it served in this case.

In 1981 the plan was matured. Government insisted that the Sectorised railways produce – by 1985 – a 5% return on the value of the assets employed, irrespective of how well the economists were managing the national economy. It was an odd, hybrid system. There were to be five Sectors: InterCity, Provincial, London and South Eastern, Freight, and Parcels. Each of these would have a Sector Director and each Sector would be subdivided into several businesses operating particular routes. The primary purpose behind it was to make the Sectors keenly aware of the detail of running costs and overheads, to reduce costs and thus retain more of the revenue earned and take less subsidy from the taxpayer. This would remove government objection to the railway and so make its future secure.

These Sectorised trains ran over routes managed by the Regional General Manager (RGM), who still controlled safety matters and the operating, locomotive and engineering staff, but the Sector Directors controlled the Regional budget. The prime-user Sector paid for the upkeep of the track and signalling and the other Sectors that might run over those tracks got a free ride. The Freight Sector was thus able to use the routes of all three passenger Sectors, and unless there were some costs that were specifically attributable to Freight, the latter – throughout the 1980s – went toll-free. Thus Freight was heavily subsidised by the three passenger Sectors and by InterCity in particular.

Regional General Managers could and did overrule Sector Directors on safety matters, yet they were subordinated to the Sector Directors where the business side and the spending of money on infrastructure was concerned. It is easy to imagine the discussions that took place – especially when a Sector Director was impatient with the engineering standards that the more cautious RGMs and chief engineers were attempting to maintain. There was a divide between the modernisers and some senior Regional officers. Not just because their jobs were being abolished but because they saw that this partial fragmentation would destroy the strong, clear, chain of command that was essential to maintain a safe railway. Maurice Holmes, BR Director of Operations, Leslie Soane, General Manager Scottish Region, Leslie Lloyd, Western, Frank Patterson, Eastern, and Peter Rayner, LMR Regional Operations Manager, and several other high-ranking railwaymen were sceptical of the divided system. They were a thorn in the side of the railway modernisers but gradually they disappeared from the scene – retired, died, sent on sabbaticals – or were removed for standing up for the old values.

But the problem was how to keep the railways open when they were under attack from people in supreme power that saw them as an expensive Victorian survival that should be abolished as soon as possible. The least used lines in the country were of course the most under threat – and the most loved by everyone – including the thousands who never used them. These were placed into Sector Provincial Railway in 1983 under the overall Directorship of Sid Newey. Newey had started at Oswestry as a management trainee, loading reluctant goats into passenger train brake vans, in 1962.

Through its sub-sectors, Provincial operated from the North of Scotland to Cornwall, from Aberystwyth to Yarmouth. It consisted of lightly used branch lines, urban commuter lines similar to Network SouthEast, and cross-country lines similar to InterCity. Total revenue from these residual railways covered only 25% of the operating costs and 46% of outgoings were due to signalling and engineering. Newey's overriding priority was to reduce maintenance and infrastructure costs in order to reduce his requirement for subsidy, then to increase traffic. Fare rises, advertising and clever ticketing arrangements can only do so much. All railways are most influenced by the general economic state of the country and by the increasing congestion of roads – brought on by the peculiar policy of expecting roads to carry all traffic. The demand for Provincial Trains services increased through the 1980s as the general economic well-being of the country improved, together with increasing traffic jams on the roads. In 1984 Provincial had a 2% increase in passengers compared with 1983 and 3 to 3.6% a year until 1989. Increased revenue and reduced overhead costs reduced Provincial's requirement for public money. This enviable state of affairs was brought about by very careful management of a vertically integrated, non-contracted-out railway. And, it has to be said, by an 'a maintenance holiday' for a time on the tracks. In late 1989 a severe recession developed, following the 1988 stock market crash in the USA, and in 1990 inflation was at 10%. Unsurprisingly, the revenue of Provincial Railways fell and its subsidy required to be increased. (Monopolies & Mergers Commission Report, April 1988, Ch 10.1)

All Sectors bore down heavily on maintenance *and* made technical staff – permanent way and Signal & Telecommunications – redundant if that was at all possible. One money-saving idea was to replace the conventional double-track junction with a facing crossover from main to main then, after a short distance, a single facing point onto the branch, which then divided back to double line. This reduced some of the complexity in the junction track components but produced a situation where, for example, an Up train ran on the Down line, head-on to down trains, for a certain distance. Mr Ivor Warburton, Director of Operations, BRB, and Mr Knox, Signalling and Safety Officer, ScotRail, both said that this formation was no more dangerous than the conventional junction, which did not produce this risk. In quick succession three head-on crashes resulted from single-lead junctions, then no more: Bellgrove in 1989, Hyde Junction in 1990 and Newton in

1991. (See Department of Transport Report into Bellgrove Collision. Publ 1990, page 10.)

In 1983 Driver Only Operation (DOO) and 'flexible rostering' of train drivers was proposed by the BRB to reduce costs and increase productivity. This caused ASLEF to go on strike. The strike lost the BRB an estimated £175 million of revenue and did not achieve ASLEF's purpose. After the strike the introduction of DOO proceeded, although more slowly than management had hoped. The Government, smarting from the show of worker power, now ordered a 'Review of Railway Finances'. From the resulting review, this seems to have been coded language for 'How can we close down the railway and break the union?'.

The survey was undertaken by a civil servant, David (later Sir David) Serpell, a *Permanent* Secretary (no redundancy for him) at the Department for Transport. Co-authors with Serpell were Leslie Bond and James Butler, with a minority report by Alfred Goldstein. Bond was a Director of the Rank Organisation and formerly of Trust House Forte, Butler was Senior Partner in Peat Marwick, accountants to the Treasury, and Goldstein was Senior Partner of Consulting Engineers Travers Morgan. Their brief was to 'examine the finances of the railway and to report on options for alternative policies … designed to secure improved financial results in an *efficiently* run railway over the next 20 years.' (Gourvish 2. p161-162.) In the event he only looked forward 10 years, but in the ensuing uproar over his findings everyone was glad he had not looked 20 years into the future. With research done by Goldstein's company, Travers Morgan, the reviewers advocated five options for the railways. Option A – which would require no subsidy from taxpayers – was a rail network of 1,630 miles, which would charge higher fares and which, according to the far-seeing reviewers, would make a profit of £34 million by 1992. It would have consisted of the East Coast Main Line terminating in Newcastle, with a branch to Leeds; the West Coast route to Birmingham, Edinburgh and Glasgow, with branch lines to Liverpool and Manchester; Paddington to South Wales with a branch line to Bristol from Stoke Gifford; London to Norwich; London to Bournemouth; and a very few routes in the South East. How *efficient* would this network be for the people of Weymouth or Plymouth or Oxford or Cambridge? But the new capitalists were/are not concerned with service to the population – only with making a profit – but for whom?

At the time of the review the BRB was buying from the private sector 50% of the components required for its trains and locomotives. This, said the review, led to difficulties in designed compatibility and delivery. There were also the contractual complexities inherent in employing outsiders – negotiations to be conducted, penalties to be paid, litigations to be undertaken.

The highly standardised railway companies and their coal-fired successors never had to worry about compatibility of parts or contractors or of suing anyone for not doing what they said they would do because the companies, and later BR, did it all themselves. But in 1983 the facilities that allowed them this efficient standardisation were being run down as 'unprofitable' and 'inefficient' on the advice of the same kind of economist/accountant as those in the Serpell group. Back in the 1960s, when BR workshops had wanted to make containers for 'liner' trains, the private enterprise dogmatists – in the Tory Party – had refused to allow it.

Serpell normally approved of everyone buying from the private sector, but in view of the serious disadvantages of non-standardisation on railways and the split responsibility inherent in contracting out, even he abandoned the sacred principle of 'competition' and urged close co-operation between parties! So why not leave it as a unified 'BR'?

It is entertaining to witness outsiders coming to 'sort out' the railway, full of their great knowledge of economics, only to find that the railway was a special case that did not answer their 'one size fits all' system for running the world.

The BRB wanted to electrify to Norwich and King's Lynn, part of the Palmer plan, but Serpell, in another paradoxical statement, said that such projects were 'high-risk investments born out of a misplaced optimism as to the rate of return'. All the best capitalists enter into 'high-risk' investment as a way of making greater profits, and the BRB had constantly been accused of not being 'entrepreneurial', but now here was Serpell advising BR not to follow best capitalist practice. Instead it was advised to invest in things that would save money – like installing more automated level crossings. These earn no cash at all, and in any case BR was doing this as fast as its limited resources would allow. If the BRB could not invest in electric trains and power signalling, there would never be any increase in income or reduction in costs.

Goldstein's report laid emphasis on the lack of knowledge of 'where the railway wanted to go'. This was a favourite cliché from ignorant outsiders contracted to sort out the railway's problems. It is quite remarkable how many investigating economists and part-time members of the Board said they did not to know the direction in which BR was going. Was this because they did not understand what a railway was for? What they did all agree on was that 'BR is a very large consumer of taxpayers' resources and the amount has grown *greatly* over the last decade. To what degree this consumption should continue into the long term is the crucial issue to be decided.' (Serpell Report) In fact, the railway was receiving less subsidy – in real terms – than 10 years earlier.

Ian Campbell, an unusual part-time member of the BRB in that he was a career railwayman, said of the Report: 'The team demonstrated in part a complete ignorance of the most elementary fundamentals and in part a knowledge derived from minor, overseas railways operating in completely different circumstances.' The BRB Response to the Serpell Review said it was "confused, not coherent, disappointing, inaccurate, implausible and

Above: The track was regularly checked for deterioration of quality using a coach carrying detecting equipment, hauled at high speed. Here No 7025 *Sudeley Castle* waits for the 'off' at Cardiff with a six-coach high-speed special to Swindon in April 1963. I rode in the test coach and saw that we achieved 97mph at Hullavington and would have reached 100 but for a 5mph restriction over a bridge under repair. *Adrian Vaughan*

Below: The Western Region used the GWR track testing coach, W139, a 1906 Churchward 'Toplight' carriage with the detecting instruments inside. It is seen here at Swindon at the end of the run in April 1963. *Adrian Vaughan*

misleading".' (Minutes of BR Council, 18 January 1984, *The Times*, 21.1.83)

Serpell's Review cost the taxpayers £627,000 – a grand example of private enterprise. And the BRB was being told by these people to reduce its overheads!

The Government claimed that reducing the amount of financial support had helped the railway move towards profitability. Logically then, all subsidy should have been withdrawn and the railway would have become a goldmine. There was a feeling amongst the Sector Directors that the railway had been for decades 'over-maintained', there was plenty of 'fat' to be removed. Staff numbers were cut by 30%. The locomotive fleet was reduced by 49% – although some new locos were purchased, and the number of carriages was reduced by 36%, though some new carriages were purchased, the total number of seats fell by 21%, which must have had an overcrowding effect.

Another remarkable vehicle was the 'slip coach'. This was a gung-ho bit of railway work going back to the 1850s. The coach was detached, usually at high speed, from the rear of the train to serve at the station at which the main train did not stop. Many companies used them but the practice declined from 1914. The GWR kept the practice going quite enthusiastically after that war and the Western Region continued to use slip coaches, although at a declining rate, until, on 15 September 1960, the very last coach was slipped. This was off the 5.10pm Paddington-Birmingham express at Bicester. The 'slip guard' became the driver of the 70mph coach after he had detached it and here we see the coach free-wheeling to a stand, under the action of the guard's vacuum brake, at Bicester. The engine of the local train then went out onto the Down Main and collected the coach. *Mike Mensing*

In December 1984 a BR press release stated that InterCity (IC) had made £47 million profit that year, of which £31 million was due to cost-cutting and the rest due to increased revenue. Very roughly, one-third of the profit was due to reductions in staff and maintenance. (BR press release quoted in Note 163, Gourvish Vol 2, p.558) New ticketing policies such as 'Capital Card' and 'Network Card' helped to increase the use of the trains in the period from 1986, when there was national economic growth and relative prosperity. In 1988/89 InterCity – directed by John Prideaux from 1986 to 1992 – made £57 million profit and took no subsidy from the taxpayer. The extent to which the railway's profit depends on national economic activity can be seen in the fact that in 1991/92, during the second recession of the Thatcherite period, InterCity made only £2 million profit but took no subsidy. The Railfreight and Parcels Sectors also took no public money at that time (1986-89). In 1982 London & South East (NSE) was judged to have lost £310 million carrying out its vital function of getting London's working population to work each day. In 1989 that loss was a mere £98 million. But if NSE had been closed as a result of its losses, what would have been the cost to London in general? So how does one judge 'profit'? The Provincial Sector lost £489 million in 1982 and £509 million in 1989. Given the depreciation in the value of money over those seven years, this might actually represent a slight improvement. The Public Service Obligation grant for Network SouthEast and Provincial lines was 45% of income in 1983, and by 1989 it was 25%. This was due in part to rising prosperity nationally but also to the new managers' success as businessmen cutting costs and sweating the assets.

The skill of BRB management and engineers was shown in the electrification of the East Coast Main Line and the extension of electrification from Colchester to Norwich, both on time and within budget. The electrification of the East Coast Main Line was a particularly great feat of engineering and management of the vertically integrated railway. The Thatcher Government did, with evident reluctance, lend the BRB taxpayers' money to supply the taxpayers with a superbly improved railway. The BRB also used its own revenue and borrowed from banks to buy the rolling stock and erect the overhead catenary. The reluctance is evident in the grudging budget that the Treasury allowed. Lack of quite enough funds obliged the BR engineer, Don Heath, to space the catenary support masts more widely than he would have liked, thus producing an 'Achilles heel' in the power supply: there have been several occasions when high winds have brought down the wires. For an increase of 15% in the budget a stronger, and therefore cheaper, catenary could have been erected.

The BR men completed the work from King's Cross to Leeds in 1988 and to Edinburgh in 1990, for a fraction of the cost that the same work would cost today – prices being equal. During the construction trains could use diversionary routes, which would be very difficult or impossible under the privatised system of franchising. The BRB's costs were not inflated by the obligation to pay compensation to a train operating company for delays occasioned as a result of the works of improvement. It seems very unfair that Network Rail should be obliged to compensate a train operating company because of delays to its trains caused by works to improve the track. There was another cost advantage that the BRB enjoyed in 1985 – the Health & Safety Executive had not yet realised the full extent to which they could persecute the railway. On four-track sections, Up and Down trains could use one pair of tracks while the workmen could be working on the other two, well out of harm's way.

In spite of the unpleasant aspect of cost-cutting, the likelihood of being killed during a train journey steadily declined. In the period 1974-77 there was 0.98 of a significant train accident for every million train miles. In 1988-90 there was 0.61 of a train accident per million train miles. Deaths to passengers and staff due to rail accidents were:

1979	13
1980	3
1981	5
1982	6
1983	2
1984	7
1985	0
1986	2
1987	4
1988	36

The total number of road deaths in the United Kingdom in 1987 was 5,300, while casualties amounted to 315,700.

There were two train crashes in 1988: a derailment at St Helens on 11 November where one person was killed, and the Clapham disaster on 12 December, where 35 were killed. The latter triple collision took place during the 'Waterloo Area Resignalling Scheme', when the absolutely worn-out electric signalling, with its thousands of miles of wiring and its thousands of electric relays dating back to 1936, was finally being renewed. The new equipment was being wired up preparatory to removing the old installations when the accident happened. (See my *Tracks to Disaster*)

Mr Anthony Hidden QC was commissioned to investigate the causes and make a report and recommendations. He stated that the deaths were the result of a wiring error by S&T technician Mr Hemingway, but, he wrote, 'Hemingway had one sole day off in 13 weeks. I find this to be totally unacceptable and to be conducive to the staleness and lack of concentration which has been manifested in the evidence. It was a practice which had been going on for years and was well known to management. It should not have been allowed and it was a contributory cause of the accident.' (Hidden Report, para 16.11) The London area S&T department was so short of men that seven technicians were drafted in from Eastleigh. (Hidden, 16.35) And while all available men were working on the new installation, who was carrying out the 'spider chasing' maintenance on the rest? Renewals deferred over decades to save money, and cost-cutting by getting rid of staff, had contributed to this awful smash.

The Secretary of State for Transport, Cecil Parkinson, challenged on this in Parliament by John Prescott and Peter Snape, absolutely denied the connection. Parkinson said:

'British Rail made it clear in its evidence to the inquiry that its spending on safety had never been constrained by the shortage of funds. The Hon Member consistently fails to understand that British Rail's revenue has increased more quickly than the grant has decreased. Therefore, the cash resources available to British Rail for investment have been growing. British Rail is pursuing the biggest investment programme for 25 years.' (Hansard, Vol 159, col 838, 7.11.89)

But clearly *not* in replacing the decayed wiring at Waterloo years earlier or by allowing the numbers of its skilled technicians to decline. Parkinson blamed the railway trade union for the lack of technicians:

'The Hon Gentleman keeps on talking about management's contribution. Management does not shirk its responsibility, but I draw his attention to at least two occasions in the report when the unions' attitude is quoted by Sir Anthony. He says that unless the unions start to adopt a more flexible attitude and to negotiate more carefully with management, British Rail will continue to be short of the skilled staff that it needs. In other words, co-operation is needed between management and unions.'

So it was the union that had been making its members redundant.

To Peter Snape, Cecil Parkinson said: Investment in safety … is not required to produce any sort of return: safety is justified as safety. The idea that it has to pass a profit test is quite wrong.' (Hansard, Vol 159, col 835, 7.11.89) But the fact remained that between 1984 and 1988 the BRB felt obliged to cut S&T staff by18%, on an already reduced establishment. In the same period Parkinson's Government had reduced the Government PSO grant support by 51%. The resultant laying off of the local permanent way gangs made track inspections less frequent and the linesides a jungle, scattering leaves on the lines in autumn to the detriment of adhesion between wheel and rail. Passengers waited in their trains while scarce S&T technicians drove miles to rectify a points failure, and train fleets were reduced to match the standard timetable with little or no spare capacity. The BRB was unable to pay sufficiently high wages to retain all the technical staff the job required. BR S&T men left for BT and were even found maintaining automatic barriers in NCP and local council car parks.

Sector managers and BRB members achieved Government targets in the reduction of subsidy required but were criticised by Government for achieving them with fare increases to avoid even greater cost-cutting. And as soon as those cost reductions were achieved, the Government ordered the BRB to make similar reductions over the next five years. Government apparently wanted a first-class railway, free of charge.

Or perhaps they just wanted it closed down.

The most perfect track laying was required where water troughs were laid. All done by skilled hand and eye, the track descended onto the trough on a gradient of 1 in 360 for 180 yards, giving a 6-inch fall. The track was then maintained on a water-perfect level for 500 to 700 yards, then rose off the trough at 1 in 360 for 180 yards. The trough ends rose up the slopes so that the extreme ends were 6 inches higher than the main level. The water in the trough was regulated at 5 inches deep so it would not spill out. This is a view of Basildon troughs, between Pangbourne and Goring, looking west from the farm lane overbridge.
Adrian Vaughan Collection

CHAPTER 6

'Organising for Quality'

As already mentioned, in 1980-83, under Sir Robert Reid as Chairman of BRB, the railway was reorganised into Sectors running within and between Regions. The 'business-led' Sector Directors were very good managers but were exceedingly cost-conscious because they were under constant pressure from reductions in government support. The business-led side thought the engineers were spending too much – they were overdoing the maintenance. The railway became more cost-effective, although it might be said that the cost-cutting process ran down the quality of the track, and the number of skilled staff was a contributory cause of the Clapham disaster. Track maintenance and renewal cost a lot, so cutting back in that area saved a lot. As a result there were times, by 1990, when miles of trunk line nationwide were scattered with temporary speed restrictions – at one stage almost the entire route from Plymouth to Penzance was littered with them, when the engineers became nervous of the state of their track.

During the same period the Thatcherites – but not Margaret Thatcher – were wondering how best to privatise the system. Margaret Thatcher 'disliked trains and avoided travelling in them. She regarded them as a dirty and inefficient corner of the public sector and was shrewd enough as a politician to rest happily on her other privatisation laurels. Her instinct was that a railway sell-off

No D814 *Dragon* coasts towards the Up Main platform at Reading in 1959. Reading Main Line West signal box, seen in the background, had levers numbered to 222. The gantry outside the box has signal arms routing as follows, from left to right: to Up Bays 1, 2 or 3 (indication of platform given by route indicator); Down Main to Berks & Hants line; Down Main to Engine Shed; Down Main; Down Main to Down Relief Line; Up Main; Up Main to Up Platform. A signal below the gantry is lowered for a Down train out of one of the bay platforms to the B&H line. On the right, the four-'doll' bracket signal reads: Down Relief Line to B&H line; to Down Main; to Down Relief; to Down Goods. *John Ashman/Adrian Vaughan Collection*

Reading Main Line West's Up B&H line Home signals, seen here in 1956, routed as follows: to Up Relief Line; to No 7 Bay (with a 10mph speed reminder); to Up Main; to Bays 1, 2 or 3. Below are two 'slipping Distants' to reassure the driver and slip guard that the road is clear through the station. The slip could not be detached if the train did not have a clear road through. On the left is the Shed Exit signal, a GWR ringed arm with a route indicator. On the right is a GWR Backing signal and route indicator for reversing Up the Down line into the station. *Peter Barlow/ Adrian Vaughan Collection*

would be politically very unpopular – and tremendously difficult to carry out.' (Simon Jenkins quoted in *Margaret Thatcher* by John Campbell, p.239) She is reported as saying that 'the sale of the railways would be the Waterloo of this government'. (Quoted in *All Change: British Railway Privatisation*, ed. Freeman, p.11)

But of course that did not make her a protector of the railways. Norman Fowler, Secretary of State for Transport during 1981, had written in 1978 that 'Conservatives reject the idea that transport ought to be regarded as a social service to which the taxpayer should be forced to contribute huge and continuing subsidies … the best way to ensure the public interest is to promote competition between the providers and free choice between the users.' (Norman Fowler, *The Right Track*, 1978) I wonder what he thinks of the 'huge and continuing' subsidies that go to his 'privately-owned' railways since privatisation. Nicholas Ridley had been since at least 1955 a fundamentalist believer in the efficiency of free enterprise for every aspect of the nation's life. He was at the Treasury between 1981 and 1993 and Secretary of State for Transport from 1983 to 1987, followed by Environment. It is reported that he advised Mrs Thatcher against selling the railway, but this too was because he could not see who would buy it in its then unprofitable state, as well as knowing that such a proposal would be deeply unpopular with the electorate.

In 1984, Malcolm Gylee, an economist at the Adam Smith Institute, proposed a state-owned track authority to sell 'paths' to privately owned train operating companies working as short-term franchisees. (Gourvish, Vol 2, p.368) David Starkie, also published by the Institute, went a stage further and proposed that the track authority be

privately owned. The idea of separating track and trains probably dates back to this paper.

Keith Irvine, who had once been a BR management trainee, had written *The Right Line*, published by the Adam Smith Institute in 1986. He revised this as *Track to the Future*, published by the Institute in 1988. Irvine wrote: '…the central theme to privatisation is that private firms perform better than their public sector counterparts. Privatisation makes the best use of naked self-interest. In the private sector, one improves one's lot by satisfying the needs of the customer otherwise the competition will step in and bankruptcy or take-over will result.' What relevance that had to British Railways is difficult to see, except that young Mr Irvine was playing to the gallery and hoping for a medal. 'Naked self-interest' is the opposite of what is required to run a public service. The railway was satisfying its 'customers' to the best of its ability on a very restricted income and was doing a good job of it. No-one else could 'step in' and do a better job under the same restrictions.

The enthusiasm of the people advocating a free-for-all on rail was inflamed by the ruthlessness displayed by some individuals after the deregulation of bus services in October 1986. This policy was energetically advocated by Professor John Hibbs, among others. It was to bring about competition where before there had been a calm determination to provide a public service. 'Capitalism is based on greed,' said Brian Souter, founder of Stagecoach. He destroyed competition with methods that the Monopolies & Mergers Commission described as 'predatory, deplorable and against the public interest'. But he was only employing normal bus company tactics and nothing he did was illegal – which is an interesting commentary on the morals of free-market economics.

The outcome was that soon there were just a few large operators nationally and a few local bus operators, rather as there had always been – and Souter owned a large part.

The assertions made by the privatisers seem to me to be no different, in general principle, from the assertions of Karl Marx – neither took any account of human nature. 'If only people were to do A, B and C, D would happen and that would be wonderful.'

What competition did Brian Souter tolerate? What did Irvine think BR had been doing if not carrying people from A to B? What else can trains do? Irvine wanted to keep a state-owned 'infrastructure company' to be responsible for the track and signalling, but he also wanted to 'abolish the monopoly of BR's civil, mechanical and electrical engineers' by making the 'in-house' departments compete with outside firms. Abolishing a *monopoly* was more important to these dogmatists than preserving skill, knowledge and experience.

Brunel – the doyen of the free-marketeers – had used

In this picture of the Didcot end of Reading Main Line West signal box, Ken Morton is nearest the camera, Inspector Tom Rixon in the centre and Ted Blackall at the far end. I can't recall the middle signalman's name. The Lad Telegraphist, a species of genius, aged 16, who recorded every bell code received or sent – several per minute – and dealt with all the telephone work, sits in his cubicle. *Adrian Vaughan Collection*

contractors to maintain the track on the early GWR. Usually, the contractor who built a section of line took over its maintenance. Brunel found out that contractors quoted a 'competitive' price for the job, won the contract, then had to make a profit out of their underestimated – i.e. competitive – budget. The last GWR track maintenance contractor to be dismissed by Brunel was Brotherhood of Chippenham, in 1850. Brunel saw that the quality of 'in-house' work could be better controlled with less administrative cost.

Irvine wanted to sell off the Sectors as train operating companies, which would then buy 'paths' from a track authority. This would create a gulf between the wheels and the rails, and the legislation necessary for this fragmented sell-off, he wrote, 'would be simple'. Irvine wrote that the 'established demand patterns would remain, keeping customers happy'. So the BR train services had been keeping passengers happy all along!

Irvine and Starkie, and Foster and Robson at the treasury, were excited by the so-called 'privatisation' of Japanese Railways on 1 April 1987. The Japanese called what they did to their railways 'restructuring'. Mr Suga, Deputy Director of Japanese Railways, said that 'there was a general consensus in Japan that the railway is an *integral whole*. To achieve high speeds and a better ride you have to improve the operational and the infrastructure side of railways.

It would be very, very difficult to separate infrastructure and operations.' (Quoted in Second Report of Parliamentary Committee on the Future of Railways in the light of the Government's White Paper proposals, HC 246-1)

The Japanese restructuring was successful because that government did not do what Starkie, Irvine, Foster and Robson urged. The President of Japan Central Railway, Yoshiyuki Kasai, published a book in 2000 about the Japanese process. It was translated into English and it was then that the word 'restructuring' was replaced with 'privatisation'. The President wrote:

'The UK Government spent substantial sums on subsidising train operating companies but because of vertical separation there was no guarantee that an adequate share of those funds would be invested in the infrastructure. In order to use public money effectively it is critical to have a vertically integrated railway.' (*Japanese National Railways. Its break-up and privatisation*, p.194)

Somehow this was missed by our economic dogmatists.

The London Stock Exchange and all the City of London financial institutions were 'deregulated' in October 1986. All the different financial houses, banks and stockbrokers were now open to global competition and take-over. This was seen as a necessity for London because financial markets globally had been thrown open to unbridled competition. US money poured in as the vast money-lending power of America was used to purchase British financial organisations. Fortunes were made. What a wonderful thing competition is – a triumph for greed and avarice.

On 19 October 1987 the US stock market collapsed. The New York Stock Exchange lost $500 billion dollars of value in a day, a 22.6% fall and the greatest financial 'crash' of the 20th century, double the severity of the legendary 'Wall Street crash' of 1929. This triggered a worldwide recession and a loss of purchasing power of money, otherwise known as inflation. The British financial collapse took place in 1989.

Inflation following the failure of expert economists ideas, caused the BRB to increase the costs of, among others, season tickets on its InterCity routes in July 1988. A very small number of 'seasons' were increased by as much as 75%. These few instances created a media and political uproar along the lines of 'what else can be expected of such a dreadful thing as a state-owned industry?' The Wall Street crash, being an error of private enterprise, was exempt from blame and could not possibly have any bearing on the railway's problem. The brilliant Tory MP for Wyre, Keith Mans, a man who would certainly have wanted to reduce the BRB's subsidy, and disregarding any of the economic/competitive factors that were already beating down on BR, believed that *competition* on the rails was the only way to bring down fares (which would then increase the need for subsidy), and instigated a full-scale debate in the House of Commons. (Hansard, 28 July 1988, col 661)

The signal levers in all signal boxes were interlocked with each other to prevent incorrect movements, and the interlocking was usually effected by mechanical means. The first really successful compact system of interlocking, capable of development to work any complexity of layout, was the 'tappet' system, invented by Mr James Deakin, employed by Stevens & Son, and patented in 1870. There were other systems, designed to get around the Stevens patent, but eventually the tappet system became the standard. It was a mechanical computer – a logic machine. Here is a small section of one interlocking mechanism, underneath Minehead signal box on the West Somerset Railway. Each lever has a vertical steel blade attached to it, with 'ports' cut into it. Brass 'tappets' fit into or move out of the ports as the levers are moved, locking or unlocking that or other levers. *David Harris*

In 1988, Andrew Gritten, working for the Thatcherite Centre for Policy Studies (CPS), suggested selling BR as 12 integrated companies, running passenger and freight, responsible for track, trains and maintenance. This was altogether too stable and too calm a proceeding to find favour with the fundamentalist privatisers. (Andrew Gritten is Chairman of the Central Railway project to build a freight-only railway from Liverpool to Lille. He proposes to use the trackbed of the former Great Central Railway south of Nottingham and intends to take five million lorry journeys a year off the M1, M2, M6 and M25.)

From 13 June 1987 to 24 July 1989 the Secretary of State for Transport was Paul Channon. In November 1988 Channon ordered a major study of all the options for railway privatisation. Coopers & Lybrand were as usual commissioned to act as consultants for the BRB. Their study cost the BRB £1.5 million and told the Board, more or less, what they already knew; the expensive study was in general agreement with the plans that the BRB had developed in April of that year. The railway would have a small headquarters holding company, which would devolve authority to subsidiary Sector companies on a 'line of route' basis, and these Sectors would be vertically integrated, taking responsibility for their track, signalling, stations and trains. Nothing came of this because it was not in line with the Treasury's ideas on 'markets' and 'competition'.

In July 1989 the working-class Tory, Cecil Parkinson, replaced Channon as incumbent of the revolving chair of Transport. His father had been a member of the Carnforth permanent way gang, and he was an enthusiastic supporter of the Starkie/Treasury approach of fragmenting the

Right: Signal boxes had detailed diagrams of the layouts they controlled. Some railway companies went to some trouble to make them akin to works of art. The GWR, of course, was one such, and even the Western Region tried to continue the tradition, its diagrams being more detailed and more pleasant to look at than some others. This was the layout controlled by Westbury North box in 1973.
Adrian Vaughan

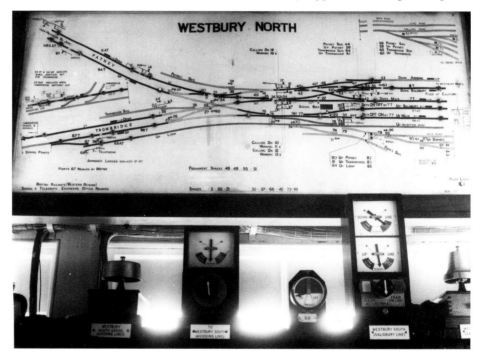

Right: This gantry, controlled from Westbury North, routed trains from the Down Trowbridge and Down West of England main line into the station. The left-hand group of signals, for trains off the Down West of England line, routed as follows: to Down Avoiding; to Down Salisbury; to Down Main. The other group routed to Down Goods; to Down Salisbury; to Down Main. The small arms with indicator screens alongside gave a driver permission to pass the main signal at Danger and proceed under the 'Calling-on' or the 'Warning' rule.
Adrian Vaughan

Left: Newbury Middle box, a GWR building dating from 1910, contained a 45-lever frame. It was closed in perfect working order due to modernisation in March 1978. *Adrian Vaughan*

Below: George Chandler was the jolly signalman of Newbury Middle box. In 1963 the box was still fully equipped with its 1910 signalling instruments – beautiful!
Adrian Vaughan Collection

railway – train operating companies paying to operate on tracks maintained by a privately-owned 'track authority'. Professor Terry Gourvish tells us in his book, *British Rail 1974-1997*, vol 2, p.369, that on 9 March 1989 Mrs Parkinson was travelling in the cab of the 15.50 King's Cross to Leeds train. Whether she had a permit or was just a friend of the driver, Gourvish does not say. During the journey she gave it as her opinion that the best form of privatisation for BR would be a privately owned track maintenance company hiring the rails to private operators and contracting out all rail maintenance and renewals. By coincidence, Mrs Parkinson's family owned a building company, Jarvis, based then on the site of the old Wheathampstead station.

In the first half of 1989 the railwaymen were offered a 1.8% pay rise, which insult caused them to stage seven one-day strikes over a period of six weeks ending in July 1989. Government considered bringing a law forbidding public service workers from going on strike, but settled for ordering a report into another reorganisation of the railway. The BRB was incensed that railway union leaders had put the union's case before the public by speaking to the BBC and newspapers, so, after the strike, all railway workers were presented with a gagging contract. It was an entirely inequitable contract binding the employees to silence, but not their employers. Many brave railwaymen and women refused to sign away their ancient right of free speech. There is also an important safety aspect to a gagging clause – it prevents an employee from exposing dangerous working practices.

In June 1989 Coopers & Lybrand and Sir Christopher Foster issued their report for the *simplification* of the railway organisation. As 'simplification' was the aim, the title was inept: 'The Future Structure for Railways: A de-centralised, market-based structure'. The Chairman of the BRB, Sir Bob Reid 1, accepted the recommendations at once, and in July John Edmonds, an extremely forceful BR senior manager, in whose path no-one stood, was brought onto the Board from his job of running the Anglia Region to develop the policy of 'radical decentralisation', which was seen as the way to 'organisational *simplification*'.

The signalling instruments inside Barnetby East box, ex-Great Central Railway, look very similar to the 'peggers' used also by the Midland and the Great Northern railways. They were photographed in 1984. *Adrian Vaughan*

(Gourvish, Vol 2, p.373) This was given the positively Orwellian title 'Organising for Quality' which was immediately rendered into plain and derisory English – by the troops who had to suffer it – as 'OfQ'.

The railway's Regions were to be abolished and instead five groups or 'Sectors' would be established according to the business that they were to undertake: InterCity, Regional Railways, Network SouthEast, Trainload Freight and Parcels. These major 'Sectors' were then to be subdivided into areas: InterCity Great Western Main Line, or Regional Railways Wales and West. It was a huge upheaval as the entire railway changed rooms, worked for a new organisation with new colleagues and went on training and team-building courses. Sector Directors were given 'ownership and bottom-line responsibility for the assets they use' in a system of organisation that would 'move responsibility for decision-making as close as possible to the customer'. Would the 'customers' want to be close to the railway's decision-making? Were they not simply expecting a train? The language is weird and business-macho, but its use proves that the railway really had become 'business-led'. The removal of 'excess' rolling stock required to cope with 'peak' demand and the introduction of overcrowding was on the way.

In October 1989 Parkinson intended to give a speech at the Party conference promising the faithful a sell-off of a fragmented railway. He showed the text to Mrs Thatcher, who told him, 'I would be grateful if you would leave the subject alone and not say anything.' (Freeman, p.15) It ought not to be inferred from this that Mrs Thatcher was a defender of railways – she would as soon have closed them down altogether, saving perhaps a couple of thousand miles. At the October Party Conference Parkinson contented himself with saying that 'privatisation studies are continuing', but in February 1990 he told Sir Bob Reid 1, that 'railway privatisation was no longer a matter for urgent consideration'. Sir Bob was at that time coaching his replacement, the coincidentally named, Sir Bob Reid, formerly Chairman of Shell. He was appointed a non-executive Director of the BRB in January 1990, became non-executive Chairman in April and full-time Chairman in October. The advice that railway privatisation had been shelved was welcome news because now the BRB, which included John Welsby, John

Edmonds and David Rayner, could concentrate on 'Organising for Quality'.

At the start of the OfQ process the BRB employed 101,000 in the Regions, 3,000 in the Sectors and 17,000 at HQ, a total of 121,000 people. In April 1992, at the completion of OfQ, the increased number of businesses had increased the staff total to 126,000, but by April 1994 this had been reduced to 109,000. BRB HQ staff numbered 640. (Gourvish, Vol 2, p.383)

The declared purpose of OfQ was to make the railway profitable by making it into lots of businesses, each with a 'simple, decentralised' management structure. The objective of each business was 'to permit power and authority to be brought as close to the customer and to the workplace as possible'. How much closer can the passenger be to the railway than when facing the booking clerk, the station staff or the station manager? And yet it was during 'Organising for Quality' that many stations became unstaffed after normal office hours – or even completely. From Newbury to Church Stretton, passengers and customers stood on unstaffed stations of an evening or rainswept night, their only company often being shadowy figures and strange smells from burning substances, as they waited anxiously for their train. The 'simplified, decentralised' management meant that managers and back-up staff were removed to locations remote from the stations, and indeed remote from the lineside.

OfQ introduced an *internal market* to the railway, Sectors paying each other for the use of facilities and track access. This introduced an unheard of rigidity into operating. Locomotives belonging to one Sector could not readily go to the aid of the broken-down train of another Sector, the result being long delays to the 'customers', for whose benefit this system had been adopted. Platforms at large stations became the sole prerogative of the owning Sector, which reduced track capacity and caused delays outside the station, waiting for the right platform to become available.

All costs were squeezed some more. Safety had to take a chance. Trains entered service with faulty AWS gear and when drivers complained they were told that the AWS was merely an 'aid' to drivers and not to be relied on. (Dennis Herbert, *Birmingham Footplateman*, p.254) The AWS had always been regarded as essential, vital. Installation of AWS was commenced in 1956 after the catastrophic Harrow and Wealdstone triple collision – which would have been prevented by AWS – in October 1952, when 112 people were killed and 340 injured. In 1994, after a head-on collision on a single line in Sussex, the 'non-essential' AWS equipment was minutely examined. It was clearly considered to be of the utmost importance. But AWS was, apparently, too expensive, so the OfQ Sector unloaded its responsibilities onto the driver. If anything went wrong it was his fault, not the faulty equipment. InterCity passenger trains on the routes from the South Coast to the North,

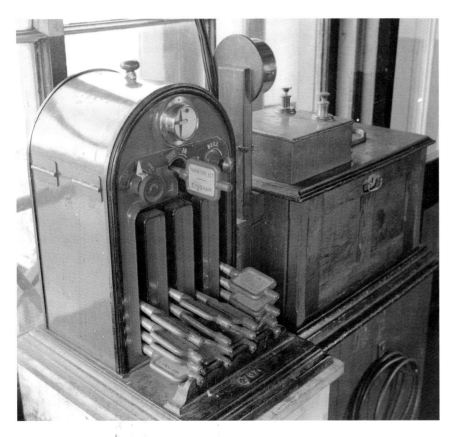

The preceding pictures show instruments for signalling trains on double lines where the two or more tracks are reserved specifically for trains travelling in 'Up' and 'Down' directions. On single tracks trains run 'Up' and 'Down' on the same line, so to avoid head-on collisions rather special instruments are required. Here in Yarnton Junction signal box is a GWR/Tyers Electric Train Token instrument, invented in 1914, which has just, in 1954, replaced a Tyer's No 4 Electric Train Tablet instrument. They both do the same job. One tablet or token can be removed from the instrument – with the co-operation of the signalman at the far end of the section – and given to the train driver. It is his guarantee that he will not meet a train coming the other way, because once a token has been removed it is not possible to remove another until the first one has been replaced in the instrument at the far end of the section, or in the instrument from which it was taken. There had only ever been one head-on collision on a single line due to the malfunction of this type of instrument – at Parkhall, near Oswestry, in 1916. *Peter Barlow/ Adrian Vaughan Collection*

through Oxford and Birmingham, had run with eight to 12 coaches, but under 'Organising for Quality' the loads were reduced to six coaches while the timetabled speed remained 90mph. Quite apart from the discomfort caused to 'customers' by inevitable overcrowding, there was a serious problem of safety in that there is less brake power with six coaches than with 12. Every engine driver knew from experience that this was the case, but the managers denied it and could produce mathematicians to prove it. But the mathematicians did not drive trains, nor have their hearts pounding fit to burst as they went past a signal at danger because the shorter train could not stop. Eventually InterCity was forced to add an extra coach – but this was usually locked and included only for additional brake force. (*Birmingham Footplateman*, p.252)

The homogenous, co-operative railway with a hierarchy of command from top to bottom was converted into six

Invented by Mr Thompson of the London & North Western Railway in 1890, these cast-iron pillars hold and dispense an Electric Train Staff. Their purpose is identical to the train token or tablet instruments – the varying designs were born out of a desire to circumvent earlier patents. These two instruments were photographed at Llanybyther in September 1962. The left-hand one works with the signal box at Maesycrugiau, the other with Lampeter. *Adrian Vaughan*

separate, self-interested railway businesses, and they were each sub-divided into four 'profit centres'. A 'Safety Validation Panel' had to be formed to oversee the safety procedures of all these businesses. On 20 February 1991 the OfQ reorganisation team met the Safety Validation Panel members and failed to get approval for the fragmentation from that Panel. Clearly there was serious doubt about safety, but approval was given in the end. John Edmonds, driving OfQ, was a very determined man.

Peter Rayner, the Operations Manager of London Midland Region, Britain's largest single chunk of unified railway, which was to be scrapped under OfQ, wrote a critique of what was being done, which he handed to the BRB and the press. It was for his wholehearted public defence of 'old railway' attitudes (labelled 'overbearing' by the modernisers) that Peter Rayner was sacked in 1992. He was in charge of safety on the Royal Train at the time.

In his critique Rayner pointed out that, before OfQ, the Area Manager West Midlands Passenger was solely responsible for running all the services in the West Midlands PTE area. Under OfQ, Regional Railways Central (RRC) was responsible for running the local trains, but without 'ownership' of the principal stations or the two power signal boxes for the area. RRC was running on InterCity tracks in some places and on its own tracks in others. Between Birmingham Proof House Junction and Walsall via Aston, RRC was responsible for incident management but the signalling was owned variously by the InterCity West Coast and Freight Sectors. There was a divided loyalty and responsibility.

He referred to a bomb scare at St Albans in 1990 when that station was under the Area Manager St Pancras and was staffed by BR men who were multi-functional, competent in all the necessary Rules and Regulations procedures. Rayner pointed out that under OfQ an incident at St Albans would be 'owned' by InterCity Midland Main Line, which was based in Derby. The nearest Manager would indeed be at St Albans, but he was the *retail* manager employed by Thameslink and therefore would have no safety responsibilities for St Albans station. Leadership would have to come from Derby. This was definitely 'decentralised' management, but it was neither simple nor efficient.

There was a shortage of maintenance staff owing to the earlier cost-cutting drives and under OfQ these were to be scattered between many more organisations, each one of them working for its own interest, not for the good of the railway as a whole. An InterCity signal technician would not attend a fault on Regional Railways signalling equipment, even if it was yards away from him. How's that for efficiency? Prior to OfQ, drivers and conductors were all under one management; they were handed their Weekly Operating Notices when they signed on, supplied from Regional HQ. With OfQ, the compilation of these safety notices was taken away from the Operating department and given to 'Planning and Marketing'. Train conductors were part of 'Retail', and

the Retail side is not concerned with the safe working of the railway. There was fragmentation even within a Sector.

One Sector of Regional Railways would not make special stops to pick up the passengers of another Sector of Regional Railways when a train had been cancelled or heavily delayed. Every Sector looked out for its own interest – the commonwealth of the railway was lost, which was hardly of assistance to passengers. The electric train heating system was removed from Class 90 locomotives working for the Railfreight Sector and their top speed was reduced to 75mph. These engines could not then assist a failed InterCity train. Railfreight Sector trains were not allowed to run through the Manchester Piccadilly area even though there were 'paths' available. The fragmentation worked its way down into the smallest crevices of operating, and produced ridiculous situations, or at least situations that appeared ridiculous to those who recalled the unified railway.

Regional Railways hired a tamper from InterCity in the summer 1992. It suffered a broken gearbox in early July and

Ystrad Mynach signal box, seen here in 1974, was built in local stone by the signalling contractors McKenzie & Holland for the Rhymney Railway, and was ledged up on the mountainside, requiring a complex rod-and-crank system to take the drive from the levers down the bank to track level, then out to the points. The northbound track used to split three ways here. The Victorians never let engineering difficulties stand in the way of their schemes. *Adrian Vaughan*

was parked on a siding at Evesham, in view of the signalman. It stood there for three weeks before a group of five men arrived in a lorry from Derby and held a 90-minute 'prayer meeting' over the stricken tamper. Never a word they spoke to a soul at the station, and went away as mysteriously as they had come. After another three weeks it was still there, then, one day, it was gone. For six weeks, kit worth £250 million waited for attention. InterCity and Regional Railways were arguing over who was going to pay for the repairs.

On 18 July 1992 the 18.20 Paddington-Hereford train was held at Oxford station for an hour because the axle counter had broken on the single track between Wolvercote Junction and Ascott-under-Wychwood. This important trunk route had been singled to save money when the Oxford area signalling was being modernised in 1973 – saving money was more important than the capacity to run trains. Axle counters are used on automatically signalled single-track railways to ensure that the section is clear of trains before another train is allowed to enter it. The machine counts the axles in and counts them out at the other end. If it counts an equal number in and out, all is well, but, not so infrequently; the machine decides that there was one less axle going out compared to coming in and shuts the shop. The train must then be ascertained – by human observation – to be in possession of all its axles and a tail lamp, then, until a scarce technician can be obtained to rectify the fault, a Pilotman is required to act as a human Train Staff to ensure that only one train at a time occupies the single track.

Regional Railways (RR) owned the Worcester line, but the 18.20 Paddington belonged to InterCity (IC). RR did not want to pay one of its men to conduct an IC train, and IC didn't have a man handy. An hour passed. The customers sat there, tired and homesick. Finally these customer-focused 'businesses' agreed a deal and the train set off. The following train for Worcester was cancelled.

Because of the OfQ policy of 'ownership' of routes, other Sectors wanting to use the line had to pay a fee. Rather than pay that, trains would be parked overnight where they finished their journey and braved the weather, the risk of vandalism and a lack of proper servicing. The last InterCity HST of the day from Paddington to Hereford would be stabled in the open at Hereford because its depot was Bristol Bath Road, and IC would not pay RR £300 each way to take an empty train from Hereford to Newport (en route for Bristol) and back in addition to the other costs of moving an empty train. IC provided a taxi to take its crew back to Bristol. Meanwhile the HST would stand for the night on the Hereford siding, maybe leaking coolant or with its batteries dangerously low so that every

The solutions to Victorian engineering problems called into being thousands of skilled craftsmen. A lot of mechanical signalling required blacksmith work by metal workers, fitters and turners. Here is the forge of the Divisional Signal Works at Worcester on 13 November 1957; a blacksmith is heating metal to create a piece of ironwork that will be part of a signal operating rod, or point rodding. *Adrian Vaughan Collection*

Once the metal had been heated and hammered into a blank shape, it could be taken to the vice and filed into its precise shape. Here the craftsman is forming the detector blade as part of the mechanism that detects if a set of points has been moved correctly into position before the corresponding signal can be lowered. *Adrian Vaughan Collection*

now and again its engines would not start ready for the first Up London service. There was no spare set – the accountants and efficiency experts had seen to that – so the sacred customer, turning up for his 'service', found that, because it had been saving money, IC had cancelled his train. So what was in actual fact more important to IC – serving its customers or saving money?

The main drive of OfQ was cost-cutting in engineering, and it is easy to imagine an engineer feeling unhelpful towards a man who wanted him to lower standards. Provincial Railways actually enjoyed a 'maintenance holiday' in this period, while overall there was a deferring of track renewals and a getting rid of middle managers and technical staff wherever possible. Getting rid of the people who keep the railway running safely and smoothly and with absolute regularity seems to be counter-productive to a 'customer-friendly' railway, but the business railway managers believed that the railway was 'over-engineered'. The engineering departments, and especially the civil engineers, were well behind in the reorganisation process – some in the financial departments of the Sectors thought the 'civils' were still in the 19th century. Maintenance and renewals were expensive – the work must either be done more cheaply, or not at all. Indicative of the animosity between the business-led railway and the engineers is this note from George Buckley, Managing Director, Central Services, to John Prideaux, Managing Director, InterCity:

'I must express the view frankly that the break-up of the Divisional Mechanical & Electrical Engineering Department was long overdue, or at least, the injection of real management into a department which was bloated, inefficient, unhelpful, over-bearing and overstaffed. Even those smaller numbers now coming to Central Services will need a heavy dose of attitude adjustment. However, the price we have had to pay has been dear, with BR costs inflated dramatically and the skill level lower.' (Quoted in Gourvish, Vol 2, note 57, p.654)

After abusing the engineers who kept the railway in one piece, Buckley admits that the policies he approved of raised costs and lowered skill.

CHAPTER 7

Towards privatisation

On 28 November 1990 there was a 'palace coup' and John Major replaced Margaret Thatcher as Prime Minister. Cecil Parkinson – Thatcher's great favourite in spite of his disobedience over the railway privatisation – departed with her. John Major appointed Sir Malcolm Rifkind in Parkinson's place. On 13 May 1991 the BRB was informed by the new Secretary of State for Transport that 'I have now reached the point at which I am clear about the definition of the main structural options for privatisation, namely: selling BR as a unit; selling by Sector; separating BR into track and train operating companies.' Rifkind told the BRB to reconsider its 1989 review and begin a new set of studies to determine the 'practical implications and feasibility' of each option. (Gourvish, Vol 2, p.384) He told BR that he had no preferences except that he required a solution that would encourage 'diversity, innovation and competition', which seems like a heavy hint towards privatisation and fragmentation.

An orgy of expensive consultancy now took place. The BRB commissioned five consultancies – Lazards, Samuel Montagu, Putnam, National Economic Research Associates and Leicester University – to investigate the implications for the railway of being split up, the financial prospects, and the contractual arrangements necessary. The BRB paid £375,000 to its consultants and handed their report to Rifkind. (Gourvish, Vol 2, p.385) The Department for Transport carried out its own investigations.

The DfT report recommended splitting infrastructure from train operating, and establishing as much

The first full-scale power-operated signalling in Britain was undertaken by the London & North Western Railway. This was the 'all electric signalling system', 110V DC and battery powered, designed by the company's Signal Engineer, A. M. Thompson. The initial installation was at Crewe, starting with the 57-lever Gresty Lane box brought into use in February 1899. There were a further eight boxes around Crewe with this system, all installed by 1907, three at Camden/Euston in 1905 and three at Manchester London Road in 1909. The Crewe North Junction power frame had 266 levers and Crewe South Junction 247 levers. These pictures of the 1907 installation were taken on 22 July 1940.
Adrian Vaughan Collection

competition as possible within the railway industry. When making this recommendation the economists actually recognised that a policy of even greater competition would make it more difficult to engineer major improvements over the network, would make the maintenance of safety more difficult, and would raise administration costs. The competing elements of the new railway would be following their own profit in true Adam Smith fashion rather than looking to the good of the whole business. To ensure that the fragmented, privatised system performed at least as well as BR's public service had done, it would be necessary to create a complex system of contracts *and* a government-run regulatory office to act on behalf of the rail users. There is a wonderful irony in the fact that, in order to turn the railway into a free-market paradise – a 'vibrant market place' – a great deal of legally binding state regulation would be necessary to maintain national coherence.

The economic fundamentalists within and outside the Tory Party and at the Treasury desired 'competition' – they believed in this as the universal cure-all as dogmatically as a Marxist believes in his economic nostrums. But competition does not work on railways. They are a special case and this is what the economists would not accept. They were so besotted with competition that they said they would auction each train path. Any 'monopoly' within the railway industry

The interior of the 247-lever Crewe South Junction signal box. The very large levers, for a power box, are arranged in a double bank. On the instrument shelf are the block instruments for the acceptance of trains, and the 'Train ready to depart' indicators. The signalmen operating these places had to have the whole timetable for Crewe station in their heads in order to work the box! Men who left very ordinary schools at 14 or 15 years of age were not very ordinary men. The North and South Junction boxes were replaced by a new power system housed in a building like a concrete bunker to withstand the bombing that the planners knew would come. Today, that signal box is preserved and open to the public. *Adrian Vaughan Collection*

was, in the minds of these people, a very bad thing, yet it was good for Tesco, Walmart, Coopers & Lybrand and Lehman Brothers, to name but a few global near-monopolies.

The Minister of Transport from 1990 to 1994 was Roger Freeman, Lord Freeman from 1997. A great advocate of railway privatisation, Freeman was a partner in, and Managing Director of, the American investment bankers Lehman Bros until 1986, when he entered politics. Lehman Bros was expanding rapidly in 1986. It understood the benefits of huge size and vertical integration. According to its website before the recent economic crisis:

'…the "One Firm" mantra is no joke. The emphasis is co-operation between divisions, and in practice this does seem to happen in that people are committed to helping others beyond their immediate team and job description. The culture is almost cult-like and is taken very seriously; in particular the "One Firm" approach.'

That sounds like an identical 'culture' to that of BR, but on rail there had to be total fragmentation – a perfect 'market place'.

The idea of auctioning each and every train 'path' separately crashed on the rock of practicality and the idea gathered strength of grouping all the passenger trains of a certain area or line of route into a 'train operating company' and offering that as a business franchise. The competition would be in the bidding for the licence. How much subsidy would the franchisee require? How much would the franchisee pay the Government for the licence? What benefits would he confer on the travelling public if he got the contract? Having obtained the franchise, the train operator would have a monopoly of passenger traffic on those routes. The inherent nature of a railway would reassert itself.

From a fundamentalist Adam Smith point of view this would be an unfortunate outcome. To counteract this tendency towards a modicum of common sense it was also part of the extreme privatisers' plan that 'open access'

operators should be allowed to run over the franchisee's routes. After all, any losses this caused the franchisee would be made up by the taxpayer. It is a remarkable thing how the free-marketeers are never backward in coming forward for public money when they need it.

In July 1991 the European Union brought out Directive 91/440. This obliged all EU countries to separate the *financial accounts* of the track and the operation of trains. The purpose of this was to have the proper figures of cost available to ensure that fair tolls were charged by each country as inter-European passenger and freight trains traversed their tracks. It *did not* order the separation of track ownership from train operating, but the Treasury extremists distorted the Directive so as to justify their previously taken decision to physically separate the track from the train in order to introduce competition to the railway.

The BRB was trying to assist the Government with its privatisation but, being more knowledgeable on the subject of railways, it tried to persuade Malcolm Rifkind, the Transport Minister, to take a 'unitary' solution. The Board pointed out to the Government that its vertically integrated, 'OfQ', business-led Sectors were performing very well while still retaining the operational integrity vital for safety and co-ordination. On 27 September Bob Reid 2 strongly urged Rifkind to make his intentions clear to the

The competitor to electric operation of points and signals in 1900-20 was the compressed-air system of the British Pneumatic Signalling Co. The system required a large building to house the compressor and there was a lot of plumbing-type piping to the cylinders driving the points and signals. Compressed air snaps points over several seconds faster than an electric motor, and that was useful in a marshalling yard or a very large and busy station. Keadby Canal Junction signal box, seen here, was a GCR installation of May 1916 on the line from Scunthorpe to Doncaster. It replaced an earlier mechanical box that controlled sidings and a swing bridge. The bridge became inadequate for wartime traffic, so a deviation line was built, with a stronger bridge over the canal, this signal box housing an electro-pneumatic power frame. The signalman controlled the trains on the main line, access to the sidings and the operation of the sliding bridge over the Stainforth & Keadby Canal. The semaphore signals operated by this frame were of the three-aspect variety.
Peter Barlow/
Adrian Vaughan Collection

Left: Bristol Temple Meads station was re-signalled in 1932-35 with all-electric frames. East box, brought into use in 1935, had 336 draw slides; West box (1935) 328 draw slides; and Locomotive Yard 32 slides. The GWR had pioneered the all-electric 'route setting' system, which, in principle, is still in use today. One lever was required to set up a whole route, moving all necessary points and signals, but after installing the system in two signal boxes, Winchester and Newport (Monmouthshire), the company reverted to individual operation of each point and signal using a General Railway Signal Co (GRS) system at Cardiff, Paddington and here, at Bristol Temple Meads East. *Adrian Vaughan*

Left: A detail of the GRS system in Temple Meads West. Out on the line there was ordinary block working with bells, block indicators and two-aspect signals. Note the large number of bells – remember that every bell code sent or received on each of the these bells was recorded in the Train Register by the booking lad. *Adrian Vaughan Collection*

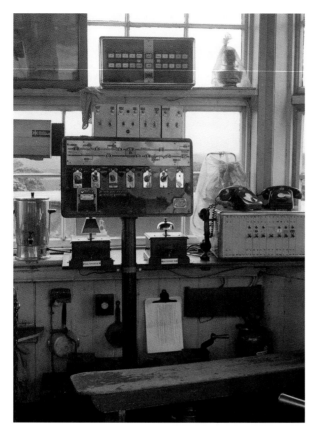

The control console in Goole Swing Bridge signal box, seen here in 1984, was the pioneer 'entry-exit', or 'NX' for short, route-relay method of signalling. It was designed by Westinghouse and installed here in 1933. A button pressed at the entry and exit of the route causes the points and signals for that route to be set into their correct position. *Adrian Vaughan*

BRB and to pursue a pragmatic approach to railway privatisation, retaining a 'National Railway Authority' as a holding company, which would own the infrastructure, maintain a coherent, national, safety and development policy and contract out train operating on selected routes. The response was such that Reid came to the conclusion that what was important to the Government was to *sell* the railway – the practicalities were a minor issue by comparison. (Gourvish, Vol 2, p.385)

While all this argument and indecision was going on behind the scenes, involving the BRB in much distracting work, the Board had to finish off the project 'Organising for Quality', rearranging the railway with a modern 'business-led' system. There was nothing inefficient about the Board or the senior management of BR in pursuit of the government's wishes. The gigantic upheaval of total reorganisation was complete by April 1992. The promoters said that the new Sector organisation had brought about a 'leaner and meaner management' with 'flexibility' while 'focusing on core competences'. Whether

it was 'flexible' is a moot point; at large stations it was more of an operational strait- jacket, as platforms were strictly segregated between Sectors. But at least the route-owning Sectors were vertically integrated and looked after their own tracks. The total cost to the BRB of creating the OfQ organisation was estimated by Board officers at around £65 million. (Gourvish, Vol 2, p.383) That would have purchased a lot of new track and signalling.

In January 1992 an election was in the offing, and in March the Tory Party Manifesto was published. This stated in general terms the intention to leave BR in charge of the track and signalling while the trains would be operated by privately financed franchisees.

When the New Labour Manifesto was published, it contained no statement absolutely opposing privatisation, but implied a public-private finance system for a state-owned railway.

The Tory Manifesto stated that, 'We believe that the best way to produce profound and lasting improvements on the railways is to end BR's state monopoly.' British Rail never had a monopoly: it was in total competition with roads and, increasingly, with internal airlines.

'We want to give the private sector the opportunity to operate existing rail services and introduce new ones, for both passengers and freight. A significant number of companies have already said that they want to introduce new railway services as soon as the monopoly is ended. We will give them that chance.'

What services can a railway run other than trains? The BRB had already sold its ships and hotels. The manifesto had a loose definition of what constituted a 'significant number'. In early 1992 there were only two passenger operators interested, Gloag and Souter's Stagecoach bus company and Branson's Virgin organisation. On the freight side, private enterprise had not up to then been a success. 'Charterail' was formed in 1990, and hired trains and crew from BR to carry cat and dog food from Melton Mowbray to Glasgow, and china clay from St Blazey. The former was a new traffic flow, the latter BR had been doing for decades. Unfortunately for this Manifesto, Charterail was declared insolvent later that year, owing £1 million to British Rail.

The Manifesto continued:

'We believe that franchising provides the best way of achieving that. Long term, as performance improves and services become more commercially attractive as a result of bringing in private sector disciplines, it will make sense to consider whether some services can be sold outright.'

It wanted to improve rail travel in the long term, yet the Government intended only short-term franchises, around seven years. The franchisee would be the bidder that agreed to pay most for the licence and take the least amount of subsidy from the Government. Oh yes! The BRB was being closed down because it 'took too much money' from the taxpayers, but these 'private enterprise' organisations would also have a subsidy without any government grumbles. Why would railway carriages become more attractive because they were supplied by 'private enterprise'? What increased 'discipline' could 'market forces' bring to the railway? Market forces are essentially the impulses of self-interest – we have Souter's word for that. Individualism is not the principle on which to base a national railway.

Then, having dispensed with an – apparently – ill-disciplined British Rail Board, an Office of Rail Regulator would have to be established to ensure that these new – and disciplined – private companies would 'honour the terms of their contract'. So where was their discipline? No such regulatory body had been required for the BRB.

The Manifesto asserted that a series of short-to-medium-term franchises would 'reflect regional and local identity and make operating sense. We want to recover a sense of pride in our railways and to recapture the spirit of the old regional companies.' How could it be operationally sensible to hand the railway over to a large number of short-term franchisees? Through routes would be broken where the franchise ended. How could 'the spirit of the old companies' be 'recaptured' by a mere franchisee, a creature with no assets and bearing no resemblance to the 'old companies'. The Government knew that what they were proposing was deeply unpopular and were playing a rather cynical nostalgia card.

Anyone who previously had expressed affection for railways was routinely denigrated as 'a trainspotter', 'a nostalgist', an 'anorak' or some other derogatory term – now the Government said that it wanted to re-create affection for railways! Sir Christopher Foster, one of its chief advisers on privatisation, has written that it was the British people's affection for its railways that has prevented them from becoming profitable – not governments making them work for nothing and withholding funding for their modernisation. The old companies, to whose memory the Tories made their hypocritical appeal, had owned the freehold of their railways for generations, which

is what made those companies great, national institutions.

At the bottom of the 'Railways' section of the Manifesto, looking very much like an afterthought, was the single sentence: 'The Railway Inspectorate will be given full powers to ensure the highest standards of safety.' Thus was announced the most impractical, ill-thought-out project in the history of Britain's railways – announced, not with a carefully thought-out White Paper, but in a mere election Manifesto, seemingly on the back of a fag packet. And these proposals, when brought into effect, would lead to the collapse of the entire national railway system. Perhaps that was what was intended.

The General Election took place on 9 April 1992 – the 183rd anniversary of the birth of Brunel. Most opinion polls and political pundits forecast a Labour victory, and to most people's surprise, not least that of the victors, the Tories were re-elected under John Major. They had a majority of 22 seats in Parliament, with 58% of voters voting against them. John Major appointed his Minister of Agriculture, John MacGregor, a history graduate, MP for South Norfolk, as Secretary of State for Transport. MacGregor's Under Secretary of State for Transport was Steven Norris. Norris had always taken a keen interest in transport – as a VW-Audi franchisee and as Director-General of the Road Haulage Association. Here was a man to take a keen interest in developing trains to get people

With apologies for the poor quality of the photograph, this is the track diagram for Gloucester Road Junction, part of the huge Norwood/Selhurst junctions complex. This fantastic layout was equipped with electrically-operated points and colour light signals, controlled by two signalmen using a Westinghouse 'L' frame of miniature levers set at 2-inch centres. This layout had been controlled by three mechanical boxes, Norwood Fork Junction with 65 levers, Selhurst Junction with 78 and Windmill Bridge Junction with 48 and three draw slides. Between them they controlled 17¼ miles of track. The preparatory work for changing from semaphores to colour lights and motor points was perfectly planned. On the night of 20/21 March 1954, 600 technicians from Westinghouse and British Railways arrived on the site, and were all detailed off to the jobs they had to do. The change-over was effected, and all connections wired up, in 6¼ hours. No trains were cancelled and no buses were used.
Michael Sadler/Adrian Vaughan Collection

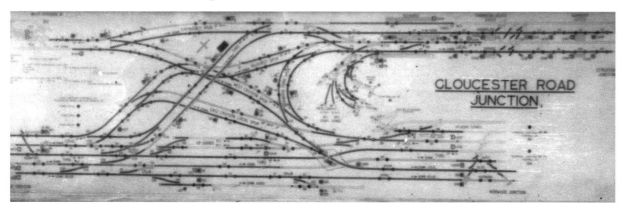

Above: The North Eastern Railway signal box at Belford, 15 miles south of Berwick, was taken out of use in February 1962, its area of control taken over by an 'NX' panel in the new signal box on the left.
Peter Barlow/
Adrian Vaughan Collection

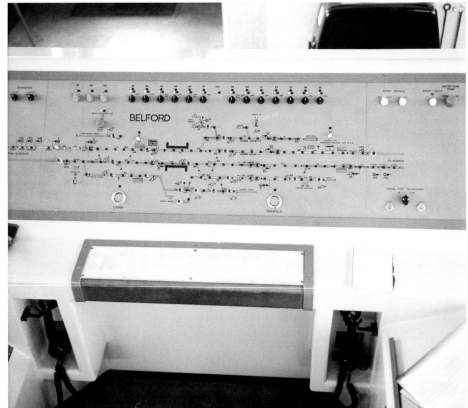

Right: Belford panel was a Westinghouse production and the first 'NX' panel in the North Eastern Region. It was replaced in 1990 by the Tweedmouth control centre.
Peter Barlow/
Adrian Vaughan Collection

By 1965 'panel' boxes were being brought into use to cover very wide areas. This is Swindon panel, an 'NX' type, which came into use in March 1968 and took over operations from Challow to Thingley Junction, Badminton and Kemble. Ronnie Astridge is nearest the camera, with Colin Baldwin. *Adrian Vaughan*

out of their cars. Apart from the sketchy Manifesto pledges, the Tories – and John MacGregor in particular – had very little idea of how to go about privatising the nation's railway. MacGregor said, 'There was not quite a blank sheet of paper as our election commitment but very close to it. Just a few outlines about how it might work.' A party official said, 'We had nothing drafted at all.' (Quoted by Jon Shaw in *All Change: British railway privatisation*, p.21)

MacGregor set to work at once to commission reports to go over all the ground that had been raked over since 1989. In this he was assisted by Sir Christopher Foster, pioneer of the 'Poll Tax', Chairman of the Royal Automobile Club and a partner in Coopers & Lybrand. They were paid £5,000 a year for ten years for Sir Christopher's advice and, apart from years of previous consultancies, they were paid £1.6 million between December 1991 and November 1993. (Parliamentary answer given by Minister of State for Public Transport, Roger Freeman, 25.11.93)

The BRB had already developed a practical answer – an answer that had put InterCity into profit and reduced the amount of subsidy required by the rest – with Coopers & Lybrand advising them. But after all the expense, this was the wrong answer. It was not sufficiently extreme. Competition within the railway was The Policy, never mind about practicality. Fragmenting the railway would allow dozens of companies to get a share of public funds through contracting to the railway.

In his paper 'The Economics of Rail Privatisation', Sir Christopher Foster wrote with an assumption of infallibility previously monopolised by the Pope. He began:

'My aim is to set out the case for rail privatisation and to show that it reflects a coherent approach. The policy's objectives were set out in the White Paper that initiated it. They have not changed. They are: "To see better use made of the railways, greater responsiveness to the customer and a higher quality of service and better value for money for the public who also travel by rail."

Foster's use of the word 'coherent' in a plan to shatter the railway into more than 100 pieces is bizarre. The privatisers said that BR was 'too big' and 'unmanageable'; Sir Christopher was a Director of one of the largest accounting and financial consultancies in the world, but that was not unmanageable. What the privatisers were proposing would introduce such a patchwork of companies, contracts and complexities that it would require far more management than Sectorised BR and would therefore be more expensive – quite apart from the implications for efficient train operating in times of emergency and for safety. Sir Christopher wrote his paper with the absolute conviction that the railways would – quite as a matter of course – become more efficient when they were in fragments, and privately owned. There would be subsidies to franchisees on the lesser routes and some lines would be closed because no subsidy would save them under private enterprise.

All types of engineering work, rolling stock, track, signalling and anything that the railway needed would be contracted out to any number of outside agencies, each one of which would need to make its profit. Thousands of contracts would have to be written, competing bids vetted, and the successful contractors – who would be taking day-to-day safety decisions – had to be supervised by Railtrack, which would have got rid of a large part of its engineering expertise. A railway nirvana would be achieved by disorganising the railway, by selling off chunks of it and creating a complex of self-interested parties that were then supposed to look out for the common good. It was so illogical that I should not be accused of paranoia if I suggest that there was some ulterior motive.

Two weeks after the election, on 28 April, the British Railways Board was summoned to meet its executioners. John Welsby (Chairman), James Jerram (Finance and Planning), and David Rayner (Safety), among others, met John MacGregor, Secretary of State for Transport, his 'Special Adviser', Sir Christopher Foster, Roger Freeman, Transport Minister, and Steven Norris, Director-General of the Road Haulage Association and member of John Major's cabinet. The BRB people tried to tell the economic fundamentalists that their plan required far more planning than they had given it, but John MacGregor would have no argument, no delay. The break-up had to be achieved as quickly as possible. And the BRB men, characterised as nationalised incompetents by Margaret Thatcher, were instructed to get on with bringing it to fruition! (Gourvish, Vol 2, p.390)

In July 1992 the hastily written White Paper, 'New Opportunities for the Railways', was published. This was to be the blueprint for 'increased efficiency' on the railways, but it was in itself an inefficient document. It was no more than a sketch of what was to happen. It was a rushed job, lacking the usual preceding Green Paper consultation document. This was because the Tories had to sell the railways before the next election in 1997. Their concern was not so much to improve railways but to carry out a politico-economic experiment on them – and using the thoughts of the 18th-century savant Adam Smith as their base premise. Robert Adley, Tory Chairman of the 1992 Transport Select Committee, said: 'The Secretary of State, the Minister of State and the Department of Transport have appeared before us and it seems to me that none of them have a clue about how all this is going to be worked out.' (Quoted by Jon Shaw in *All Change: British railway privatisation*, p.25) John MacGregor admitted in Parliament that 'in working through some of the proposals, it is clear that much work remains to be done.' (Ibid, p.25) The Minister of Transport, Roger Freeman, said that to have worked everything out in detail *before* establishing the system would have taken ten years and they might not win the next election. So these

The automation of signalling at Westbury involved colour light signals controlled from the panel signal box replicating the indications of the old semaphore gantry in a less interesting way, but easier to see at night. The photograph is dated 6 August 1985.
Adrian Vaughan

This gigantic building, known locally as 'Colditz Castle', was built to house the Westbury signalling panel and interlockings. It was brought into use on 13 May 1984. *Adrian Vaughan*

people, who had no experience of running railways but who thought they perceived in them a lack of efficiency, rushed an inefficiently thought-out process into law.

The New Labour Party now assured Sir Bob Reid 2, and the country, that if New Labour was returned to power the privatisation project would be abandoned. The Government, on the other hand, was offering to double senior railway officers' salaries to secure their co-operation in the privatisation.

The White Paper stated that railways have 'substantial strengths', and listed some of them, but the most important – the strength that comes from of unity of organisation – was not mentioned. Section 2 stated:

'2. The railways have substantial strengths. They have unrivalled city centre to city centre connections. They are particularly cost effective for long distance and heavy freight. They can be energy efficient. They often cause less environmental damage than road transport. But the railways cannot play their full role unless they give passenger and freight customers the services they expect. The key to success is a reliable, efficient operation offering high quality services to users. The introduction of competition through greater involvement of the private sector and the ending of BR's monopoly in the operation of services will be instrumental in achieving this.'

British Rail was already running high-quality, frequent services. The White Paper acknowledged that:

'3. British Rail has made significant improvements in

recent years. Its efficiency compares well with that of other European railways. The productivity of the BR workforce is among the highest of any European railway. Intercity services and BR freight operate without direct subsidy. The amount of taxpayers' money used to support BR fell from 1975. If 1975 be taken as 100 then:

BR	SNCF	DB	FS	
1979	79	122	131	96
1983	94	121	104	179
1989	44	131	95	243
1991	65	114	79	207'

Section 5 stated:

'However, regular users know that the performance of the railways is not good enough. Too frequently, and on too many lines, the quality of service fails to meet the travelling public's expectations. BR's staff and management work hard to improve services. But they are limited by the structure of the industry in the public sector. The industry is more insulated from the demands of the market than its private sector airline, coach and road haulage competitors. It therefore has fewer incentives to improve its performance and less freedom to respond to what the customer wants. Radical changes are needed.'

'19. Improved services for passengers and freight customers will come from: (a) more concern for the customers' needs. Management and employees in the private sector have greater incentives to provide the services which the consumer wants. The profitability of their company – and at the end of the day their jobs – depends on providing a service which attracts custom. Nationalised industries do not face such acute pressures.'

In spite of lacking the alleged disciplines and incentives of the private sector and being unpressurised, BR had delivered its millions of commuters, every day, for decades, and, in the most favoured operational area of long-distance express trains, had become very successful.

The White Paper stated:

'34. Intercity has been one of BR's successes. It has improved its services, with increases in frequencies and speeds on many routes. It has proved increasingly popular with the public, with the number of passenger kilometres increasing from 11.8 billion in 1981 to over 13 billion in 1990. Every week more than a million people travel on Intercity. These improvements have been matched by better financial performance. Intercity has made profits since 1988-89.'

The very next paragraph stated:

'35. The Government has, however, decided not to move to outright sale of InterCity services at this stage. The first priority is to improve the service to customers by introducing private sector management, culture, disciplines and incentives. Moreover, it is not clear that the business as a whole could improve its performance sufficiently to allow sale in this Parliament. It remains the Government's intention that in the longer term Intercity services should be sold.'

Another advantage of BR's unitary organisation was a simple system of tickets. People before had never even considered 'tickets'. 'Through ticketing' and the ease of buying tickets was taken for granted by the entire nation – even as travellers groaned under the 'inefficiency' of BR. The White Paper acknowledged this virtue of vertical integration and that some problems might arise under the system of fragmentation that would cause difficulties for 'customers'. But no advantage like simplicity and good service was going to stand in the way of the application of their free-market dogma.

'91. Rail passengers now benefit in some important ways from being able to deal with a single railway operator. They can buy through tickets, travelling on trains operated by different business sectors. With the exception of certain services open only to full-fare-paying passengers, they can generally turn up at the station and catch the next train. The system is flexible enough for

This is Westbury panel box on 6 August 1985, still an 'NX' panel as 20 years earlier but rather more lavishly laid out. At the booking desk is Chriss Burden, on the phone 'Daisy' Richards. *Adrian Vaughan*

them to change the route of their journeys.

92. The Government wishes to retain these advantages for passengers when different services are under different control. It will require that train service operators cooperate in providing a through-ticketing system.'

Having said that, the White Paper appeared to contradict itself by continuing:

'93. It will be for train service operators to make arrangements to accept each others' tickets.'

But where would be the much-desired competition if franchises had to co-operate in setting fares?

Track and signalling would become the responsibility of a state-owned company called Railtrack.

'16. One part of BR will become a track authority – Railtrack – with responsibility for operating all track and infrastructure. The other part will become a residual operating company responsible for operating passenger services until these are all franchised to the private sector. When franchising is completed BR's only function will be to provide track and associated infrastructure.'

So Railtrack would be state-owned – BR in disguise. This seemed like a sensible acknowledgement of the need for unified command, to keep together at least part of the experienced team running the job, which is especially important to ensure the standardisation of equipment and safety of the railway. However, the White Paper went on to the let-down:

'18. In the longer term the Government would like to see the private sector owning as much as possible of the railway. Powers will therefore be taken to allow the future privatisation of all BR track and operations.'

Section 23 laid down the outline form of Railtrack:

'23. Railtrack will be responsible for timetabling, operating signalling systems, track investment and maintenance. The Government believes that revenue subsidies should be targeted directly to provision of services. Railtrack will not therefore be subsidised (although it will be eligible for capital grants in certain circumstances, see para 43) and will be expected to make a return on its assets and to charge operators for the use of its track. Within this policy framework Railtrack's charges and allocation of train paths will be overseen by the Regulator. Separate detailed accounts will be prepared for Railtrack: this will assist the Regulator in his task of policing charges and access.'

The Government fatally undermined Railtrack's supervisory/unitary role by ordering it to contract out the work of renewal and maintenance. This was in the interests of their dogmatism about competition, of course.

'24. Railtrack will be required by the Government to contract out its own support functions, for example track maintenance, where that offers value for money.'

There would have to be expensively negotiated and drawn-up legal contracts and Regulators to 'ensure' that all work was carried out correctly, but in the end handing over engineering works to a third party was an abdication of responsibility.

Section 19b was headed 'Competition and Ending the Monopoly':

'New operators will be allowed to provide services, giving customers a choice and stimulating improved services and value. Already a number of companies have indicated an interest in introducing new freight or passenger services.'

Treating BR as possessing a monopoly of transport in Britain must be one of the major errors of privatisation.

Passenger services would be managed and operated by private companies who would be awarded their franchise after a competition with other hopefuls for certain routes. Forty franchises were at first considered viable – clearly not from any railway operating logic but simply because 40 would make for a lot of competition. In the end the number 25 was agreed upon. These franchises were to be eligible for state subsidy. The successful franchisee would be the one who agreed to work the trains for the least subsidy and who agreed to pay the highest rent to the Government. It was the Government's fond hope that money would flow into its Treasury from the franchisees. There was also the unpublicised hope that, by these fragmentary means, the power of the trade unions would be broken. The chief economists driving the policies of competition and markets expected that the Government would stand aside from the railway and allow Adam Smith's 'invisible hand' to work its wonders – which could only have been wholesale rail closures and more road-building. There was, in fact, nothing in these arrangements that would make the railway work better than it was doing under the BRB. Rather the reverse.

What was perfectly obvious in 1992 was that the trains were a national necessity and therefore, should a franchisee get into financial difficulties, the Government would be obliged to render financial support above and beyond any agreed subsidy.

Section 59 stated the obvious difficulties into which the Government intended to descend in order to re-create the railway in accordance with the best practice of economists. There is a kind of childlike innocence, a naivety, in the stating of the obvious, as if the writer had only just discovered the pitfalls and was really quite surprised:

Underneath the control room of Westbury Panel, the racks and racks of switching relays are a vital part of the circuitry to interlock the points and signals and thus prevent conflicting movements of trains when the panelman upstairs 'calls' a route. *Adrian Vaughan*

'Regulating access to the network raises complex issues. To ensure safe and efficient operation, rail services have to operate in accordance with a very detailed timetable. The timetabling process is of key importance in deciding which services should have priority in the allocation of paths. There are difficult issues, too, about how different types of passenger and freight services should be charged for the use of infrastructure and related overheads. For passenger services, provision will need to be made to reconcile the requirements for franchised services with the opportunities to be provided for liberalised commercial services. The Government has commissioned a major consultancy study to address these issues.'

The Government spent £450 million on privatisation consultancies. (Parliamentary answer, 15.11.96)

Besides the subsidised franchisees, there would be 'open access' train operators. The impractical theoreticians who envisaged all this really thought that there could be as many operators on the railways as wanted to come forward. Timetabling, junctions and platform arrangements meant nothing to the economists, stockbrokers, bankers and lawyers who were selling their

exorbitant advice to the Government. The privatisers had candidly admitted the difficult and expensive complexity of their plan, yet were determined to go ahead and apply their 18th-century theories to the 21st century. I recall my jaw-sagging disbelief, in 1992, listening to the BBC News and hearing politicians talking about the railways as if they were roads and betraying their total lack of understanding of what running a railway involves.

The White Paper stated:

'33. Having to purchase rolling stock outright before commencing operations could prove a formidable barrier to entry for operators entirely new to the market. That barrier should be lowered if they are able to lease new rolling stock from private sector leasing companies or if a healthy second-hand market can be developed. Most franchisees will wish to commence operations using the existing rolling stock, and this will be available to them to rent.'

The locomotives and carriages had to be sold off because of the concept of franchising the train operating function. People thinking of taking on a franchise might be put off by the capital cost of buying their trains outright – then again, when they lost their franchise they would have the problem of selling their vehicles. Franchising required a rolling stock leasing system.

In April 1993 Roger Freeman, Minister of Transport, announced that BR's 11,260 locomotives and carriages would be transferred to three BRB-owned subsidiary 'ROSCOs' – rolling stock companies – by 1 April 1994, and at some later stage offered for sale. The three ROSCOs created another set of middlemen – always expensive people to have around – and another set of companies that could hold the Government to ransom with regard to railways. They would have a captive market. The job of advising the BRB on how to structure the companies, of setting a value on the rolling stock – and therefore on the cost of renting it and finding buyers for it – then went to Hambros Bank.

In 1996-97 Hambros was engaged by Andrew Regan to assist him in his attempt to purchase the Co-operative Wholesale Society (CWS). The CWS, like BR, is a survivor from a more humane world and, like BR, was a target for the eagles of individualism. Documents confidential to CWS were improperly obtained by Hambros for the advantage of Regan. In August 1998 the Securities & Futures Authority severely reprimanded Hambros, and the company was fined £270,000 and costs of £80,000. Messrs Pantling and Large (Directors) were each reprimanded, fined £20,000 and made to pay costs of £10,000. Mr Salmon was reprimanded, fined £8,000 and made to pay costs of £10,000. Hambros apologised to CWS. In 1999 Hambros was sold to a French bank for £300 million. Simon Leathes, Hambros Finance Director, received a 'success fee' – shares worth £252,000 – in addition to his wages of £275,000 per annum, with an annual bonus of

£100,000. Hundreds of staff at Hambros lost their jobs. (Financial Services Authority Report, 16 September 1999.)

The BR fleet was on average 16 years old (Gourvish, p.420) and this included six ex-London Underground trains, built in 1938, which were running on the Isle of Wight. The BRB's accounts valued the whole fleet at £2 billion. Given the Treasury's order to make an 8% return, that indicated a total rental value of £160 million. Hambros' calculations valued the fleet at £4.341 billion, 8% of which was considered to be too high for train operators to afford – so they simply said the value was £3.5 billion. It is wonderful how economists can create their own reality. The three ROSCOs, each with a mixed selection of vehicles to hire out, were called Angel Trains, Eversholt, and Porterbrook. Not names which would 'recover a sense of pride in our railways and recapture the spirit of the regional companies'. How tritely promises slip off the tongues – or the pens – of politicians – whatever serves for the moment. These became subsidiaries of the BRB on 1 April 1994 and were transferred to the Department of Transport in August 1995 prior to the final offers being made.

The New Labour Party made thunderous threats of re-nationalisation should they ever be returned to power, which must have had a dampening effect on potential bidders. At the October 1994 Party Conference Tony Blair promised that

'…education … cannot be left to the market. Nor can our health service. Or our armed forces. Or our police. Neither should the railways or the Post Office.

These are public services – they should be run for the public; and they should stay in public ownership for the people of this country. And if the Tories say there is no money to fund better public services, then let us tell them the cuts they could make. They could save 700 million pounds on the costs and fees and city charges of railway privatisation. 700 million could have been used to build a high-speed link from London to Manchester and Liverpool, upgrade lines between there and Hull and Middlesbrough, and still have enough left over to improve commuter services on Network SouthEast.'

The Tories blamed these dire warnings for the low price they got for the BR fleet. But as the same government *guaranteed* 80% of any buyer's subsequent income until 2004, it seems unlikely that Blair's posturing had much effect on price. The BR fleet was sold cheaply because there was no rush of eager buyers – and the weeks and months were passing. The entire privatisation project had to be sold before the next election.

Only three groups came forward. Dr John Prideaux, whose consortium purchased one-third of BR rolling stock under the title 'Angel Trains', stated in a lecture to the Institute of Logistics & Transport on 11 November 2003 that the price paid was 'not based on any accountancy mechanism but on the purchasers' notion of the earning potential of the assets procedures.' In other words, the Government was so desperate to sell the fleet before the next election that they took whatever the buyers offered – in total £1.743 billion. As a measure of the future earning potential of the vehicles, the price was seriously pessimistic, and, for people supposedly committed to business efficiency, to have accepted it was truly remarkable – except that it was a political decision, not a commercial one.

Angel Trains and Porterbrook were sold in January 1996 for £527 million and £528 million respectively. Eversholt went in February, to a management buyout, for £518 million. They were all sold with a government guarantee of a certain level of income from leasing their existing locomotives and carriages to the train operating companies. In August 1996 Porterbrook was sold to the Stagecoach train operating company for £830 million. This bit of vertical integration – which evaded the notice of the High Priests of Fragmentation – lasted four years. Then Souter, having somewhat over-reached himself in the USA, and also looking to the time when his guaranteed income on the leasing business would come to an end, sold out to Abbey National for £1.4 billion, a profit of £773 million. Eversholt was sold on to Forward Trust, a subsidiary of HSBC, in February 1997 for £726 million.

Since then all three ROSCOs have gone on to become very profitable companies. In his November 2003 lecture, John Prideaux stated that fierce competition between the three ROSCOs has 'driven down the price of new trains by 30%. Rents for new trains are set by direct competition between the ROSCOs and the lessors.' But this surely is the disadvantage of competition to the proprietors of the competing companies? It reduces their profits. Robert Stephenson, railway engineer and Tory MP for Whitby, had discovered this in the 1840s and had complained bitterly and at length about it in a speech in January 1856. (See my *Railwaymen, Politics & Money*, pp.120-2) When competition reduces profits, companies amalgamate, or at least cool their competition. By November 2006 the competition was so cool that the Rail Regulator announced that he was 'minded' to refer the lack of competition to the Competition Commission.

CHAPTER 8

The Railways Bill

On 4 July 1992 John MacGregor made a statement to Parliament with the publication of the White Paper on the future of British Railways:

'British Rail has made significant improvements in recent years. Investment in the railways has greatly increased. The productivity of the British Rail workforce is among the highest of any European railways. I pay tribute to the considerable efforts of everyone in British Rail in bringing that about … common objectives have been the harnessing of the management flair and enterprise of the private sector, the application of the disciplines and incentives of the marketplace, the opportunities for private finance and for greater competition and choice which privatisation brings, all to provide better services for the public.'

That was very kind of him, but one might ask the old question, 'If it ain't broken, why fix it?' The answer to that was the mere assertion that: 'Private sector involvement will help develop the quality and quantity of rail services even further.' There was no reason, beyond political dogma, why BR could not do that – indeed it was doing that.

The Parliamentary debate on the Railways Bill was initiated by John MacGregor, on 29 October 1992. What comes out is the blind faith he placed in the workings of 'management', 'the market', 'private enterprise' and 'competition'. The value of and the vital need for railway experience was never specifically mentioned by his side of

In 1936 the Great Western, very early on the diesel scene, introduced seven 350hp Hawthorn-Leslie/English Electric diesel-electric shunters. The Southern Railway introduced three English Electric 350hp machines in 1937. The LMS took 30 in 1939, another 36 starting in 1945. The LNER had four in 1944. The British Railways diesel-electric shunters were introduced in 1953 – later coded as Class 08 – and were almost identical to those of the GWR. They were the most successful diesel locomotive BR ever had, with nearly 1,000 built, spread all over the system. This is No 08250 at Lowestoft, and behind it the 4.40pm DMU to Norwich in the summer of 1985. *Adrian Vaughan*

The English Electric Type 1 1,000hp diesel-electric was introduced in 1957 and proved the most reliable of the early, low-powered main-line diesels. They became Class 20 under the TOPS scheme and 228 were built up to 1968. This example of the type is very much at home here on the North London line, working a transfer trip from the Western Region at Acton to Dockland.
Adrian Vaughan Collection

the House, not in three debates. The nearest approach to this admission was in a later amendment to the Railways Bill, allowing BR to give a free grant of £100,000 (Hansard, Vol 218, col 42, 1.11.93) to any individual or group of BR managers, or persons who had once been BR managers, who felt like mortgaging their houses to raise the money to buy into a franchise. Even then, BR managers' railway operating experience was not mentioned – only their good fortune to be freed from the shackles of the past – which consisted of steadily and securely providing train services as part of a unified, experienced industry – and to join the glossy new world of self-interest, gambling, and unstable private enterprise, which was to be trusted to bring unspecified 'new products' to the railway and the commonweal.

Mr MacGregor said:

'BR is not financially viable and our task has been to find ways to maximise the amount of outright privatisation and – short of that – to maximise private sector involvement. Many services do not, some perhaps cannot ever, pay, thus we cannot provide an entirely privatised and competitive passenger railway. *The main attraction of privatisation is that it allows the private sector to take management and financial responsibility for service. Secondly it creates some competition to provide the service.*' (Hansard, Vol 212, col 1164-65, 29.10.92)

The only way to get someone to buy your unprofitable railway is to promise subsidies in order that shareholders could receive their dividends. BR's subsidies went into the track, trains and signalling, the new subsidies would also be required to maintain dividends to shareholders. Thus the railways would cost more to run, not less. Competition is not necessary to provide train services in an organisation devoted to the public as BR was.

Mr MacGregor followed this with the curiously contradictory statement that, 'Pouring more and more money into the system will not necessarily provide a railway system that meets modern customer requirements.' BR was already providing a very high quality of service on a budget that could not be described as 'more and more money', as MacGregor had acknowledged at the start of his speech. In fact, it was his declared intention to pour more and more money into the railway – once it had been sold off:

'The Public Service Obligation subsidies in the current year amount to about £1 billion. We intend to continue those subsidies … [but] we intend that as much risk as possible should be transferred to the private sector.' (Hansard, Vol 212, col 1166-67, 29.10.92) Subsidies to franchises were immediately greater than those previously paid to BRB.

It was clear that breaking up the railway was going to make the maintenance of safety difficult because of the number of different operators that would be involved. Mr MacGregor talked about safety on the railway.

'We are committed to ensuring the safe operating of railways and our proposals were drawn up with the expert advice of the Health & Safety Commission [HSC], which will continue to have a role. Primary responsibility will rest with Railtrack, then with the train operators. All standards of safety will have to be met and the HSC will monitor and enforce those standards across the industry. Rail operators will have to demonstrate their ability to

The Class 20s were operationally reliable and on passenger trains had a top speed of 60mph. They could also be worked in multiple like this, coupled nose to nose, to overcome the shortage of power of single engines and the steam engine's lack of visibility when drivers had to look for signals with all that engine casing in their sight. This was a regular scene at Skegness, on 10 June 1984. *Adrian Vaughan*

comply with safety regulations before being allowed access, and the powers of the HMRI will be extended to ensure continued safe rail operation.' (Hansard, Vol 212, col 1170, 29.10.92)

Confident words, which might have returned to haunt him.

At the second reading of the Bill on 2 February 1993 Mr MacGregor again paid tribute to the real and existing efficiency of BR:

'British Rail has improved considerably in recent years in many of its services. But most people agree that there is still much room for further improvement.'

Both statements were true. Sir Bob Reid 2 modestly agreed that the BRB could do better – any organisation can do better. The issue was, could better railway work be done by breaking the railway into dozens of little bits?

Having emphasised how well BR was operating, Mr MacGregor went on to dogmatically assert how much better the new system would work when all the horrors of nationalisation were removed. He now described BR as if it was a dismal failure; he made unjustified assertions and statements the only purpose of which was pejorative.

'As an organisation, BR combines the classic shortcomings of the traditional nationalised industry. It is an entrenched monopoly. That means too little

The Brush/Mirlees 1,250hp Type 2 diesel-electrics were introduced in 1957, with a top speed of 90mph. The original engine and generator were not entirely successful and from 1964 the class was re-equipped with English Electric power. They went initially to the Eastern Region but spread later to the LM and Western Regions. Here, in its original colours of green with a white stripe, D5848 stands in Ripple Lane yards in 1960.
Adrian Vaughan Collection

responsiveness to customers' needs, whether passenger or freight; no real competition; and too little diversity and innovation. Inevitably, it also has the culture of a nationalised industry: a heavily bureaucratic structure; an insufficiently sharp awareness on the part of employees that their success depends on satisfying the customer — indeed, on attracting more customers; and an instinctive tendency to ask for more taxpayers' subsidy and to feel that public subsidy will always be there as a crutch whenever things look difficult. Inevitably public ownership also brings with it the constraints of public finance, not least given the many competing demands on the public purse.' (Hansard, Vol 218, col 156, 2.2.93)

The 'private ownership' system he was going to introduce was designed to take public money, and because there were so many organisations to take the money, more of it would be required. The new system would suffer from other, more expensive, illnesses, from which the solidly organised BR could not suffer. And as for '…to feel that public subsidy will always be there as a crutch whenever things look difficult', that was highly ironic. It was perfectly obvious that the said crutch was part of the sale! As the railways would be crippled by being severely broken up, the crutch was bound to be bigger.

The whole point of breaking up the railway was to introduce 'competition', yet even the privatisers could see that a certain monopoly was essential in operating trains. On 22 March 1993, in the House of Commons, Bob Dunn, MP for Dartford, asked the Minister of Transport, Roger Freeman, 'when will open access for operators of new services come into effect, following enactment of the Railways Bill?'

To which Mr Freeman replied:

'We have already announced that there will be restrictions placed on open access, to the extent necessary to allow the successful transfer of British Rail's passenger services to the private sector. If open access operators apply for train paths in advance of invitations to tender for the franchise concerned, they will be informed then of the terms of competition which will apply.'

The franchisees had to be sure of a monopoly to get them to bid for the franchise. The successful franchisee was also guaranteed a monopoly for a number of years.

Mr MacGregor said that a vital part of the new plan was to divide responsibility!

'Responsibility for track will generally be split from responsibility for operating trains. A new public sector organisation called Railtrack will be responsible for track. That split has a number of advantages, on which I will expand later. Railtrack will be required to contract out as many of its services as it reasonably can. That, too, is a vital point and is laid down in the Bill. It will be vital in improving its efficiency and thus keeping its prices down.'

(Hansard, Vol 218, col 159, 2.2.93) Again, the same blind assertions, contracting out, *will* be 'more efficient'. Why, when Railtrack would have to pay the contractor to make his profit, would that be cheaper than keeping the work 'in house'? Would it be more efficient work when jobs would be sub-contracted, subjected to the full benefit of private enterprise wrangling.

The Secretary of State cited the success of British Airways (BA) as proof that fragmenting BR would be highly successful.

The history of BA up to 1993 was not particularly edifying but was a classic example of the piratical attitude that can accompany private enterprise. Under Lord King, BA's public 'image' was changed by the use of glossy adverts, while costs were reduced by making 23,500 people redundant. The £545 million of inducements paid to employees to forsake the industry were contributed by the British taxpayer and, with that indirect subsidy, BA moved towards profit. In 1984 Richard Branson set up Virgin Atlantic with one plane, but very quickly became a serious rival to BA. Lord King was no more enthusiastic, and after Branson scored a huge public relations coup in 1991 by flying aid into Baghdad and hostages out just before the start of the 1991 US-Iraqi war, Lord King decided to undertake a 'dirty tricks' campaign against Virgin Atlantic and its owner. Branson was obliged to sue Lord King for libel in 1992. King settled out of court for £500,000 compensation to Branson and £110,000 to his

In BR standard blue, No 31110 is waiting at Whatley Quarry Junction while the guard re-sets the junction leading to the Quarry from the Radstock branch on 14 June 1975. The train consists of 'cripple' wagons for the repair shops. *Adrian Vaughan*

airline company. Branson divided his compensation among his staff, the so-called 'BA bonus'. That was kind of Mr Branson, but it also illustrates that these great egos are not suitable people to be running public services.

A practical, orderly, co-ordinated railway was of less importance than a railway disorganised to conform to an economist's theoretical 'model'. Mr MacGregor said in Parliament:

'One issue which has surfaced in public debate is that of vertical integration – the management and control of both track and trains by the same body – as against horizontal integration – separating the track authority from the operators.'

It would have been nice, at that point, to ask him how a thing can be integrated when it has been separated.

'We concluded, and we made it clear in our election manifesto, that full vertical integration was neither practical nor desirable across the great bulk of the railway network. That is why we propose Railtrack as the national infrastructure authority.' (Hansard, Vol 218, col 165, 2.2.93)

He went on:

'Operators who run both the track and the trains would inevitably face a conflict of interest when others applied to run services on their line.'

This had never been a problem in the 'glorious' past of the old companies, on 'joint' lines and lines where 'running powers' existed.

Above: In 1958 BR introduced what became known as the Class 40 Type 4 diesels. They were the next generation of main-line diesels, developed from the LMS/English Electric Nos 10000 and 10201-3. They had 2,000hp to work with, a weight of 135 tons and a top speed of 90mph. Owing to their huge weight, their acceleration was little if any better than an express steam engine, but of course they were far cheaper to operate. They went to work out of King's Cross, Liverpool Street and Euston on the best expresses. Here, No 332 emerges from Kilsby Tunnel in 1962, when barely a year old. It was scrapped in 1987. *Peter Barlow/Adrian Vaughan Collection*

Below: No 40096 – originally D295, built in 1960 – is seen at Manchester Victoria on 17 July 1979. This one was withdrawn in 1983; the last to go were withdrawn in 1984. *Kevin Connolly/Adrian Vaughan Collection*

'We want to give everyone, including freight operators, a fair crack of the whip – they regard this as very important – but we could do it on vertically integrated lines only if we adopted intrusive regulation to ensure fair treatment for all.'

During all these debates in 1992-93, MacGregor talked as if he had the system cut and dried, but in fact the Government's policies were constantly being changed. They did not know, for instance, how the access charges for the yet to be discovered train operators would be calculated. The main objective was to get it all sold off before the next election and – perhaps – the return of a government opposed to privatisation.

Rothschild Consultants had been involved in the sell-off of all the British nationalised utilities since 1985. One of their employees, Simon Linnett, working on the privatisation of the railways, wrote in November 1992, when privatisation was being forced through Parliament: 'There is no [previous] sale which has reached this stage in the legislative process in anywhere near the same level of government confusion as we perceive at present. (Quoted in Gourvish, p.408) During the whole time that the Railways Bill was being drafted, then debated in Parliament, the privatisers behind the scenes were still developing their ideas on what the privatised railway would look like.

But even the Tories, who were so eloquent upon the virtues of private enterprise, acknowledged that self-interest required more regulation (and therefore more expense) to produce a public service than a nationalised railway would require. There was going to be regulation from a Rail Regulator and a Franchise Director under Mr MacGregor's plan. He went on to express his optimism on the outcome of having a track authority divorced from the trains.

'One of our key priorities is to secure suitable levels of investment in rail infrastructure. Investment on that scale requires a strategic view of the kind that only Railtrack can provide. Railtrack will focus infrastructure investment on the parts of the network where it is most needed. It would be unrealistic to expect individual franchisees to do the same.'

But a railway company owning its freehold and running its own trains would have a strategic view.

'Railtrack will have the key role in ensuring the safety aspects of track and signalling. The existence of a national track authority will ensure that safety standards and procedures are coordinated across the track in a clear and systematic way. [This was] a point that was of particular importance to the Health & Safety Commission in its consideration of our proposals. It would be much more difficult to achieve that if track responsibilities were spread across a large number of local operators.'
It would have been safer, therefore, if the railway had remained an integrated whole.

A 1,160hp Sulzer-engined, BTH generator Type 2 diesel-electric brings the 4.25 pm Marylebone to Nottingham train past Aylesbury South box and into Aylesbury station in 1963. In all, 151 of these were built between 1958 and 1961. Their top speed, with the right load, was only 75mph, and they were developed into the Class 25, the first of these appearing in 1961. They were also Sulzer Type 2, but had 1,250hp, and were geared to run at 90mph. *Peter Barlow/Adrian Vaughan Collection*

Not only was the railway to be fragmented into short-term operators, but Railtrack itself would be no more than 'a supplier of infrastructure services to the operators of train services' and would contract out all its maintenance and renewals. This was a tremendous abdication of responsibility, and clearly those who proposed it – while invoking the nostalgia of the 'old companies' – had no idea of the sense of responsibility possessed by the Directors of those old companies. Contracts do not guarantee good workmanship. Loyalty to one's district and pride in a public service ethos are required – but this was a BR 'culture' that it was the declared purpose of privatisation to destroy. Unspoken but very much intended was the dispersal and thus weakening of trade unionists. Trade unions are concerned with maintaining standards, if only for the safety of their members.

Mr MacGregor was not even certain about standards of safety. On 5 February 1993 he told Parliament that Railtrack would 'maintain the infrastructure at *appropriate* levels'. What were they? MacGregor believed that because Railtrack would eventually become be a privately owned, shareholder company it could raise whatever money it wanted without the Public Sector Borrowing restrictions of a nationalised concern. But if Railtrack was busy borrowing and spending rather than making huge profits through the tried and tested method of cost-cutting, then the profits would not be there, the share price would go down and people would not want to invest in Railtrack shares.

During 1993 the entire civil, mechanical, signal and telecommunications engineering capacity of BR, including seven drawing offices with 37,000 employees, was being planned to be divided into 14 businesses – seven maintenance and seven track renewal companies called British Rail Infrastructure Services Companies (BRISCOs). It was estimated that they would in total have an annual gross income of £1 billion. This chopping up and re-packaging was carried out by a small body of BR managers. The ultimate aim of government was the sale of these businesses to the private sector – perhaps management buy-outs – but meanwhile they were to be contractors to the still-nationalised Railtrack. By the time the various BRISCOs were sold in 1994, 14,500 staff in these technical departments had been made redundant or not replaced when they retired. These were new losses of staff, after years of job cutting. (Gourvish, Vol 2, p.404) More than 100 contracts were rushed together to enable the businesses to carry on doing for Railtrack what they had been doing without contracts for BR. One of the features of these contracts was that the contractor agreed to reduce its charges to Railtrack annually during the term of the contract. Constant cost-cutting was built into the system. The new businesses were rushed together and operational on 1 April 1994.

This is one of the 2,000hp 'D600' class of five diesel-hydraulics foisted upon a reluctant Western Region by the British Railways central management in December 1957. They were powered by two German MAN diesels and German Voith hydraulic transmission, which had worked well in Germany. This equipment was mounted in a massively strong chassis designed and built by the North British Locomotive Company, the total weight of the locomotive being 117 tons. They worked all the best trains out of Paddington to the West, but performance-wise they were little better than a 'King' with a keen crew. *John Ashman/ Adrian Vaughan Collection*

The 'D63xx' diesel-hydraulics – or Class 22, as they became – were half-size D600s, first introduced between 1959 and 1962. They were fitted with MAN/Voith equipment and had a total weight of 65 tons. The first four were 1,000hp, but the rest – 52 units – were 1,100hp. They all had a top speed of 75mph. They were unreliable and the traffic they were built to haul melted away. Withdrawal of the whole class took place between 1967 and 1971. D6316 is seen here at Ranelagh Bridge yard, Paddington, in 1962. *John Ashman/ Adrian Vaughan Collection*

The sale of the 14 BRISCOs – with their estimated total revenue of £1 billion a year – generated for the public purse £169 million, out of which came deductions for consultants and lawyers' fees. James Jerram, a full-time Director of the BRB, was unhappy with the projected cost of consultancy – put at £3 million by Coopers & Lybrand – and he demanded that the work be put out to tender. (Gourvish, Vol 2, p.409).

Mr Brian Wilson MP said in Parliament in November 1993:

'Seldom can a piece of legislation have been so thoroughly discredited before even reaching the statute book. Yesterday the final depths of farce were plumbed. We learned that the Department of Transport working party on restructuring British Rail had told Ministers that a £2 billion public service obligation grant will be required for next year. That is £1.15 billion more than for the current year, and it is just the first instalment in the cost of privatisation.

At a time when everything worthwhile in our society is under threat and when the nation's economic plight is so dire that Value Added Tax is to be added to the cost of domestic fuel, the Government are considering spending an extra £1.15 billion not on improving the railways but on financing the privatisation of the railways. As a result of that extra £1.15 billion, not one extra train will run, not one extra passenger will be carried and not one extra

tonne of freight will be transferred from our roads. The phenomenal increase in the taxpayers' subsidy will not go towards developing our railways. It will go towards paying for the gargantuan additional costs inherent in rail fragmentation and privatisation.' (Hansard, Vol 231, col 43-45, 1.11.93)

The last debate on the collection of untried – and clearly unworkable – assertions called 'the Railways Bill' took place on 3 November 1993 under a 'guillotine' motion, so that the debating time was strictly limited. John Biffen, a Conservative politician who had once described Mrs Thatcher's style as 'Stalinist' (*Sunday Telegraph*, 5 July 1987) said of this guillotine debate, 'no House of Commons having even a modest regard for self-respect would be presenting Members with such an extensive Bill to be dispatched in two days.' The son of a tenant farmer in Somerset, he had voted against the 'Poll Tax' and the Maastricht Treaty, voted for a referendum on the EU Constitution, and was sacked from cabinet by Mrs Thatcher.

The Royal Assent was given to this most unpopular Bill on 5 November 1993. To become law on the day of commemoration of the man who tried to blow up Parliament is quite apt, as was the day on which the Act was to take effect – 1 April 1994. But the joke was on the electorate.

Above: The Western Region management was very impressed with the technical details and operational performance of the Deutsche Bundesbahn 'V200' class and saw no reason why the machine should not be translated into Western Region practice. These became Classes 42 and 43 – the 'Warships' – introduced in 1958. They had tubular main frames in a light alloy and stressed sheet metal bodies. Within, those built at Swindon had two 1,000hp Maybach engines driving Mekydro hydraulic transmissions. Those built by North British had MAN/Voith equipment. One, No D830, was fitted with two 1,250hp Paxman Ventura engines. The 'Warships' were very fast and very technically advanced, weighing 79 tons for 2,000hp, and were carried on two four-wheel bogies. The Class 40 needed eight axles to carry its 2,000hp and 135 tons. The BRB decided in 1967 to standardise on diesel-electrics, so the withdrawal of the 'Warships' began. Here No D838, an NBL-built engine, passes Reading on the Up Main in 1962. *John Ashman/Adrian Vaughan Collection*

Left: The cab of a 'Warship', successor to the 'King' class steam engines.
BR/Adrian Vaughan Collection

Above: The Class 35 'Hymek' was the most powerful single-engined diesel on British Railways. It had a 12-cylinder Maybach engine developing 1,750hp and driving a British Mekydro hydraulic transmission, and 101 of them were built at Beyer Peacock's works, Gorton, between 1961 and 1964. Because of the policy of standardisation they were all withdrawn from service between 1971 and 1975. Here we see No D7021 on the Up Relief Line, passing New Junction, east of Reading.
John Ashman/
Adrian Vaughan Collection

Right: A 'Hymek' returning 'light' to Oxford North Junction from Bletchley after taking the Cardiff-Corby coal train in 1970.
Adrian Vaughan

CHAPTER 9

'Safety is justified as safety'

In November 1992 the Managing Directors and Profit Centre Directors of BR's various passenger sectors met with John MacGregor at Euston House. MacGregor was told 'in no uncertain terms' (Gourvish, p.394) that, if the railway was to be sold, it should be sold as the vertically integrated Sectors then successfully operating. They foresaw that a privatised railway would want to cut its costs and quality of service in an attempt to make a profit, hence there was to be a government regulator to oversee standards on the railway and the railway would therefore be more strictly controlled – interfered with – than was the case under BR. On 1 January 1993 MacGregor appointed to the BRB Sir Robert Horton, Archie Norman, a supermarket genius, and Jennifer Page, sacked Chief Executive of the Millennium Dome, to be 'shadow' Railtrack Board members. In March John Edmonds moved from the BR Board to the shadow Railtrack Board, and in August Christopher Jonas, a banker, was added.

Sir Robert Horton had spent most of his working life with British Petroleum, becoming Chairman in 1990, and, as profits fell, being ejected in a boardroom coup in 1991. He said of himself, 'Because I am blessed by my good brain I tend to get the right answer quicker and more often than most people. That will sound frightfully arrogant but it's true.' (Alastair Osborne, *Electronic Telegraph* No 1373, 27.2.99)

Horton's Chief Executive was the extremely untypical career railwayman John Edmonds. A Lowestoft lad, he had entered the railway service in about 1965 with an Oxbridge degree as a management trainee. He became known for his iconoclastic attitude towards BR's traditions of engineering excellence. His thoughts were that railwaymen were over-cautious and the railway over-engineered – cost-cutting was his forte. For long he had wanted to see the whole business sold off, contracted out, made into a flagship of free-market enterprise.

Swindon Works dump: as the diesels flood in, the steam engines are displaced. Acres of scrap boilers lie on the ground in 1963 and provide smokebox hidey-holes for scrapyard staff when they want a fag, or their lunch, or should it come on to rain. *Adrian Vaughan*

The tearing apart of the railway at this time must have contravened the obligations laid on the railway by Anthony Hidden's 'Recommendations'. In his Report on the Clapham crash, issued in November 1989, he made 92 recommendations. In every one, the word 'shall' was used, suggesting an order rather than a recommendation. The Recommendations were addressed to 'BR' and to a unified authority. Railtrack agreed to be bound by the Hidden Recommendations but it was not possible – for instance – for Railtrack 'to give technical training as necessary to ensure that efficient and safe practices are carried out by all technical staff.' (Recommendation 14)

The task of improving safety on a fragmented railway is much more difficult than on a unified railway. Sir David Davies, President of the Royal Academy of Engineers, made a study of Automatic Train Protection (ATP) in 1999 at the request of the Government and made the following observation.

'Such trials impact upon the operational and financial performances of the different sections of the industry. The current machinery … has been criticised for its long delays in establishing safety cases and proving trials … owing to multiple interfaces between different organisations … they may be incompatible with the current franchise agreements.' (Sir David Davies CDE, FREng, FRS, 'Automatic Train Protection for the Railway Network in Britain', January 2000)

Hidden's Recommendation No 46 obliged the BRB to install ATP on a large percentage of its passenger lines within five years, after selecting which ATP system would be used. Under the ATP system, if a train approached a danger signal or a junction too fast the system would apply the brakes and stop the train before it got into danger – and the driver could not cancel the braking.

In January 1990 the BRB formed an ATP Project Management team under Bob Walters, and two versions of ATP were installed for comparative trials. The British Westinghouse 'SEL' system was installed on the Marylebone-Bicester North route, and the Belgian system, designed and manufactured by ACEC of Charleroi, on the Paddington-Wootton Bassett-Bristol Parkway and Bristol Temple Meads routes. ATP equipment was installed at 455 signals from Bristol Temple Meads and Bristol Parkway to West Drayton, with the exception of some deliberate gaps between Bath and Bristol. Eighty-seven HSTs of Inter City Great Western and 34 Class 165 DMUs on the Chiltern route were equipped with the ATP pick-up equipment; the existing AWS equipment remained in place throughout. The trials or Pilot Scheme began in May 1991 and were to last two years. They were under the unified control of the BRB and under the Board's validation procedures.

The trials were disrupted as soon as they started by the semi-fragmentation under OfQ, and no sooner had OfQ been completed than they were again interrupted by

The Southern Region placed an order with the Birmingham Railway Carriage & Wagon Company for 65 of its 1,550hp Sulzer-engined diesel-electrics in 1959, to replace all their steam engines in Kent. They came into service in 1960-62, and were so successful that the SR increased the order to 98 while the first batch was still rolling out of BRC&W's Smethwick works. Only the loss of their freight work and their passenger turns going over to DMU operation caused them to be withdrawn, from 1985. Of the original 98, 30 are still at work, preserved or with main-line locomotive companies. Here, one of the class comes powering down the hill out of Oxford, past Hinksey North signal box, with a Washwood Heath to Southampton express goods in June 1970.
Adrian Vaughan

Rumbling over the Usk Viaduct into Newport (Monmouthshire) is No 6606, an English Electric Type 3 diesel-electric, powered by a 1,750hp Mirlees engine driving the English Electric generator. They must surely be the most successful of BR diesels, with 28 of them still in use today on the national rail network and 40 in store or preserved. *John Ashman/ Adrian Vaughan Collection*

Railtrack taking over from the BRB in 1994. After that came the disruptions and distractions of outright sell-off. The ATP Project Director, Bob Walters, took part in a management buy-out of the project in 1996 and this was subsequently purchased by AEA Technology, a branch of the Atomic Energy Authority.

Page vii of 'The Formal Evaluation of the APT Pilot Scheme', published internally in November 2001, stated:

1. BRB internal re-organisation into Business Sectors 1992-4 disrupted ATP project management and the working relationships between organisations.
2. Government policy to privatise the railway in 1993 generally distracted from ATP implementation and lowered staff morale.
3. ATP was not a consideration in government privatisation policy.' The hidden recommendations on safety were pushed aside by the government's rush to political dogma and a great safety measure was seriously delayed.

Messrs Jacobs and Insell of the GWR Signal Department had patented their Automatic Train Control in July 1905. It was brought into use at the various Distant signals on the double-track Henley branch in January 1906. Installation at all Distant signals on the four tracks

between Reading and Slough was completed in November 1908, reaching Paddington some time in 1910. The Great War intervened, but afterwards the GWR steadily got on with almost universal application – without any government help – and all double-track routes were equipped by 1930. The GWR employed all the engineering personnel required and did not have to ask permission from any outside body – it just got on with the job.

This GWR system of management was how BR operated – but the privatisers said that BR was inefficient and what we needed was to get back to 'the glories of the past'.

In March 1994 the BRB submitted its report on the ATP Pilot Scheme. In it the Board advised the Government that the cost – even of a partial application of ATP – was not justified by the benefits in lives saved. The BRB reckoned a life at around £3.5 million. The Health & Safety Commission thought the true value was at least three times greater, but it would not name a price. (Cullen Report into the Ladbroke Grove disaster, Annexe 26B) In the Parliamentary debate following the Clapham crash, Cecil Parkinson told the Commons that 'investment in safety is not required to produce any sort of return: safety is justified as safety.' (Hansard, Vol 159, col 848, 7.11.88).

The Health & Safety Commission's advice was sought. The HSC read the BRB Report and agreed with its conclusions, although if a life was valued at at least £10 or 11 million maybe the ATP was cost-effective. A three-cornered discussion then took place between the Chairman of BRB, Railtrack and John MacGregor, which ended on 21 November 1995 with the decision to bring the existing pilot schemes into operation, but that for general use the Train Protection & Warning System (TPWS) would be developed together with improvements to train braking systems. TPWS will bring a train to a stand at a red signal provided that the train is not travelling at more than 70mph.

So the excellent ATP was restricted to the existing pilot scheme routes, and the 'Heathrow Express' trains – owned by the British Airports Authority – were fitted with the equipment during their construction. This was in contravention of Anthony Hidden's Recommendation for near-nationwide fitting.

The ATP system had been validated by BR and was working very well for a pilot scheme at the end of 1993, although there were still faults to be put right. After Railtrack took over that company, it would be obliged to re-assess and validate the ATP all over again, according to its own safety case. The shadow Railtrack knew it would have insufficient technical staff to make such an evaluation, and in December 1993 asked the manufacturers to produce 'Proofs of Safety' and hired as consultants large numbers of ex-railway signal engineers and other technical experts to carry out the new validation. Railtrack put the value of a life at £2 million.

The price of a life is not the only saving brought about by ATP. It was not given monetary value for cost reduction due to the simplification of layouts, without reducing the traffic capacity of that layout. Layouts that would have been dangerous without ATP became harmless with it installed. It could be said that ATP actually allowed the signal engineers to get a quart into a pint pot, safely, always providing that all the different train companies had got around to fitting their trains with the ATP equipment.

Chapter 13 of the Uff Report on the Southall crash, paragraph 13, page 160, states:

'While Railtrack were generally in favour of continuing the pilot [scheme] both Great Western Trains(GWT) and Angel Trains regarded it with a degree of disfavour and would have been content to see the project abandoned.'

The Class 37s, as they became, were always thought of as freight engines. Here a pair of them bring a long train of air-braked 'Procor' stone hoppers into Westbury, en route for either Whatley or Merehead quarries. *John Ashman/Adrian Vaughan Collection*

No DP2 was built by English Electric as a demonstration model to entice BR to buy more of the type. It was erected on the same assembly line and simultaneously with the 'Deltic' diesels. It has the external look of a 'Deltic', but is actually the forerunner of the Class 50. DP2 carries a single, 16-cylinder, 2,700hp English Electric engine driving an Electric English generator. Although its service speed was 90mph, it had been built so that it could easily be tweaked for 105mph. It was given on loan to BR(LMR) in 1962 and worked WCML expresses – it is seen here passing Rugeley. It was a great machine but was heavily damaged in a collision at Thirsk in July 1967 and scrapped. *Peter Barlow/ Adrian Vaughan Collection*

Neither GWT nor Angel Trains, which owned the HSTs concerned, had any legal obligation to cooperate with the ATP project. On 6 September 1996 the GWT representative stated that his company would not pay any part of the antennae development costs. At a meeting between Richard George of GWT and David Rayner of Railtrack on 28 January 1997, the possibility of abandoning ATP was seriously discussed, but in July 1997 GWT agreed that it would co-operate but still without any legal obligation to do so. A Parliamentary Transport Committee investigating the effect of privatisation on ATP found GWT's position 'deeply disturbing'. (Uff Report, p.155)

There were difficulties with fitting the ATP antennae and cabling to the underside of the leading end of each HST power car. The HSTs had been designed years before and there was very little room under the cars in which to mount the electrical equipment, because of the fuel tanks.

Railtrack decided, in the second half of 1996, to commission an investigation into the problems of the antennae. The work of making the report was not given to recognised experts in the field but put out to competitive tender. Weeks were wasted waiting for someone to bid for the job, so the investigation was not begun until April 1997.

Late in 1996, while Railtrack was looking for a contractor to investigate the existing antennae, a new design was brought out by ACEC. This was approved by Railtrack in December and, without knowing who was going to pay, Railtrack told Bob Walters of the ATP Project Management to order 100 of the new antennae from the Belgian company. ACEC was not sure if it had received a valid order, since no-one knew who was going to pay, but they got on with manufacturing them anyhow. In March 1997 the ATP maintenance contract between ACEC and GWT expired and was not renewed by GWT, but ACEC continued repairs and maintenance to its train-borne equipment on a 'gentlemen's agreement'. In August 1997 the funding had still not been found and Bob Walters tried to cancel the order, but by then ACEC had completed it. GWT, repenting after the calamity at Southall in September 1997, agreed to pay its share of the costs and placed its official order for the improved ATP equipment. The new antennae were fitted progressively during 1998. The Uff Report into the Southall crash states:

Above: The 'Deltic' engine was a German invention from the Great War. The Germans forfeited their patent rights after that war and they were given to the Napier Company of England. Napier produced engines for the Royal Navy, using the 'Deltic' principle, until the company was purchased by English Electric after the Second World War. EE used the 'Deltic' principle to produce a 3,300hp, 18-cylinder diesel engine for BR. It was/is not only remarkably compact, due to its shape, but also operated on the 'two-stroke' principle. The engine has no cylinder head, no valve gear and therefore no camshaft. The converging piston heads compress and fire the fuel. However, the advantage of the simplicity in these areas is somewhat lost by the complexity of the gearing required to bring the power output of the three crankshafts into one transmission shaft. The locomotive has an excellent power-to-weight ratio – 3,300bhp available for an all-up weight of 105 tons. They were timed to haul trains at 100mph. Until the 4,000bhp *Kestrel* was built by the Brush company, the 'Deltics' were the most powerful diesels in Britain. *Kestrel*, however, remained an unrepeated prototype, whereas 22 'Deltics' were built. The 'Deltics' were non-standard and were withdrawn between 1980 and 1982. Six have been preserved. This view shows No 55007 (the former D9007) *Pinza* (one that was not saved) at King's Cross on 22 March 1980. *Kevin Connolly/Adrian Vaughan Collection*

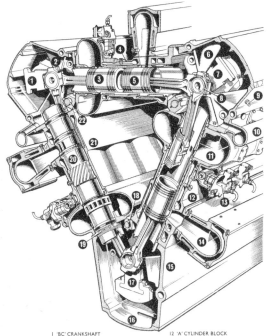

Right: The amazing 'Deltic' engine. *BR/Adrian Vaughan Collection*

1 'BC' CRANKSHAFT	12 'A' CYLINDER BLOCK
2 'BC' CRANKCASE	13 FUEL INJECTION PUMP
3 INLET PISTON	14 EXHAUST MANIFOLD
4 'B' CYLINDER BLOCK	15 'CA' CRANKCASE
5 EXHAUST PISTON	16 'CA' CRANKCASE COVER
6 'AB' CRANKCASE	17 'CA' CRANKSHAFT
7 'AB' CRANKSHAFT	18 'CA' FLEXIBLE DRIVE SHAFT
8 CONNECTING ROD	19 CASTELLATED RING NUT
9 CRANKCASE TIE-BOLT	20 CYLINDER LINER
10 DRAIN OIL MANIFOLD	21 'C' CYLINDER BLOCK
11 AIR-INLET DUCTS	22 BLOWER DRIVE SHAFTS

'This whole episode well illustrates the lack of priority and lack of commitment which undoubtedly contributed to the serious delays suffered by the ATP project since its effective downgrading in 1995.' (Uff Report, 13.13-16, pp.158-9)

The company chosen to investigate the problems of the old antennae was called Electrowatt, and the actual investigator and author of the report was Andrew Johnstone. Railtrack – which had already ordered new antennae – made a peculiar specification for the inquiry. It did not require any engineering assessments but instructed Johnstone to conduct interviews and look at documents. Johnstone reported in July 1997 that Railtrack was in favour of continuing with the trials but that GWT was not. He was deeply impressed with the capabilities of ATP and, while he recognised that, according to conventional statistical methods, ATP was not cost-effective, he heartily recommended the urgent installation of the system as he thought that there was a one in four chance of an ATP accident occurring within the next ten years. Two months later, on 19 September 1997, came the Southall crash, which ATP would have prevented. The train was fitted with ATP but the driver was not properly trained in its use. Seven passengers were killed and 150 injured.

The immediate cause of the Southall crash was the failure of Driver Harrison to look where he was going, but there were contributory factors due to privatisation, Harrison's lack of training being one.

The sale of the Great Western Trains (GWT) franchise had taken place in February 1996. There had been worries about the standards of maintenance at Old Oak Common prior to GWT being franchised in a management buy-out. The cost-cutting attitude was reinforced after privatisation.

On 8 September 1995 a Down HST leased to and maintained by GWT at Old Oak Common suffered the loss of a fuel tank at high speed near Taplow. All four securing nuts came off, the tank fell onto the track and the contents exploded, causing a fire. The train stopped on the Thames Bridge, some passengers jumped out of the burning coach, and one was killed by an Up HST.

The 'D1000' class 'Western' diesel-hydraulics were designed at Swindon. They were Type 4 2,750hp machines, using a pair of Maybach engines to drive a Voith hydraulic transmission. They had two six-wheeled bogies, and all wheels were powered. No D1000 *Western Enterprise* entered service in December 1962, and 74 were built between 1962 and 1964. The first withdrawals began in 1973 and by 1977 none were left in service on BR, although seven have been preserved. In this picture, D1070 *Western Gauntlet* stands in Ranelagh Bridge yard, flanked by the as yet unnamed Nos 50015 and 50037 on 9 September 1975. *John Ashman/Adrian Vaughan Collection*

As a result of this – and nine other incidents that were thought to be indicative of poor maintenance at Old Oak Common – an audit of GWT maintenance procedures at the depot was carried out in November 1996 and a report issued in January 1997 discovered 'Significant areas of non-compliance' with the GWT's Safety Case. (Uff Report, 14.12)

The Fleet Director of GWT, Mr Cusworth, believed that the audit had revealed plenty of staff resources at Old Oak Common. He was therefore, in 1997, carrying out 're-structuring' to 'increase efficiency' and his scheme had passed a risk assessment carried out independently. The fleet maintenance men were 're-structured' to abolish 'job demarcation' but without a 'substantial' reduction in the number of tradesmen employed overall at the depot. 'Substantial' is a qualification that seems to suggest that a few men were made redundant. The 'spare capacity' was supposed to exist if any man could tackle any job of maintenance. The retraining of tradesmen to be competent in new skills was not carried out in any regular way. Staff were trained in some tasks but not in others, and records of who had been retrained to do what were not properly kept. When the risk assessment was delivered, did the assessor know that the men would only be retrained to multi-tasking on an ad hoc basis? (Uff Report, 6.7; 6.8; 6.10) The size of each maintenance team was reduced and the smaller teams were 'overstretched, disorganised and inadequately trained', and were reduced to 'delivering the minimum service that could be got away with.' (Uff Report, 6.7, 64) But that statement tends to blame the men. It could be reversed to say that GWT had so arranged matters that they could get the greatest amount of work from the least number of people. Hidden's Recommendation 14 said: 'BR shall give technical training as necessary to ensure that efficient and safe practices are carried out by all technical staff.' The successors to BR were bound by the Hidden recommendations.

On 18 and 19 September the maintenance of the HST that was to go out on the Paddington-Swansea service was in the hands of men who did not know their job, and therefore did not carry out maintenance routines properly. The Automatic Warning System at the western end of the set was working, but that at the eastern end was not working. The driver who took that HST down to Swansea knew that on the return journey, east end leading, there would be no AWS, so he asked for the train to be turned around on the Landore triangle so that the western end of the train would become the leading end. His message was ignored due to the railway ignorance of a seriously under-trained member of staff in the control office, but even if the driver's message had reached a controller with some basic railway knowledge, that turning manoeuvre could not readily have taken place because GWT had not paid to use those tracks and there were private enterprise procedures to go through to gain access. These are obstacles to efficiency, to flexibility.

On an integrated railway the Platform Inspector would merely have phoned the signal box and told the signalman 'that one on No 3 needs to turn on the triangle'. At a place today where there is a triangular junction – I need not tell you where – the train crews and signalling staff remain

No D1010 *Western Campaigner* approaches Blatchbridge Junction 4 minutes early with the 11.30 Paddington-Penzance 'Cornish Riviera Express' on 27 May 1975. *Adrian Vaughan*

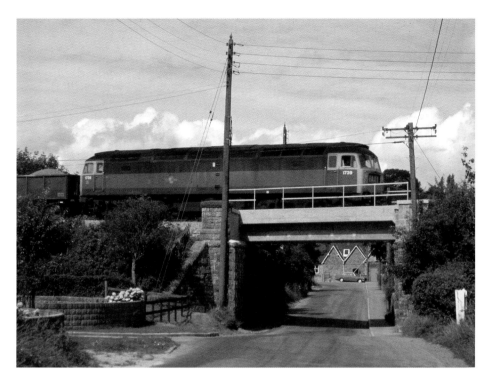

The Brush/Sulzer Type 4 (Class 47) 2,750hp diesel-electric was one of most successful of the BR diesels. They were equally at home on express passenger trains – with a top speed of 95mph – as on freight trains at 30. Between 1963 and 1969 512 were built, and by 1986 507 were still in service. In 2007 between 30 and 40 were still at work on the national network. Here is D1739, in two-tone green livery, crossing the Wanstrow bridge on the single-track Cranmore branch, bringing a train-load of stone up to the main line at Witham in 1966. *John Ashman/ Arian Vaughan Collection*

unofficially BR-integrated and trains are turned, on request, should the need arise. 'Management flair' seems more to have been hobbled than harnessed by the system put in place by the privatisers.

John MacGregor, selling the privatisation to Parliament on 29 October 1992, made the following remarkable statement:

'Anything to do with BR is complicated. It is important we get the *practical* details right. Our objective is to improve the *quality* of railway services by creating many new opportunities for private sector involvement. This will mean *more competition*, *greater efficiency* and a *wider choice of services more closely tailored to what customers want*.' (Author's italics)

Anything less practical than what he proposed could not be imagined. Railways are not the place for self-interested free-for-alls and groups doing only what their contract states. They require the human warmth of experienced common sense directed towards serving one's passengers.

The railway, when 'engineering-led', traditionally had had a good margin of safety – or was 'over-engineered', according to iconoclasts like John Edmonds – so there had been plenty of 'fat' to cut off. By 1994 engineering costs had been seriously reduced, but still 90% of track was in a 'satisfactory' condition. Mr Hidden's Recommendation 50 stated: 'BR shall ensure that the organisational framework exists to prevent commercial considerations of a business-led railway compromising safety.' That recommendation proves that Mr Hidden was aware that the profit motive

was not likely to foster a culture of safety – and this Recommendation was undermined by the fragmentation of the railway at privatisation. Railtrack, which would 'never compromise safety', improved its profits – partly – by cutting maintenance. And those reductions were in addition to the cheeseparing that had been going on for years under pressure from the Treasury, then the wondrously named 'Organising for Quality' regime.

As an aside, Recommendation 14 stated that 'BR shall give technical training as necessary to ensure that efficient and safe practices are carried out by all technical staff.' One wonders who was ensuring that the contractors made sure all their technical staff remained as well trained as under BR.

Good railwaymen in 1994 were genuinely fearful of what their new masters might do, drunk on their theories of private enterprise and their contempt for the 'culture' of BR. They would want to show how much more bright and efficient private enterprise was than the dull, social democratic, over-engineered British Rail.

The privatisation of the railway could not turn railway men and women into super-heroes of capitalism – nor would it make contractors stop working for their own profit (which is only natural) and start to work for the public good. Privatisation did alter the railwaymen's perception of right and wrong. 'We would never compromise safety' was an oft-repeated declaration from Railtrack after privatisation, but Railtrack's 'arm's length' responsibility for the infrastructure through contracting out of maintenance and renewal put safety in jeopardy. The loss to Railtrack of experienced railway people, and the basic need of private companies to make a profit, all tended to compromise safety.

Above: No 1902 has been creeping from signal to signal through 'Daffodil Junction' – so named because of the number of yellow lights a driver got on his passage through – and has now been brought to a stand at a red. The driver now waits for the road to clear through Gaer Tunnel, Newport (Monmouthshire), with a heavy freight. *John Ashman/ Adrian Vaughan Collection*

Right: The English Electric Type 4, 'D400' class, 2,700hp diesel-electrics were put into service, under a leasing agreement between English Electric and BR, from 1967. They had a top speed of 100mph and were used on the Euston-Carlisle run. They became the property of BR in 1973 and became Class 50. After a hiatus when they all had to have new cylinder heads, they worked well on the main lines of the Western, where they displaced the 'Western' class, and in the 1980s on the ex-Southern Region, later known as Network SouthEast. They were withdrawn from service between 1989 and 1994, and several are preserved. Here is No 50001 at Paddington on 10 September 1975. *Adrian Vaughan*

Above: A '50' passes Fairwood Junction off the Westbury Avoiding Line with the 15.30 Paddington train on 15 May 1974.
Adrian Vaughan

Left: The Class 56 Type 5 has a Ruston-Paxman 3,250hp engine geared for a top speed of 80mph. A total of 185 of them were built between 1976 and 1983, designed primarily for heavy freight. They were good engines but their maintenance costs were high, relative to diesel costs available in the USA. With privatisation and the American take-over of freight working here, the cheaper to maintain US locos, which became Class 66, displaced them. However, such is the demand for railway motive power that five are still at work, and four are preserved. Here No 56046 and another of the same class are on a heavy Down freight train, seen from the 9am Norwich-Liverpool Street train on 12 March 1985.

CHAPTER 10

Railtrack: 'an "engineering-free" railway corporation'

It would be reasonable to suppose that Railtrack was established directly by Act of Parliament. That was the way in which every one of the 'old private companies', to which the privatisers paid such homage, had been formed. But at the time the Bill was being debated, the Government still was not sure of what it wanted in a privately owned railway. The 1993

Railways Act makes no reference in its 132 clauses to 'Railtrack'. That Act was an enabling device. Nick Harvey, Liberal MP for North Devon, put it very well when he observed in Parliament that, instead of the large tome that was the Act, the Government needed only to have brought out a single sentence, thus: the Secretary of State can do what he likes, how he likes, when he likes and where he likes. (Hansard, Vol 218, col 155-255, 2.4.93)

On 1 April 1994 Railtrack moved out of the 'shadow' of the BRB to become the state-owned and regulated company legally responsible for the proper maintenance of the tracks, signalling and stations in prime condition. But Railtrack would not actually carry out the work of the renewal and maintenance of the track, signalling and stations. Railtrack would not even decide when rails needed changing.

Andrew McNaughton came to BR in 1973 to work as a manager in the civil engineering side of BR. He contributed greatly to better track maintenance techniques. He was Railtrack's Head of Production from 1993 until, under Network Rail, he became Chief

The Railway Executive set out to create a fleet of diesel-mechanical multiple unit trains in 1952. Trial runs with a two-car set, powered by two 125hp Leyland engines under the floor, took place in April 1954. Manufacturers and railway workshops were then invited to tender to build vehicles 57 feet and 63ft 6in long, with various seating arrangements in each size. Rolls Royce, AEC and Leyland built the engines and transmission, which were then sent to Derby, Eastleigh and Swindon for fitting to the vehicles built at those railway works. In 1955 these multiple unit diesel trains were taking up their work in the most needy places – East Anglia, Lincolnshire and Northumberland. Units with a external door between each pair of seats were intended for 'high-density' commuter areas where rapid entry and exit by passengers would assist in time-keeping. Seen here is a Class 117 'high-density' unit heading into Sonning cutting on the Down Relief Line during the bitterly cold winter of December 1962. *Adrian Vaughan Collection*

The interior of a 'high-density' carriage, with a door between each pair of seats.
Adrian Vaughan Collection

Engineer and became Professor of Railway Systems Engineering at the University of Nottingham. He told the *International Railway Journal* in August 2002 that 'we contracted infrastructure maintenance companies to carry out inspections, hold the data and make decisions based on that data.' Surely this was an abdication of Railtrack's legal responsibility?

Railtrack was still a nationalised organisation in 1994. Its Board of Directors were all devotees of 'free markets', and were at one with the free-market fundamentalists at the Treasury and in the Tory Cabinet, and fully intended that it should be sold as soon as possible. One of the most important drivers of the policy was Sir Steve Robson, a 'mandarin' at the Treasury whose life's mission was to remove government from business. The method supported by Robson for railway privatisation was not business-like – but of course he was working from his 'one-size-fits-all' textbook rather than from any knowledge of railways. He was, it seems, blinded to the realities of what he was proposing for the railway by his views of the nationalised industry – as, indeed, were all these people. In an interview with the *Daily Telegraph* on-line on 21 March 2001, he is reported as saying, 'We absolutely should have privatised railways. As one Chief Executive put it to me at the time, "British Rail was an organisation in which the tiller was not connected to the rudder. Management could not manage."'

Railtrack was Robson's model of good management, where the decision to replace dangerous track was left to a third party. By contrast, the methodical, economical and highly effective management of the electrification of the WCML in 1966 was carried out by a rudderless organisation. Robson's statement at this interview then conceded that he hadn't managed too well himself. 'We probably broke it [the railway] into too many pieces. We should reduce the number of train operating companies. They are incentivised to cut costs but not on customer service.' He was, however, absolutely certain that, whatever the shortcomings of the private sector might be, they were nothing compared to those of British Rail.

BRB Headquarters continued to function under John Welsby, and it was due to the capabilities of the much-denigrated BR men at Headquarters that the Government was able to sell Railtrack only two years after it had been formed. There were rooms full of contracts, floor to ceiling. Paper everywhere. The change to Railtrack was absolutely revolutionary for the railway, not only in the dysfunctional arrangements that were created but also in the new attitudes that had to be adopted. Any method of working that pre-dated 1 April was 'BR', and to be forgotten. BR equalled inefficiency, and this was Year 1 of the Revolution. James Meek, in his *Guardian Unlimited* article of 1 April 2004, 'The £10bn rail crash', quotes Welsby as saying:

'All my lads had about three jobs. Firstly they were running a railway, secondly they were breaking it up for sale, thirdly they were often preparing a management buy-out at the same time. People were working 12 hours a day, seven days a week. Our advice was passed across but then it was up to Railtrack to take the advice or not. We were big, bad BR being broken up and done away with because

The DMU was very successful, hard-working and long-lived. In 1976 a refurbishment scheme was very welcome and the restored trains re-entered traffic with a silvery kind of white body paint emphasised with a broad blue or green band. Here is a refurbished Class 117 unit at Ealing Broadway in 1977. *John Ashman/ Adrian Vaughan Collection*

we were anathema to the government so the New Order was not going to look very favourably upon us.'

Christian Wolmar, on page 4 of his book *Broken Rails* (1st edition), tells of a remark made in 1994 by the Railtrack Board to a very senior BR engineer at the time that he was offering his services to Railtrack. 'Get yourself a proper job. This is the real world now. We'll call you if we need you.'

The railway was deliberately made dysfunctional, yet these arrangements were based on the advice of the best economic brains in the country. Their system split the railway between so many different companies to create 'a vibrant marketplace', but then the same people felt that they could not trust their privatised railway system to carry out its contradictory role of private profit and public service, so expensive regulatory – government – controls had to be established. The private railway had to be regulated to an extent unknown in the days of BR.

Railtrack – set up in the belief that it would attract private investment in the railways – could only attract investment from the private sector if it could make a high profit in order to pay a substantial dividend so as to maintain its shares at a high value. Banks would be more enthusiastic to lend large sums to a rip-roaring success and would charge less interest if the risks of lending were low. How would Railtrack, taking over the direction of a loss-making industry, (with the exception of InterCity in the last years) make its profits? British Rail had held the

advantage of an integrated organisation to enable it to do as well as it had.

By order of the Government all maintenance and renewals had to be contracted out to whoever had bought the 14 BRISCOs. Between them, these infrastructure maintenance companies comprised the engineering and technical staff, and *records of the infrastructure*, tools and depots previously part of British Railways. The purchasers included the contractor Jarvis, which was owned by Cabinet Minister Cecil Parkinson's in-laws and with Cabinet Minister Steven Norris on its Board. Other purchasers were contractors Balfour Beatty and Amec.

To make these vital railway infrastructure companies attractive bargains, the sale prices were very low relative to the value of the assets and the guaranteed profit. They had a 'dead cert' customer – Railtrack – just as did the ROSCOs. Debts were written off, capital values written down and any monies existing within those businesses at the time of purchase – and there were many millions overall – were given as a free gift. Just to allow freight trains to use the tracks they had always used required 224 separate contracts had to be drafted, discussed, amended and finally approved. The BR managers who had purchased Freightliner were encouraged to do so by the Government's promise to pay their track access charges at the rate of £75 million a year for five years. This was another free gift of public money rather than a competitive marketplace, and in fact the arrangement was criticised by the National Audit Office.

Railtrack was unique in the world: an 'engineering-free' railway corporation, owned by shareholders, but under government regulation.

BR had, in the past, employed, for a wage or salary, men experienced in every possible skill required. 'Organising for Quality', while it made InterCity profitable and reduced the need for subsidy to other Sectors, did so at the expense of expertise – a lot of talent had been dispensed with, but what was left was there for the good of the railway. OfQ was the railway 'business-led', and in 1993/94 involved the BRB in the employment of an expensive army of consultants. Railtrack had contracted out just about everything that BR would have done itself, and did not have the engineering expertise within its ranks to supervise the people it was employing.

Railtrack was hastily thrown together like a tin hut in a shanty town, yet its creation had cost as much as a 400-acre country estate with a 40-bed mansion. The Swedish Government had separated the track from the trains in 1988, as the apologists for Railtrack have pointed out, but there was one huge difference. The Swedes had taken five years of careful and detailed planning before bringing their arrangements into use. John MacGregor had thrown his shanty together in great haste for political reasons. The results of this were to cost the nation the price of a dozen more country estates – and all this by people who believed they were great businessmen who had the single answer for all problems and denigrated the nationalised railway as 'expensive', 'inefficient', 'unbusinesslike', 'not responding to the needs of the customer' and so on, ad nauseam.

John MacGregor insisted that under these arrangements the railway was a competitive market and *therefore* was more efficient, more cost-effective, than integrated nationalisation. That seems a tolerably dogmatic assertion. Common sense pointed another way.

Clare Short, the Transport spokesman for New Labour, speaking in Parliament on 17 April 1996, just before the sale of Railtrack, stated that the New Labour Party was 'committed to a publicly owned, publicly accountable railway'. This statement was included in the prospectus offering shares in Railtrack to the public. According to S. G. Warburg, one of the banks that handled the share sales, without her pronouncement the shares would have sold for £4.50, but that still undervalued the assets of BR.

Short observed that the Railtrack prospectus announced that Railtrack would be obliged by law to pay compensation to the train operators if their trains were delayed or unable to run as a result of Railtrack's actions: 'A single day's cessation of train services will cost Railtrack about £12 million. According to my rudimentary calculations Railtrack has enough money put by in the £75 million allowance for fewer than seven days' loss of services.'

The diesel-electric multiple unit prototype No 210002 was designed to take current from the third rail and also had a diesel engine for use on non-electrified lines. A lot of space was taken up by the engine room, and passenger seating adjacent to the engine was very noisy. The design was abandoned and BR moved on to the diesel-hydraulic 'Sprinters'.
No 210002 is seen entering Paddington at 17.15 on the murky evening of 24 March 1986. *Adrian Vaughan*

It is slanderous to say that BR was lacking vision. The Executive always tried to improve the trains and the service. However, it is difficult to invest in the future when the money to do so is in short supply. Given that one fact, BR did extremely well. Its diesel-electric 'Blue Pullman' was part of the 1955 Modernisation Plan. Design, building and trials take time, yet on 23 July 1960 a six-car train was brought into public service on the London Midland Region, and on the Western Region an eight-car set began work on 17 October. There were power cars at each end containing 1,000hp North British/MAN engines driving GEC traction motors. They had Pullman-quality interiors and ran at a top speed of 90mph. The ride was rather hard but they were still a revolution in train travel, and from September 1964 they formed almost a high-speed shuttle service from Paddington to Birmingham/Wolverhampton, Bristol and Cardiff/Swansea. They were withdrawn from service in 1973. Here the 2.30pm Weston-super-Mare to Paddington Pullman waits to leave Bristol Temple Meads at 3pm one day in 1964. *Adrian Vaughan Collection*

To assist in selling Railtrack, the Government – the taxpayers – would pay the first £75 million of compensation that would become due under this law. Short continued:

'In summer 1994, services were lost for 18 days. After the first seven days, every additional day's lost service will cost Railtrack £12 million out of its profits. The big question is: how long could Railtrack last in those circumstances? Are Mr Horton's management skills considered so great that he can do now what he signally – if I may use that word – failed to do in 1994? Railtrack's profit last year, as stated on page 63 of the prospectus, was £189 million before tax. If one adds to that the whole £75 million additional penalty allowance, I

calculate that Railtrack's annual profit would be wiped out in 22 days.

When the Chairman of the British Railways Board – I remind the House that he is a Tory appointee – writes to the Permanent Secretary to the Department of Transport complaining that "material information for investors" on a desperately important subject has been left out of the prospectus, the country can see for itself that the Government, who have been consistently tainted by sleaze and underhand dealings, are prepared to sell Railtrack on a false prospectus.'

During June 1996 the national railway infrastructure was sold under the name of Railtrack at the rate of £3.90p per share. S. G. Warburg handled the sale for the Government and was also the Government's adviser on how the company should be sold. The National Audit Office said that there was 'a potential conflict of interest' in Warburg's role as both adviser of the price of shares to the Government and as seller of those shares. Nothing was done to rectify matters.

The sale, according to the BBC News on 14 July 1999, raised £1.9 billion for the Treasury. In the last balance sheet of the BRB for the year 1993-94, the total value of British Railways' assets – stations, land, etc – was estimated as at £6.464 billion. Deducted from the £1.9 billion were the fees to the banks that handled the sale – £39.5 million – of which £10.9 million went to S. G. Warburg.

There are many different reports as to how much the Government paid out in order to sell the railway. It depends on how many of the costs one includes, but it seems that the taxpayers made a net loss on the sale of their assets. Dr Nigel Harris and Ernest Godward, in their study *The Privatisation of British Rail*, made careful calculations and estimated that 'at least £5 billion' was spent on the re-organisation of BR from OfQ to privatisation, the costs of the relatively successful OfQ being entirely lost in the privatisation upheaval. The Chairman of the Parliamentary Public Accounts Committee, David Davis, stated that the railways were sold for £1.5 billion less than their market value.

In Parliament in March 1995 Glenda Jackson asked Mr Watts (Minister of State for Transport, 1994-97) 'what has been the cost of railway privatisation between 1/1/92 and 1/1/95'. The answer was, '£205 million including £22 million in consultancy fees. The estimated cost of privatisation from February 1995 to January 1996 will be £26 million excluding the cost of selling Railtrack.' (Hansard, Vol 256, col 12, 6.3.95)

Mr Meacher asked Mr Watts:

'Is the Minister aware that, in addition to the quarter of a billion pounds cost of preparing for privatisation that he quoted, it is also reported that the Secretary of State intends to write off £1.5 billion in debts as a sweetener in order to secure the sale of Railtrack? Is the Minister also aware that senior officers have been offered up to double their present salaries – up to six-figure levels, excluding additional share options – to secure their co-operation in

the run-up to privatisation? Is it not the ultimate absurdity that the cost to the public purse of selling off British Rail is now likely to exceed the total revenues from that sale? Does it not speak volumes for the Government that they can suddenly find billions of pounds to subsidise the privatisation programme when they have starved British Rail of desperately needed cash investment for years?' (Hansard, Vol 256, col 11-12, 6.3.95)

More millions of pounds had been spent by the BRB from 1982 to 1992 with the same consultants during the reorganisation of the railway into Sectors and finally 'Organising for Quality'. All that money was wasted when that system – which was working very well – was abandoned for privatisation.

Shortly after it had been sold, Railtrack Directors boasted that it would 'soon to be able to offer other railways the benefit of its experience'.

What if BR – which was actually performing very well, by John MacGregor's own admission – had remained in public ownership? Then all that unproductive money spent on lawyers and economics consultants could have been spent on improving the tracks, and the thousands of experienced electrical, mechanical and civil engineering staff would not have been scattered thinly across the land but remained within a solidly organised unit to improve the railway. Think of the efficiency of integrated, engineering-rich BR West Coast. Because of the 'ownership' of its own expert engineering staff, InterCity West Coast – Ivor Warburton – had been able to re-lay the West Coast Main Line track for 125mph running within

The 'Blue Pullman' races into Sonning cutting at 90mph.
John Ashman/Adrian Vaughan Collection

Occasionally the diesel Pullman was out of service and a locomotive and conventional Pullman coaches were used. Here No 1729 keeps time on the Down Main in Sonning cutting.
John Ashman/Adrian Vaughan Collection

budget. When he handed over to Railtrack in 1994 there was not a temporary speed restriction anywhere on the network. What could have been done, under such an organisation, with £5 billion?

The people rearranging the railway had no understanding of railways – their plans were based on economic theories. John MacGregor, and his Transport Minister Roger Freeman, Sir Steve Robson at the Treasury and advisers such as Professor Glaister and Sir Christopher Foster did not appreciate the virtuous nature of a unified railway. Indeed, the virtuously unified nature of a railway was what greatly offended them. There was no competition *within* BR. Oh dear!

The railway had always been a great *public* institution – the era of the great private companies not excepted – and every service a passenger might require was provided, even day trips around Dartmoor for passengers from cruise liners anchored off Plymouth or Dartmouth. BR did not go to those lengths but it did all the other things done by the much-vaunted 'old companies'. The great disadvantage of BR, in the Adam Smith fundamentalist view, was that, in giving a universal travel service to the public, BR was preventing hundreds of businesses opportunities. BR was hundreds of businesses that could be sold, hundreds of businesses to which banks could

lend money, shares to be traded, to be taken over, bought and sold. Privatisation was a huge opportunity for certain kinds of people to make fortunes at the public expense.

MacGregor's and Freeman's unrealistic outlook concerning railway work is well exemplified in their policy on railway stations. They intended that Railtrack should lease to the train operators all but the 13 largest stations in Britain, and that these 13, eight of them in London, should each be divided into three separate businesses – station operating, renting of retail outlets, and property development – and each thrice-divided station should be sold as three independent businesses. This was too much fragmentation for the strained loyalty of the BRB, and John Welsby managed to persuade MacGregor and Freeman that the nationalised Railtrack would be perfectly capable of letting kiosks and building offices over stations without having separate organisations to do it.

The greatest hole in Railtrack's shanty was the insistence by the free-market fundamentalists that contractors should be responsible for maintenance and renewal. Entrusting railway maintenance to contractors was a bad policy – as Brunel had found out by 1850 – as indeed had the Stockton & Darlington Railway 20 years before that. In the textbook, free-market, model railway envisaged by the Adam Smith-ers, the employment of contractors was said to be essential to introduce a competitive market into railway maintenance costs. Experience, competence and a conscience were what was required, but Adam Smith had never mentioned these things in his books, published in

1760. Railtrack laid onerous terms on the contractor in each contract, including an undertaking that the contractor would reduce its prices by 5% a year for the lifetime of the contract. Railtrack sought to obtain 'value for money' through competition. The contractor was paid a fixed sum for its maintenance work, so the contractor decided what needed doing and certified when that something had been carried out correctly. (Mr Don Foster MP, Hansard, Vol 356, col.89, 6.11.00) Clichés do not a superb railway make, nor competition keep the rails from breaking. The theorists got their cheap railway. The collisions and derailments followed.

Shortly after Network Rail replaced Railtrack, the Network Rail Chief Executive, John Armitt, was interviewed by John Humphrys on BBC Radio 4. Mr Armitt's replies to Humphrys' questions clearly implied contractors' self-regulation. Armitt said, 'We carry out a full regime of testing – um –' (there was a slight pause to contradict what he had just said) – 'by our contractors.' Mr Armitt continued, 'Our contractors go through all sorts of loops [sic] to be contractors.' But that had not prevented Railtrack's contractors from sub-contracting, and the sub-contractors sub-contracting when men were recruited in pub bars for weekend work on the track. Mr Armitt again referred to the self-certification of work by contractors when he stated, 'We are going to become *more interfering*, we are going to *take back some of the key responsibilities for interpreting inspections, deciding what should be done and when it will be done.*'

The dangers of employing contractors and allowing them to be judge and jury in their own case was amply demonstrated at 12.10pm on 4 February 1997. A train of loaded – some over-loaded – ballast wagons owned by Southern Track Renewals (STR), hauled by two EWS locomotives, Nos 37167 and 37220, with inaccurate speedometers, operated by Connex South Central, and driven by its inadequately trained driver, crossed Bridge 799 over Old Bexley High Street at too high a speed whereupon the bridge's longitudinal timbers, on which the tracks rested, collapsed and derailed the train. The errors mentioned so far were not held to have been the cause of the bridge failure. The reason for the collapse of the bridge was utterly inadequate maintenance by the contractor – South East Infrastructure Maintenance Company Ltd (SEIMCL), a subsidiary of Balfour Beatty Rail.

In spite of John MacGregor's, along with others, belief in the superiority of private enterprise management over that of BR, the fact was ascertained by the H&SE that SEIMCL was

'…unable to manage their organisation. SEIMCL did not have adequate systems or procedures and failed to provide sufficient resources to meet their commitments to ensure that the longitudinal timbers carrying the rails

Some of the derailed ballast wagons at Bexley on 4 February 1997. *Brian Morrison*

The High Speed Train, the most successful and comfortable train ever to be placed on British rails, was developed by tightly budget-restricted BR at Derby in the early 1970s. Fleet production of the HST (Class 252) began in 1975 with seven-car sets 'top and tailed' by power cars, each containing a 2,250bhp Paxman 'Valenta' engine driving the generator. They accelerated like rockets and cruised silently and with armchair comfort at 125mph. The Class 253 followed in 1976 with eight coaches. They were at once a huge success and remain so to this day. Here we see the prototype, No 252001, at Paddington alongside No 50011 on 10 September 1975. *Adrian Vaughan*

on Bridge 799 were replaced after they had been reported as being in urgent need of replacement.'

How do contracts assist in maintaining a safe railway? The SEIMCL contract specified that track inspections be carried out to Railtrack Group Standards as follows:

A. Weekly by a patrol man.
B. Eight-weekly by the Section Manager or his assistant.
C. Annual examination of longitudinal timbers by a Bridge Examiner.
D. Two-yearly examination by the Permanent Way Maintenance Engineer.

The records showed that weekly patrols happened only on alternate weeks. The Section Manager only managed an inspection every three to four months.

The bridge was first reported to have 'severely decayed' timbers by the Bridge Examiner on his annual inspection on 13 August 1995. The timbers were so rotten that the bases of the cast-iron rail chairs were an inch into the surface of the wood and the indentation made by the base of the chair was an inch wider than the base – the chairs were moving sideways due to the forces exerted by wheels. Rather than immediately booking the timbers for replacement the following weekend, and in the meantime placing a 5mph speed restriction on the bridge with a 24-hour guard of a permanent way man, the timbers were scheduled for renewal in August 1996. I suppose that a 'risk assessment' was carried out in order to reach this conclusion, which goes to show that a risk assessment is a process whereby one makes a judgement on how long a dangerous situation can be allowed to exist before a disaster occurs.

In January 1996 the Bridge Examiner identified 'Timbers to change at Bexley'. On 27 February 1996 the Section Manager inspected the bridge and reported: 'Bridge 799, 1450mm gauge'. The British standard gauge is 1432mm. The track was three-quarters of an inch wide of gauge because of the split and severely decayed longitudinal timber bearers. The weekly (in theory) patrolman's report for 9 September 1996 stated: 'Rotten timbers. Tie bars fitted.' These tie bars were incorrectly fitted and were only a temporary expedient. It was later noted by an engineer that 'Tie bars cannot be fitted'. On 7 November the patrolman

HST set No 253015 leaves
the Severn Tunnel by the
Welsh portal in 1977.
John Ashman/
Adrian Vaughan Collection

noted: 'Bridge timbers very bad condition'. On 17
December 'Long timbers need changing urgently', and on
22 January 1997 'Extremely rotten bridge timber requires
urgent attention'. The Section Manager's inspection reports
said the same sort of thing at other times.

Railtrack, which had the over-arching responsibility for
the safety of the railway, knew the bridge was dangerous,
SEIMC knew it was dangerous, but – apart from hiring
consultants, who reported that the bridge was dangerous
– no-one did anything about it. The only conclusion I
can come to is that under the 'vibrant marketplace'
system of running railways the disruption caused to
traffic during a speed restriction and then the weekend
replacement would have obliged Railtrack to pay
compensation for the delays to the train operating
companies so it was put off and put off.

The Health & Safety Executive solemnly investigated the
derailment, clearly reported all the failings and produced
pages and pages of 'lessons to be learned in order to reduce
the possibility of an accident from inadequately maintained
track happening again'. The safety experts did not even
mention the 17 months without an adequate speed
restriction over the rotten, wide to gauge, bridge tracks. The
line speed for freight trains was 40mph, but the condition
of the bridge required something much less than that.

The most important lesson of all, which was never even
considered, was the danger of having the contractors, for
all practical purposes, in charge and the danger of making
Railtrack liable to pay compensation to train operating
companies when their trains were delayed due to essential
engineering work.

Of course, Railtrack was at a great disadvantage at this
time in having merely the eyes of the bridge inspector and
patrolman for guidance. It was not until

'…the latter part of 1997 and through 1998 that, with
the support of [consultants[McKinsey, Railtrack
developed a range of asset management models with
which better to calculate when an asset has reached the
end of its shelf life and when it would be appropriate to
renew that asset.' (Mr Tony Fletcher, Railtrack General
Manager West Coast Main Line Modernisation Project,
speaking to the Rail Regulator, May 2000) All was
'consultant', nothing was common sense.

Railtrack and the contractors STR and SEIMC were
prosecuted by the HSE. On 26 May 1998 they pleaded
guilty to failing in their various duties to the railway and
were fined a total of £150,000. In summing up, the judge
said that it 'was merciful that nobody was killed, although
four people were injured'. He also stated that in his view
and that of the two magistrates sitting with him, 'Railtrack
has the overall responsibility of protecting the public from
any failures of its contractors STR and SEI. It is clear that
they failed to heed the warning issued in the document
"Maintaining a safe railway infrastructure". It set itself
high standards in its document "Railtrack's Railway Safety
Case" and it has failed in our view to attain them.'

Above: Locospotters examine the effects of a pigeon strike at Bristol Temple Meads. *John Ashman/Adrian Vaughan Collection*

Above right: The driver takes the necessary steps to restore respectability. *John Ashman/Adrian Vaughan Collection*

Below: The blessings of the HSTs spread to Swansea and Penzance, giving far-flung parts of the kingdom astonishingly fast services. Here No 253016 waits for the 'off' with an evening train to London, with No 47298 alongside with a cross-country service.

Above: British Railways busily set about building clean and practical servicing facilities for its new diesels. This is the barn at Penzance.

Left: Fuelling No 253016 in the new depot at Penzance.
John Ashman/
Adrian Vaughan Collection

CHAPTER 11

The West Coast Main Line and Ladbroke Grove

The modernisation scheme for the West Coast Main Line (WCML) was first made public in May 1993, when the then Chancellor of the Exchequer, Kenneth Clarke, announced in his Budget speech that the work would be undertaken as a 'private finance initiative'. On 1 December John MacGregor, speaking in Parliament, blithely made it all sound so easy. Blindingly simple. He could not envisage the hydra-headed monster he was creating – the railway was a business, like any other business, and could be managed like a factory or a water supply company.

He said with such innocent faith:

'Once the new performance standards have been set a competition will be held in late 1994 to select a private sector consortium to modernise the line … the new standards will stipulate minimum performance. Where commercially justified the InterCity West Coast franchisee (and possibly other train operators) will be able to contract for line speeds and other improvements in exchange for increased payments.'

But he didn't see that if improvements over and above the minimum were made at the request of one company, that company would pay extra but all the others using the line would receive the benefit too. This could not be acceptable under the system he was creating. He had laid a minefield in that one sentence alone. He further enthused:

'The principles have been devised to transfer risk out of the public sector to those who can control them best. This approach will bring together private and public expertise to modernise the line in a way that its full potential is realised without the capital cost coming out of public funds.'

He finished his statement with, 'The Inter-City West Coast franchise will be let at the earliest possible time.'

So, even before Railtrack had been sold, right at the start of this earthquake upheaval, changing the railway's organisation from sturdy vertical integration to something resembling jelly, the Railtrack Board, Sir Robert Horton,

John Edmonds, Chief Executive, and Norman Broadhurst, Finance Director, set out on a gigantic scheme for the modernisation of the West Coast Main Line. They were going to show the Government, which was waiting with bated breath to see the miracles their 18th century dogma would perform, the Great British Public as well as those who had voted for this that a 'marketplace' was the proper place to keep a railway.

The Railtrack shadow Board went looking for a private sector partner with whom to carry out a Feasibility Study into its 'flagship' project – the great work, the successful completion of which would prove that the free-market fundamentalists were right, and would justify all the money spent on disorganising the railway. The West Coast project was critical to the credibility of the whole privatisation project.

Forty-two groups of consultants came forward, doubtless among them many ex-BR engineers. Their plans were vetted, 14 were selected for more detailed examination, six were invited to submit formal proposals, and interviews were held during March 1994. The WCML Development Company Limited (WCML Dev Co) was selected on 24 March 1994. Was this how the GWR planned their 'New Lines' 1900-1914, or was this a new, vast bureaucracy created by a 'free market'. A bizarre contradiction. The Feasibility Study that resulted from this was kept a secret from the public until October 2003, when the *Guardian* newspaper got a copy of it under the Freedom of Information Act, and a copy was placed on the internet in 2008, whence I have downloaded my copy.

The WCML Dev Co was a complex consortium of private companies. Its members included: Babcock & Brown, specialists in transport project finance and leasing; Booze Allen & Hamilton, management and technology consultants with particular experience in advanced train control, signalling and communication systems; Brown & Root, engineers and constructors with experience in managing major multi-disciplinary projects; and Sir Alexander Gibb & Partners, a leading civil engineering and railway consultancy. Specialists from Railtrack joined the consortium to form what was described as 'a strong team'. Direction and oversight were provided by a joint steering committee comprising senior executives of the above four companies and Railtrack.

The Feasibility Study based its search for cost-effectiveness on the latest technology and was enthusiastic about the prospects. 'New technology can greatly improve reliability by removing some of the most common failures in civil and signal engineering.' There was no chance of the new technology having its own gremlins, its own common failures.

The Study looked at three signalling systems. The first was conventional four-aspect colour-light signals with track circuit block, and the second was track circuit block, the track circuits being track-mounted beacons that sent messages to the train driver's cab, thereby abolishing the need for lineside signals. Both these systems held trains apart at around 2,000 yards. The last one was the latest technology; transmission-based signalling, usually called 'moving block'. This was so new that it did not exist. One day, it was hoped, it would control trains by means of track-mounted radio beacons, radio masts along the route and a receiver/computer in the driving cab. The intended effect was that the train in front sent a radio signal to a mast and thence by wire to a computer, which in turn sent out a movement command to the radio mast that transmitted the message to the track-mounted beacons that sent a signal to the displays in the driver's cab of the following train. The driver was thus instructed as to what he must do to regulate his speed in relation to the train in front. The benefit of this system was that it allowed trains to run as close together as the braking distance – according to speed – allowed. To quote the Study, 'the only restriction on line occupation will be the ability of the train to stop'. Quite! That was ever the case.

Moving block would save the expense of much lineside cabling and lineside signals, and it would replace several large signal control centres along the route with one building and a handful of men. This would have the added effect of weakening the railway trade union, which is always considered to be a great advantage by the fundamentalist capitalists, although they do not say so too publicly.

To a safety-conscious railwayman who knows that only God is perfect, moving block seems like an accident waiting to happen. It is designed to reduce the interval between trains down to the bare braking distance –

Liverpool Street station was planned in 1865-66 under the dictatorial direction of the Great Eastern Railway's General Manager, Samuel Swabrick – not even the Chairman of the company had any say in his decisions. The station was opened to passenger traffic in November 1875 and remained unrebuilt for 110 years. To pay for the work the outer end of the station was demolished and turned into a tunnel supporting an office block, while Broad Street station next door was completely removed in favour of an office block.. The present Liverpool Street station is British Railways' last great rebuilding job, commenced in 1985 and re-opened by Her Majesty Queen Elizabeth II in 1991. Liverpool Street, like Euston and King's Cross, is down in a cutting and was abominably smoky. Here is 'Claud Hamilton' class No 8852 adding to the smog on 25 April 1931. *Dr Jack Hollick/ Adrian Vaughan Collection*

perhaps with just a bit of a safety margin for wet rails or whatever – but if you start worrying too much about safety margins you end up with block sections, so you lose the advantage. Moving block would work best on the London Underground or a TGV line where there are very few junctions and all the trains run at the same speed. The WCML is a very complicated railway with thousands of trains a day travelling on it at different speeds and coming onto it and leaving it. However, the consultants' remit was to find a cost-effective method of rebuilding the WCML network for 125mph running, and with 'moving block' they believed they had found a system whose installation costs would be two-thirds of that of rebuilding the existing signalling system, and subsequent maintenance costs would also be less.

Unfortunately there was no such thing as 'moving block' at that time. It was only an idea. The Software that could cope with the complexities of the WCML had not been designed. The Feasibility Study said that the 'Method of Mitigation' of this was 'rapid prototyping'. The development of a thoroughly reliable radio link,

The steam age station had 18 platforms, and 400 points and signals all controlled by two manually operated signal boxes with two men in one box and three in the other. The station was incredibly busy with constant arrivals and departures of loaded trains, empty coaching stock and light engines. Here 'B17' 'Sandringham' class No 2825 *Raby Castle* stands off the platform ends while the fireman cleans his fire, throws out ash and soot and waits for the next working. *Dr Jack Hollick/ Adrian Vaughan Collection*

something that passengers could depend on at 125mph, had not been carried out and the Method of Mitigation for this was to use 'off-the-shelf' equipment – but which was not designed to be railway-reliable – and to look at what European railways were doing about the problem. If the latter proved to be ineffective, then European delays would be 'off-set by Railtrack leading and guiding standards'.

The Study stated that moving block was being researched under the European Train Control System (ETCS) project funded by the EU. This was true, but moving block was only one system among several being investigated. The Study then disingenuously said, 'It is likely that ETCS will be adopted as European Network Standard.' But ETCS was the acronym of an investigation project of several signalling systems, not a signalling system in itself.

The Railtrack Board, Government and Treasury were delighted. They now believed that they would be able to have the whole thing done with private money and thereby justify their dogmatic break-up of the railway, an Act of Fundamentalist Faith in 'the market'. John Welsby, Chairman of the BRB, did his best to warn Edmonds, Horton and Broadhurst of the Railtrack Board that 'moving block' was more of a fantasy than a piece of railway equipment, and was severely shouted down for his trouble. The situation is reminiscent of Brunel's support for the atmospheric railway, which was as inapplicable to a main-line railway as was moving block: 'I have no hesitation in taking upon myself the full and entire responsibility for recommending the adoption of the atmospheric system,' he said, meanwhile ignoring his best

friends, Daniel Gooch and Robert Stephenson, who were trying to stop him making a fool of himself.

In January 1995 19 European railways issued a joint statement saying that 'moving block' was not a feasible system of signalling at that time. Although the Feasibility Study had said that European developments would be watched, this European declaration was inconvenient, and so ignored. In March 1995 Railtrack and the Government published the plan for the WCML. The cost-effectiveness of the project depended on using moving block. The Feasibility Study had warned that if moving block did not work on a complex main-line railway and conventional signalling had to be used, the rebuilding would incur 'exceptionally high costs'. This warning was not included in the Railtrack public summary. In March 1995 companies manufacturing signalling equipment stated to Members of Parliament that they *might* be able to have moving block in an operational form by 2005. But the Railtrack summary of 1995 said that the moving block technology would be operational in five years and 'most of the hardware for this train control system already exists, the technology required being relatively mature'. That too was entirely untrue – unless one counts 'off the shelf' mobile phone technology as the 'mature' system for use on trains.

The Feasibility Study recommended that Railtrack should recruit a consortium of powerful civil engineering contractors to manage and construct the entire project.

After all, that was what Railtrack was about – engaging contractors. Railtrack Finance Director Norman Broadhurst had of course read the Study and, from his recommendations that followed, apparently believed that the job was going to be such a huge success and so profitable that Railtrack should keep the project for itself. He persuaded most of the Board that this was the right course of action and Railtrack committed itself to carrying out the project, which depended for its success on the then non-existent 'moving block'. By this time Railtrack's 'in-house' signalling design team numbered about six or seven men. An expert in moving block technology was required.

In 1995 Railtrack recruited two independent groups of international civil engineering contractors to develop their own version of 'moving block' equipment, with Professor Brian Mellitt as Railtrack's Director of the project. Mellitt was already the engineer in charge of the 'moving block' system for use on the 10-mile Jubilee Line Extension from Green Park to Canary Wharf and Stratford.

In March 1997 Richard Branson's weirdly named 'Virgin Trains' company was awarded the franchise to run the InterCity trains on the WCML under the title West Coast Trains. In May the New Labour Party won the General Election by a landslide and Blair promptly reneged on his – and other New Labour leading lights' – pre-election promises to re-nationalise the railways. Virgin Trains and Railtrack then entered into a contract to jointly

Right: The platforms were connected by a meandering footbridge, photographed in July 1982. *Adrian Vaughan*

Right: A Class 86 electric locomotive, another great triumph of BR design, waits at the buffers. Above and beyond is the Station Master's office, erected on columns as a tea room around 1910.
Adrian Vaughan

enhance the WCML. According to public statements, Branson's contract with Railtrack bound his Virgin train company to invest £2 billion in the WCML. Railtrack agreed to spend £2.1 billion to install 'moving block' signalling and to relay the tracks in two stages, to enable 125mph running by 2002 and 140mph by 2005. The agreement would be effective from 2012 to 2027. When the job was complete, Railtrack and Virgin Trains would share the profits, the estimates of which were based on the ability to run at 140mph. In turn this depended on the successful installation of 'moving block' signalling, which at the time of signing did not exist. If Railtrack failed in this vast project, with a highly problematic – or even impossible – signalling system at its core, it was bound to pay very severe financial penalties to Richard Branson.

The contract between Railtrack and Virgin made them partners in the West Coast route, and created a conflict of interest for Railtrack, because it would be sharing in the profits and this could influence its decisions regarding the several other train operators who used parts of the West Coast system. The necessity of accommodating Virgin trains, travelling at 125mph and later, supposedly, at 140 mph, would monopolise the fast lines and confine other operators to the slow lines. The Rail Regulator, Tom Winsor, stated that

'The Regulator recognises, however, that approving the current PUG 2 agreement would make it impossible, on current infrastructure plans, for Railtrack to renew the existing access rights on the route for Silverlink Train Services, Connex South Central and Central Trains (on behalf of Centro PTE) after they expire.'

Then again, what should be the access fees of the other operators if their trains benefited from Virgin's investment? On the other hand, should other users pay for what they had not asked for? The Railtrack/Virgin contract brought in private money but paradoxically showed up the disadvantage of the privatisation scheme. Tom Winsor was in a quandary because Virgin would, in his opinion, be entitled to protection from competition owing to the large investment it was making in the route, but the whole point of privatisation was to introduce competition. It was a real mess. Winsor ordered Railtrack to show him how it was going to allow the other operators their full access and how it would provide spare capacity for their future needs.

The rolling stock leasing companies were aware that whoever won the West Coast franchise was going to want the best trains for the route. The necessitated 'tilting' Virgin Trains publicly claimed the honour of having 'initiated' investment in tilting trains. The company's website had this statement:

'Virgin initiated discussions with Fiat, whose Pendolino trains had been in service with FS [Italian State Railways] for over 10 years. By forming a partnership with Alstom, whose train-building capabilities were well known in Britain, the new trains could be assembled in Britain at Alstom's Washwood Heath facility in Birmingham and exploit Alstom's expertise in power equipment for electric trains. Virgin put together a very strong bid to replace every train in use on the West Coast Main Line by 2004. The new trains and the maintenance contract are valued at £1.2 billion.'

The heart and core of the 'Pendolino' is its tilting capability. This is not Fiat technology, but Swiss, and the use of the Swiss technology was initiated by two Directors of Angel Trains. The bogies and tilting mechanism of the 'Pendolinos' were in use on Swiss trains in 1994, manufactured by Swiss Industrial Geschellshaft (SIG) at Schaffhausen. The mechanism is based on a Swiss all-electric system used for the barrel stabilisation of the large gun in Swiss army tanks. The Fiat tilting system was electro-hydraulic, developed from the system used on the British APT, and has twice the number of moving parts of the SIG system.

The small group of Angel Trains Directors travelled to Schaffhausen to arrange matters with SIG, and to Turin to consult with Fiat. The deputation told Fiat that they would buy a billion Euros-worth of 'Pendolinos' built by Fiat but *only* if the trains were fitted with the SIG bogies and tilting equipment. Virgin Trains made the specifications for the interior fittings and décor. Fiat then purchased SIG. Alstom, a French company that had already purchased the British GEC with works in Preston and Washwood Heath, Birmingham, then purchased Fiat-SIG and the trains were built in Birmingham with the vital Swiss equipment. The 'Pendolinos' are the property of Angel Trains, and their maintenance is carried out by West Coast Train Care, which is owned by the Alstom conglomerate.

What is also noteworthy here is the huge contrast between the vast amalgamations creating what could be described as 'monolithic' train construction and train care organisations – because this was of great advantage to the efficiency of those companies – and the fragmentation of the railway for the sake of 'efficiency'.

In mid-1997 Sir Robert Horton left the Chairmanship of Railtrack for the less risky job of Chairman of Betfair, the largest on-line gambling business in the world. He was replaced by 64-year-old Sir Philip Beck, but whereas Horton had been the Executive Chairman, Sir Philip was semi-detached – he was a *non-executive* Chairman. How a man could be a part-time Chairman of any large-scale company is difficult to understand, much less one as peculiar and complex as Railtrack. Sir Philip became known in newspaper articles as 'the Invisible Man' because he was so infrequently seen or heard, leaving most statements to be made by his Chief Executive.

Sir Philip had been Chairman of the building contractor Mowlem. Mowlem, first registered in 1903, was re-registered as a 'plc' in 1982 to take advantage of the Thatcher Government's intention to sell off public utilities and to involve contractors in providing public services like schools.

Sir Philip was Chairman as the Government handed out the contracts. Among many jobs, Mowlem built London City airport and the Falkland Islands airport in 1983, while buying construction businesses globally. Too much expansion too fast is usually called a 'bubble', and in 1995 the bubble burst. The company had to 'downsize' and this included Sir Philip, who then took up a non-executive Directorship at Railtrack. When he replaced Bob Horton, the outgoing Chairman said, comfortingly:

'Sir Philip's great experience of the construction industry will be valuable in steering Railtrack through the next phase of development. The company faces a challenging agenda and we are fortunate that the new chairman is a very experienced senior industrialist who brings the added bonus of having served on our board since 1995.'

Sir Philip had had four years' experience as a non-executive Director of Railtrack and was experienced as a harvester of contracts, and the new railway industry unloaded everything to contractors. Now he was on the other side of the fence – supervising contractors swarming over vast railway construction projects involving many different train operators and government bodies. Nothing he had

previously experienced could have prepared him for the vast complexity of what he was taking on. Railtrack was no conventional company – no other company had been put together like a jigsaw puzzle by a gang of 18th-century economic fundamentalists.

John Edmonds, who had wanted to retire as Chief Executive in 1996, stayed on until June 1997, when the Government found his replacement, Gerald Corbett. Mr Corbett had attended business schools in London and at Harvard University. He was employed by a Boston, Massachusetts, business consultancy for seven years before joining Dixons for five years, then he became Group Finance Director at Redland and, in 1993, Group Finance Director of Grand Metropolitan. At 'Grand Met' the Burger King franchise came under his financial control. Four years later, Grand Met was taken over by Guinness; Corbett left with a £600,000 going-away present and walked into the job at Railtrack at £325,000 per annum.

He was cheerfully optimistic about his complete ignorance of railways, announcing with innocent confidence:

'To be successful in senior corporate management does not necessarily require intimate corporate knowledge. There are people at Railtrack who know the company

The platforms as seen from the footbridge in July 1986.
Adrian Vaughan

The end of No 10 Platform on 12 February 1983. *Adrian Vaughan*

intimately. I am delighted to be taking up this position. Railtrack is making enormous strides forward in the railway industry and I am looking forward to playing a part. Under John Edmonds, a great deal of work has already been done. The whole industry is becoming more customer-focused and performance-orientated. I will have a sound management team around me to continue the trend of improving performance and increasing investment. Together we will go forward to realise the Chairman's vision to create the best railway in the world.'

Mr Corbett's description of Edmonds's 'enormous strides' was unrecognised in the Office of the Rail Regulator. In January 1997 the Rail Regulator had stated that Railtrack's investment was

'…wholly unacceptable. The company has spent £330m less than planned on track maintenance and made little progress in spending £450m for modernising stations.'

Railtrack countered by promising to spend £10 billion over the next ten years. The BRB had been investing rather more than £1 billion a year between 1990 and 1994. But

Mr Corbett delighted shareholders with his strong entrepreneurial style – he dealt 'robustly' with the demands of the Rail Regulator.

On 5 October 1999, four months after Sir Philip Beck had become Chairman of Railtrack, the Ladbroke Grove collision took place.

The track layout for the two miles approaching Paddington, from Ladbroke Grove eastwards, was a good example of squeezing the assets. The layout renewal began in 1988, under the auspices of the integrated BR, as a four-track railway.

In March 1993 BR set out to build an electrified railway from Paddington to Heathrow Airport and two more tracks were required from Paddington to West Drayton. Owing to the huge difficulties in widening the embankments and viaduct west of Ladbroke Grove, the extra tracks had to commence/terminate at that place. To increase capacity all the tracks eastwards from Ladbroke Grove were to be bi-directional. There was therefore the risk of a head-on collision occurring if a westbound train on Line 3 ran past signal SN 109 and into the path of an eastbound train. After the Clapham disaster, Anthony Hidden's Report obliged BR to install automatic train protection in the track and on the trains. That process was well in hand in 1993 and the designers naturally assumed that all trains would be equipped to make use of ATP so that the apparently dangerous track layout at Ladbroke Grove would be perfectly safe.

Privatisation in 1996 brought to the route the franchisee Thames Trains and its 'Turbo' diesel railcars, which were not fitted with ATP or TPWS because there was, at that time, no obligation on Thames Trains to do so. Her Majesty's Railway Inspectorate inspected Phase 1 of the Ladbroke Grove layout on 31 January 1995 and wrote to Railtrack to express concern about the poor visibility of the signals 'which will be made worse when the masts and catenary are erected'. (Cullen Report, 10.5) In spite of the known risk, HMRI said that trains could continue running. Eighteen months later, on 17 May 1996, Railtrack replied that the erection of the catenary had had 'a negligible effect' on signal sighting. HMRI was 'simply overwhelmed with work' and 'took on trust' all Railtrack's assertions and promises.

Recommendation 93 of the Hidden Report obliged the government to 'ensure that the Railway Inspectorate is adequately staffed and resourced to match its increased responsibilities incurred as a result of these recommendations.'

At the Ladbroke Grove crash Inquiry, a spokeswoman for Railtrack said: 'We would never compromise safety. That is why we get Rail Inspectorate approval at every stage.' Railtrack had never received approval from HMRI – only criticism of the layout – but had been allowed to continue running trains on the understanding that matters would be improved.

An HMRI investigation into the collision at Watford in August 1996, in which one passenger died, made 21 recommendations. No 5 was that

'Railtrack adopt a track layout assessment method in order to identify the risk of a collision at specific locations where a signal had been passed at danger. Railtrack should then prioritise those junctions that may require re-design or the adoption of additional safety measures.'

The route between Ladbroke and Paddington was six tracks wide and ran on a serpentine route. Drivers were looking ahead at a series of constantly reversing curves where the signals appeared to move about over and beyond the lines they controlled – and where the catenary obscured the view of most signals for many seconds at a time. Here was a case for a Layout Risk Assessment, but Railtrack did not carry one out because the layout was designed before it had come into existence.

Colin Bray was Railtrack Western Zone's Signal Standards Engineer. He made several suggestions for reducing the risk to safety in the layout between Ladbroke Grove and Paddington, including making the two centre lines, 3 and 4, uni-directional instead of bi-directional. This would have abolished the use of SN 63, the signal that had been passed at Danger more than any other – including SN 109. Mr Wiseman, Railtrack's Major Projects Division Business Development Manager, said of this idea, 'The proposal to make uni-directional working

may have a significant capacity impact.' The suggestion was therefore rejected. Colin Bray suggested a reduction of the line speed so that drivers had more time to see the signals. That too was rejected. The Operational Planning Manager, Mr Wilson, wrote to Production Standards Manager Mr Mayo, 'I recognise safety is paramount but believe there must be ways of mitigating this risk *without crippling the Zone's major revenue generating terminus.*' (Author's emphasis) (Colin Bray's evidence to Cullen Inquiry, 13.6.00, p.89-94) Mr Hendy, Barrister at the Inquiry, thought this was an admission of 'profit before safety' and put it to Mr Bray. 'Now, the long and the short of it is that the recommendation for abandoning bi-directional working for the centre lines was ruled out on cost, was it not?' Mr. Bray replied: 'I do not believe that is an accurate way to put it and I think it is necessary that we look at it very carefully.'

Railtrack engineers were trying to get 'a quart into a pint pot'. They certainly wanted to mitigate the risks, but without reducing the money they could make out of the layout they planned. So no useful mitigating measures were taken. Then an under-trained and inexperienced driver, lost and confused in a complex layout he did not understand and with the sun washing out the signal aspects, drove into the trap that had been laid for him; 31 people died and 416 were injured. (In April 2004 Thames Trains was fined £2 million for failing to correctly train the driver.) This was the macho, profit-making, business-led, new railway. The cost to the NHS, to the emergency services, to the repair and replacement of track, trains, signalling, and overhead catenary must have been £100 million.

Everyone involved in the design of that Ladbroke Grove-Paddington layout knew that it was more or less dangerous and that No 8 gantry carrying the fatal signal, SN 109, was particularly badly sited. No-one with the power to act did so, not even the HSE. They all had excuses. No-one was going to stand in the way of business. That was the problem.

The Ladbroke Grove disaster occurred just as Railtrack's six-monthly report to shareholders, 'Railtalk', was being distributed. On 8 October a Railtrack shareholder wrote to the *Financial Times*:

'On Wednesday I received "Railtalk". Analysing this report in the context of rail safety is painfully illuminating… The preface highlights "performance" and "investment", there is no mention of safety… Page two is entitled "Around the Network", with no mention of safety… Page three is from a statement by Chairman Sir Robert Horton; there is no mention of safety… Page four lists the top ten issues raised by shareholders; none mentions safety… Page six says that "action to reduce train delays is the watchword throughout Railtrack"; there is no mention of safety. Safety is mentioned in "Railtalk" once… This analysis makes it clear that the management culture of the railways has shifted perceptibly towards explicit bonus-linked goals of train performance and away from an absolute safety requirement.'

Left: The scaffolding goes up, 8 May 1986.
Adrian Vaughan

Left: The rebuilt platform ends on 5 May 2008.
Adrian Vaughan

Right: Under the old roof, the 10.50 arrival from Norwich is on the left on 5 May 2008.
Adrian Vaughan

Below: A 1987 BR-built electric locomotive, No 90011, stands at the buffers with the 09.00 train from Norwich.
Adrian Vaughan

In October 2000 the Crown Prosecution Service (CPS) gave serious consideration over a period of many weeks to the possibility of charging the Directors of Railtrack with 'Corporate manslaughter', but the charge was not brought. The reason given by the CPS was that a successful prosecution would have to show that there was a 'controlling mind' behind the errors leading up to the disaster, and there was no evidence of a 'controlling mind'. That was the carefully considered opinion of the Crown Prosecution Service. Railtrack and the fragmented railway industry had been proven to be a disaster. No 'lessons' were learned.

After Ladbroke Grove Sir Philip decided that Railtrack needed management changes. Sir Alastair Morton, Chairman of the Shadow Strategic Rail Authority, and the Minister of Transport, Lord MacDonald, were of the same opinion, and thought Sir Philip Beck should resign. He stayed. Sir Philip took 13 months to reorganise his Board. The changes were announced on 21 November 2000. The following day he told the Parliamentary Transport Committee that

'…the changes which Railtrack announced yesterday are intended to strengthen and will strengthen the role of engineering at the Board level and emphasise the company's customer focus. Richard Middleton you know already; he is a Chartered Engineer with 24 years' experience in the railway industry, and has become Technical Director. The company's engineering strength at the top has been further increased with the appointment of Andrew McNaughton, who is a Chartered Engineer with 27 years' experience; he will be Chief Engineer. Jonson Cox, who is not with us today, is Railtrack's Chief Operating Officer and is currently responsible for front-line operations and will assume Board responsibility for commercial and franchising activity.'

Mr Corbett found himself in charge of a company in organisational turmoil, embroiled in a huge contract with Richard Branson and, at the core of this contract, a signalling system that was still on the drawing board, and an engineer in charge of it with whom Corbett did not get on. Professor Mellit eventually departed and in July 1998 Corbett brought in GEC-Alstom, on a nine-month contract, to define – a year after the contract with Branson had been signed – what 'moving block' was and, if delivered, what it would do for the railway. On 9 December 1999 Railtrack publicly announced 'Black Diamond Day' – its abandonment of 'moving block', which it now described as 'a high-risk project'. This left Railtrack with the problem of 'exceptionally high costs' of signalling the WCML with modern conventional signals. This necessity also meant that it would not be able to fulfil its contract with Virgin. At the same time, the Rail Regulator laid an enforcement action on Railtrack to compel it to provide sufficient capacity for *all operators* using the WCML by 2005.

The costs of West Coast modernisation were rising through the billions of pounds, while delays rose with equal alacrity. In 1966, much denigrated BR electrified the WCML from London to Manchester at the rate of £6.25 million per mile at 2002 prices – and that included the cost of BR's own workshops building the locomotives and carriages. In 2002 the cost of rebuilding the WCML under the influence of private enterprise was estimated by the appointed consultant, the US firm Betchel, at £22 million per mile. (Roger Ford, memorandum to House of Commons Transport Committee, 2002) Delays to Virgin trains were 50% on some days in 2000, and in July Railtrack was under the threat, from its quasi-partner, of a £10 million lawsuit, as was allowed for in their contract. With the costs of Railtrack's flagship project and privatisation going through the roof, and with no likelihood of the contracts with Virgin being honoured, the Rail Regulator summoned the Railtrack Board to his presence in May 2000 and spent the day interrogating them. A transcript of this event can be obtained from the Office of the Rail Regulator.

The questions from the Regulator and his men produced replies from some of the Railtrack team couched in the amazing jargon of power-businessmen, replies that, while difficult for a non-business person to understand, do nonetheless convey very strongly the incredible complexity of the situation in which these men worked. However, Mr Simon Murray, Railtrack Director of Major Projects Investments, recently brought onto 'the team' from a career in civil engineering, did speak in standard English, and one of his contributions demonstrates perfectly not only Mr Murray's astonishment at the Byzantine complexities created by the fevered minds of the great economists, but also the uniqueness of the railway as a business, something the great ones had always denied.

'It is very important in understanding the risks to explain the context in which we seek to identify, quantify and manage risk. Certainly one of the things I understood shortly after I joined the railway was that the nature of risks on railway projects are very different from those commonly found on major construction projects. The railway has its own, unique, risks.

If we are to obtain the capability from the railway which the OOR wants we shall have to rely on complex technologies. Delivering these complex technologies within a safety management environment driven by our own staff and the HMRI is more complex than I have come across in any branch of infrastructure engineering. I personally have never encountered complexity of this level in infrastructure engineering.

We have the complexity of planning and managing work on the railway, the complexity of logistics, and the complexity of the relationships between all the other stakeholders and Railtrack. I have never seen such levels of complexity.'

Mr Tony Fletcher, General Manager West Coast Modernisation, made some very interesting contributions, and at great length. At one stage he was asked how long he would like to reconstruct the WCML. His answer was lengthy and the Rail Regulator interjected, 'You are working to an answer, aren't you?' To which Mr Fletcher snapped, 'I can shut up now if you like.' But then he went on to reveal the depths of Railtrack's chaos on this issue. He said:

'What I am trying to do is to put the answer in the context of West Coast, to portray the progression of events and circumstances which has meant that this programme has never got to a level of stability [sufficient] for any party to actually process the implementation of the work, and that stability has not existed for five years.' So Railtrack had been dealing with thousands of contracts and arrangements and studies and targets – and all the time the proverbial goal-posts were moving – and actual work was almost at a standstill.'

Robin Gisby, commercial sponsor of the West Coast project, talked about the pitfalls of fragmented responsibility and the need for co-ordination – although he did not use those words. He said:

'We have not talked much about the trains, the performance of the trains, the design of the trains, and the interaction with the track. Alstom build this thing, get it tested and try and interface it with our track. It relates to signalling and it relates to safety at stations. If we had done some of these things earlier we might have built something which would actually have involved a large waste of money because the train they finally came up with may not necessarily fit it [the railway]. Clearly there is a large range of joint working between us and Virgin and us and Alstom trains and us and Alstom signalling as their train design evolves and matures and goes into service…'

Near the end of the day's meeting, Tom Winsor said, a trifle wearily perhaps, 'I have a short question for Mr Corbett. Is it reasonable that a party to a contract should expect to have that contract honoured?'

Mr Corbett replied, a little sadly perhaps, 'Yes, that is reasonable – in the real world – but in many senses the railway is not the real world.'

The stairs to and from Liverpool Street on 5 May 2008. *Adrian Vaughan*

Left: The station exterior in May 2008, which was superbly well restored by BR. *Adrian Vaughan*

Left: In memory of the station that died to give its next door neighbour a bright new lease of life: the front of Broad Street station on 2 April 1984.

CHAPTER 12

'That's not our problem...'

In March 1999 Railtrack issued its Network Management Statement (NMS), a glossy, 250-page brochure setting out a wish-list for a railway of the future – always the future – using fantasy phrases like 'A World Class Railway' and 'High Speed Inter-Urban Routes'. Just so there could be no doubt that this was no more than a propaganda exercise, on the inside cover there was a declaration couched in hard, legalistic language that read: 'The inclusion of any project or proposal in this statement does not imply that it has formal investment approval.'

This NMS talked of a £27 billion investment programme over the following ten years but, according to the House of Commons Transport Committee, less than £11 billion of that would be true investment and the rest would be required to keep up with essential maintenance.

The last of the 'Star' class, No 4072 *Tresco Abbey*, waits at the 1850-built platform at Oxford with a Birkenhead-Dover express in June 1931. A perfectly matched set of Mr Maunsell's latest carriages has been increased by one GWR 19th-century clerestory, added at Oxford to provide more seats for the passengers on a well-filled train. The station was completely rebuilt in 1972/73. *Dr Jack Hollick/Adrian Vaughan Collection*

Railtrack talked of building 'high-speed inter-urban railways' when it could not rebuild WCML, nor properly look after the existing railway. It could not even re-lay the tracks when it said it would. In the BBC Radio 4 documentary on Railtrack, broadcast on 8 June 1999, Chris Green, Managing Director of Virgin Trains, said:

'Railtrack must replace 630 miles of track in three years. Every night for three years a section of track must be coned off and in the morning the cones removed – eight hours of engineering work and 16 hours given over to the passengers. It could be done but it will require a military discipline and Japanese precision.'

Robin Gisby expressed surprise that Green was still worried. Using that special, loose, Railtrack-speak, he said:

'The first really big deadline for us is the introduction of their new train for which we have to upgrade the track and the power supply. I'm pleased to say that I think we are now making some very good progress on that and I think we'll hit those deadlines.'

The BBC interviewer said, 'Given that it's taken so long to make a start on the project, how can anyone have confidence in Railtrack delivering in the time that you are now promising?'

Gisby replied:

'Well, I think the first thing to do is sort out a specification for what we're trying to build. The arrangement with Virgin for the upgrade was not actually sorted out until early 1998. Technically work could have started in 1995 but none of the interested parties were ready to do it until last year. We have so far authorised about £600 million to be spent of which £300 million has been spent in the overall programme and you will see a rapid increase in those figures over the next two to three years so that we meet our deadline.'

English Welsh & Scottish Railway (EWS), the freight train company, was in 1999 investing £800 million in new locos, wagons and terminals, enough to triple the amount of freight on rail. But then the disadvantage of fragmentation intruded – EWS did not own the tracks. It had to share its 'paths' on rail among the other trains, and it needed more paths to take the extra traffic it intended to capture. The Rail Regulator asked Railtrack to confirm that it could provide 42 new paths on the WCML Slow Lines, for anyone, but primarily for freight. Gisby assured the BBC interviewer that 'we are committed to providing the 42 and we're coming up with infrastructure and timetable solutions over the next few weeks to meet the commitment.'

However, the Rail Regulator was not convinced and told Railtrack to produce its plans now, not in several weeks' time, warning Railtrack that it may be in breach of its legal obligations under its network licence.

A seven-car HST off the Worcester line stands at the 1990-rebuilt Up platform at Oxford in May 2008. To the rear is the capacious footbridge, also added in 1990. The train is superb, the only disadvantage being that if the seats are filled additional passengers have to stand and cram together. *Adrian Vaughan*

Railtrack had to pay good profits to keep up its share value in order that people would want to invest in the shares. The company had therefore to walk a tightrope of handsome profit across the great chasm of public service. It cut out jobs – and that meant a reduction in quality of maintenance. Railtrack Finance Director Norman Broadhurst said that Railtrack had cut costs by 4% by reducing its workforce by 600 to 10,600, and he hoped to do the same in the following year. There were few enough men to begin with. A Railtrack manager – who did not want to be identified because he was still employed by Railtrack when he was interviewed by Christian Wolmar – said, 'Railtrack does not have the power to enforce its own safety standards.' (*Broken Rails*, p.185)

Railtrack invested £960 million in 1997-98 – rather less than the BRB had done in 1993-94 – but hoped to invest £1.45 billion in 1998-99. Railtrack's profit for 1997-98 was £388 million before tax, which was £1.06 million per day, while the taxpayers were putting in £5 million a day in subsidies to the train operators, which ended up with Railtrack. The City banks were thrilled – the taxpayers were underwriting their investments. In 2000 the government had to *give a grant* of £4 billion to Railtrack. Without taxpayers' money, Railtrack would not have been able to continue its work on WCML.

Jonathan Bray, of 'Save Our Railways', said, 'Railtrack is nothing more than a gigantic money-laundering machine turning public subsidy into private profit.' (*Electronic Telegraph*, Issue 1105, 4.6.98) On 18 October 2001 the Secretary of State for Transport, David Jamieson, stated in Parliament that 'whilst no public money was paid to

No D7001 leaves Oxford with a train for Paddington in 1970.
Adrian Vaughan

Railtrack between 1996 and 2001, the company's profitability in those years was contingent [dependent] on public money [because] 85% of Railtrack's income is from train operating companies, most of which are supported by public money.' (*See table below*)

While all this money, 85% of which was derived from the publicly-subsidised train operating companies, was being shovelled out of the railways to no useful purpose elsewhere, Railtrack's debt was rising so that by mid-2001 it owed £3.5 *billion*. It will be noted that the highest dividend was paid at the time of greatest indebtedness. The £3.5 billion was the amount that Railtrack had invested in the railway in three years, about the same annual rate at which BR was investing in the three years up to sell-off. Railtrack promised a doubling of investment in the railway

– but on what was this money to be spent? Mr Broadhurst, Finance Director, said: 'Because Railtrack is beginning to improve its financial performance, it can begin to get involved in major projects like the Channel Tunnel Rail Link [CTRL], which adds to our business.' He warned that *close regulation* and *over-demanding* targets would make Railtrack unattractive to City investors. City investors – Japanese and US banks – were looking for 25% returns, so they were only interested in very major projects like the CTRL or the WCML. So the apparently large sums of money invested in the railway was going in those directions most approved of by global bankers. This procedure would eventually reduce the railway system to what Sir David Serpell had suggested in 1983. And that was really what privatisation was about.

Meanwhile there were all the ordinary railway routes to be looked after and, when spread over the network, investment of a billion pounds a year does not go far.

	1996-97	1997-98	1998-99	1999-2000	2000-01	
Directors' total salaries (x £1,000)	1,386	2,167	2,046	2,153	2,669	
Directors' other emoluments* (£) including payments in kind	16,000	11,000	10,000	11,000	26,000	
Other performance-related bonus* payments (£)	48,000	49,000	28,000	23,000	15,000	
*Bonus payments were 'based on safety, asset condition and financial targets met'.						
Payments to Directors for	292,000 (*one man*)	335,000 (*three men*)	309,000 (*two men*)	153,000 (*one man*)	594,000 (*two men*)	
Total amount of money paid in dividends to shareholders (£ millions)	180	121	133	137	138	**Total** 709

After the Bexley bridge fiasco, Mr Vic Coleman of the HSE said, 'The contractors had failed to deal with the problem although they had known about it for months and Railtrack had the information as to the state of the bridge and had done nothing.' Were the contractors brought under the strict supervision of Railtrack? No. They continued to be judge and jury with the blessing of Railtrack. Although Railtrack had the legal obligation to ensure the safety of the track, that peculiar organisation did not have sufficient engineering expertise to supervise them. When BR engineering was chopped up and repackaged for sale as Infrastructure Maintenance Companies (IMCO),

Above: In May 2008 an Up Birmingham service passes under the old signal gantry, still in use for the colour signals brought into use in 1973. *Adrian Vaughan*

Below: Looking north from the north end of the Up platform at Oxford in 1970. A train is signalled out of the Up Bay platform to the right. The bridge girders in the centre are crossing Duke's Cut, an arm of the Oxford Canal connecting with the River Isis. The ex-LNWR Rewley Road station is out of sight immediately right of view, but the presence of those tracks and the swing bridge over the Cut keeps the railway clear of all buildings. *Adrian Vaughan*

the engineers were sold with them. As late as November 2000 Richard Middleton, an ex-BR civil engineer on the Board of Railtrack, had to tell a Parliamentary Committee that Railtrack was *thinking* about employing more engineering staff. Railtrack was, under the law, responsible for safety – and they were considering whether to employ an appropriate number of engineers.

'The way that the industry is structured currently the responsibility for the engineering of the network sits with the contractors. The bulk of the engineering resource that was in BR went into those companies [IMCOs]. *If we decide* (author's emphasis) that the engineering decision-making is not being carried out appropriately within the contractual framework then we will make arrangements to move that decision-making inside Railtrack. The resources, therefore, will come in part from growing our own resources by recruiting separately more engineers. In answer to your direct question of how many more engineers that will be, it is too early to answer that question, but it is certainly not a small number, it would certainly be in the hundreds.' (House of Commons Transport Committee, Q.613-615)

But privatisation was perfectly safe. There was a Health & Safety Executive, was there not, and a Rail Regulator? For 1998 the Regulator had given Railtrack the target of reducing speed restrictions on the track by 7.5%. Railtrack fell short of that by 5%, so the Regulator made the target for 1999 a 12.5% reduction. All the boxes were ticked, targets were set, and promises were made. What a great system.

Broken rails in the Severn Tunnel had been an occurrence of extreme rarity thanks to the policy – implemented by the GWR when the tunnel opened in 1886 and continued under the inefficiencies of BR – that no rails inside the tunnel should be more than six years old. Track removed from the tunnel was then re-laid elsewhere. Under Railtrack, with that management's convictions about the 'over-engineering' of the railway, plus the super-modern policy of 'how-long-can-we-let-it-go-for?' risk assessments, this period was extended by 50% and there were four instances of broken rails in seven months during 1998. This was unprecedented in the history of the tunnel. But Railtrack allowed 125mph running through the tunnel because any speed restriction would oblige Railtrack to pay compensation to the operators.

In April 1999 the HSE had to order Railtrack to put a 20mph speed limit throughout the 5½ miles of the Severn Tunnel. This was done a couple of months after Railtrack had sent a letter to all Great Western Zone staff applauding the fact that the mass of speed restrictions imposed during 1998 on the entire South Wales Direct line, from Wootton Bassett to Severn Tunnel Junction, had been removed. Over the UK rail network there was an increase of 24% in the number of broken rails comparing 1998 with 1997.

A length of 300 rotten sleepers was found on the Erewash Valley line north of Derby for which the contractors had taken no remedial action. The HSE had to order the renewal of that track. Two foreseeable landslides occurred on the Hellifield-Carlisle line in 1999 where, in 1994 at Ais Gill, seven passengers had been killed when a landslide had derailed a lightweight diesel unit. (See my *Tracks to Disaster*, p.128)

This is Oxford station looking north in May 2008. Rewley Road station has disappeared and houses have been built on the site of its tracks and engine shed. The swing bridge is still there, just beyond the steel fencing, rusting away beneath brambles. *Adrian Vaughan*

Left: A Great Western Society excursion to Tyseley hauled by No 6998 *Burton Agnes Hall* accelerates enthusiastically northwards on 1 October 1972. It was photographed from the Walton Well bridge with the ex-LNWR line to Bletchley below and LMS signals to the fore. *Susan Vaughan*

Below: Seen from the same vantage point a 'Voyager' heads north in May 2008. *Adrian Vaughan*

A 'Castle' brings the 9am from Worcester off the Worcester line at Wolvercote Junction in 1955. *Peter Barlow/ Adrian Vaughan Collection*

Richard Rosser of the Transport Salaried Staff Association commissioned the Advanced Railway Research Centre of Sheffield University to make a study and comparison of the rate of renewal of track between British Rail, Railtrack, SNCF and Swedish Railways. The conclusion was reached that the Railtrack renewal rate was 80 years, whereas BR's had been 40 years, which was comparable to SNCF/Swedish practice. These findings were sent to the Rail Regulator, who was carrying out a similar investigation. The Regulator had already concluded that Dutch Railways and BR had the same renewal rate. The Regulator stated that, based on the higher standards of BR, 'Railtrack is spending one-third less than what is required to keep track at a constant age or "steady state". A back-log of renewal is developing.'

At Leeds in May 1999 the signalling system failed for three days in a row as steam-era wiring lost its insulation and produced short circuits. In searching for the faults the S&T men caused more short circuits. Railtrack was at the time investing in Leeds railway station – in a shopping mall and its car park. This use of railway land curtailed the possibility of expanding the rail facilities in the future. Railtrack said that when its investment in 'retail outlets' at Leeds was complete it would turn its attention to the wiring problem. The renting of shops in malls is an important part of Railtrack's revenue, and Railtrack was working hard to increase this side of its business.

So Leeds City station got a brand new retail outlet while the signalling was in a dreadful state. The BBC Radio 4 documentary *File on 4*, which covered this story on 8 June 1999, recorded Robin Gisby, Railtrack's Commercial Manager, saying: 'Bright, clean, tidy stations are as important as the signalling. The signalling – yes, we've got to get that sorted – but the Leeds incident was very unfortunate and we want to see the investment going into all aspects of the railway.' The Rail Regulator did not have a clear understanding of the condition of the track and signalling equipment and Railtrack had reservations about how much detailed monitoring of assets was required.

The Rail Regulator was of the opinion that

'Passengers, freight users and the taxpayer are paying for Railtrack to spend £1.7 billion a year on maintaining and renewing the network. The ORR needs to remove the deficiencies in their information on the condition of Railtrack's assets so that they can satisfactorily assess on the customers' behalf what is being achieved with this money.' (Ensuring that Railtrack maintain and renew the railway network, HC 397,1999-2000, p.7, 17(c), and p.9, 19(2))

Lord Bill Bradshaw, ex-General Manager at Paddington and a railwayman for 40 years, said on BBC Radio 4 on 6 August 1999:

'There is no comparison by which the efficiency or value for money of Railtrack can be tested – unlike the water companies where several companies' performance can be compared. We do not know if Railtrack is value for money but we, the travelling public and the train operating companies, do know that they are not satisfied with what they are getting.'

Birmingham New Street station had become a wedge of unpunctuality by 1994. Rail traffic had been increasing ever since Birmingham Snow Hill station was closed in 1972. The BRB re-opened the rebuilt Snow Hill and Moor Street stations in 1987 to cater for suburban trains from districts south of Birmingham and also for trains from London Marylebone. Still traffic increased – long before privatisation, be it noted. In 1994 New Street was more congested that it had ever been. The West Midlands Transport Authority – Centro – then spent £30 million on measures to reduce congestion at the station. In May 1998 Railtrack issued its new timetable. Rob Macdonald, Chairman of Centro, stated on BBC Radio 4 on 8 June 1999:

'We spent £30 million to reduce congestion and then along came Railtrack and re-sold to other train operating companies the plots we'd vacated, and now punctuality is worse than in 1994. The major investment we had made in Snow Hill was lost overnight.'

It could only happen on a fragmented railway where all the operators are thinking of themselves – but we were told that converting the unified railway into internal and external 'markets' would produce 'coherence' and 'efficiency' because 'management flair' would be allowed to thrive for the first time since 1939.

At the local level the fragmentation of the railway team leads to all kinds of inefficiencies that inflict inconvenience and discomfort on the sacred 'customers'.

One day the 'main to main' crossover at Diss, in Norfolk, failed to return to its 'Normal' position for Up and Down main-line running after being used for a shunting movement. Under the integrated BR system, the porter at Diss could have given the point blades a push with his foot and closed them the one-sixteenth of an inch necessary to 'make' the electric detection that would then clear the Up and Down main-line signals. But under the discipline-of-the-marketplace system of railway operation, where the railway is brought 'closer to the customer' and the needs of the customer come first, the porter at Diss is not employed by Railtrack and cannot go onto the track. The points are at the end of the platform, the trains are standing at red signals within his sight and as time goes by more trains come to a stand queuing behind them. Meanwhile, 43 miles away at Colchester panel, the signaller sends for that rare breed – a signal technician. He is out on some other fault, but after a couple of hours, or however long it takes, he arrives at Diss and sorts out the job in a few minutes.

The electrically operated bell used to convey train signalling messages between Carmarthen Junction and Ferryside signal boxes failed sometime in May 1999. During the time that a signalling bell is out of use, trains running on the line it signals must be stopped and the author cautioned. The Railtrack-employed Safety Production Manager (District Inspector in BR days) for the Carmarthen area applied to the S&T maintenance contractors, GTRM, to come and rectify the fault. GTRM disowned the fault because, they said, it was in the 37-core cable and that was Racal's responsibility. Racal was contacted and said that it only maintained the cable, and did not own it, and Railtrack would have to contact the owner of the cable – Global Communications. The bell was working again on 7 November.

The Ferryside fault was an illustration of the problems that arise when the once independent and self-contained railway gets involved with clever business deals and matters that have nothing to do with railways. The Ferryside-Carmarthen signalling bell – part of the safety system protecting the trains – was operated through a circuit running through a 'hybrid cable' that was not part of the maintenance contract with GTRM. These cables are not dedicated to the signalling bell

An HST forming the 11.40 Malvern to Paddington service comes past the graffiti at Wolvercote Junction in May 2008.
Adrian Vaughan

Above: Norwich Thorpe goods yards and station are seen from the Carrow Road bridge in July 1985. Signalling was then still by local mechanical boxes, the engine shed was still standing on the left, and electrification was yet to come. *Adrian Vaughan*

but are 'telecoms'-type cables, owned by Railtrack and carrying the signalling circuits, but leased to Racal for its purposes. So even the wiring in the signal boxes became fragmented! Racal was very slow to deal with the faulty cable due to the fact that its internal organisation is complex. Racal leases the cable to Global Crossings but Racal Field Force, which is part of Global Crossings, actually does the fault-finding and repair work.

An electric cable at Stratford, East London, was cut at 19.05 on 17 April 2001. There was no power to the points and signals over a wide area, including Stratford loco depot and Temple Mills yard. There was a standby diesel generator, which was supposed to 'cut in' automatically in such an event, but it did not start because it had not been maintained for years and it was a fact that Railtrack was willing to take the cost of delays rather than spend money on it. To complicate matters, the cable had been cut in contractor AMEC's area, but the standby generator was maintained by Balfour Beatty. The generator was in such a state that it could not be brought into use and a temporary standby generator was not brought into use until 18.45 on

Right: This is Norwich Thorpe station seen from the Carrow Road Bridge in May 2008. BR electrified the main line into Norwich in 1986. The goods yard and engine shed area disappeared in the early 1990s to be replaced by night cubs, supermarkets and multi-storey car parks. *Adrian Vaughan*

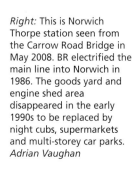

the 19th. The trains were delayed, but a coach and horses was driven rapidly through 'customer care'.

It was on 10 May 2002 that the neglect of facing points at Potters Bar, maintained by Jarvis, caused the fatal crash that killed seven and injured 70, 11 of them seriously. This would not have happened had maintenance been under the supervision of 'over-engineered' British Railways. BR engineers did not suffer under the lash of *marketplace discipline*. Their job was to maintain a safe railway, not keep investors happy. Jarvis squirmed a lot after the crash, putting forward for many months the possibility of 'sabotage' as the reason for the crash, but on 28 April 2004, after the fact was established that several other points in the vicinity were also in a poor condition, the company admitted responsibility.

Jarvis continued as contractors to Railtrack for railway maintenance. They got the contract to restore the tracks at Potters Bar. In November 2002 at Aldwarke Junction, between Sheffield and Doncaster, track workers employed by Jarvis removed the 'V' rail provided at a set of points to enable the wheels of trains on the diverging route to cross through the main line. In place of the 'V' rail they put in an ordinary straight rail, which formed a barrier to any train turning across the main line. This was done without any prior notice being given to the signalman controlling the points, and he was miles away in a power box and could not see what was happening. He had been aware the signalman could then have informed the signal technicians, employed by another contractor, who would have disabled the controls to the junction points so that no train could be routed to the diverging route. As a result of these men removing a piece of track without telling anyone, the signalman routed a coal train across the junction and a derailment took place. While Jarvis was in court over this, the company was still awaiting a court appearance for causing a derailment at King's Cross in September 2003, its men having removed a rail and then forgotten to put it back. Jarvis was losing a lot of money at this time, its creditors were restless and it was trying hard to obtain more maintenance contracts from Network Rail. The company must have had some success because its shares were up to 40p on 12 July.

On 25 August 2001 the 10.05 Yarmouth to Liverpool Street passenger train, 10 coaches hauled by No 47787 *Victim Support*, left Platform 2 and began to travel over points 20 and 47 to reach the Up Main line. As the engine's bogies curved onto the Up Main, four sleepers gave way and the rails moved apart under the trailing bogie, derailing that and the leading bogie of the first coach. The train stopped. Yarmouth station was reduced to a one-platform station on a summer Saturday. The first priority for a business-led railway in this situation is to decide who is to blame. Railwaymen from an older school would find this unprofessional, but they had not had the benefit of market discipline. The contractor for the maintenance of the line was Balfour Beatty. Eventually that company's representative arrived and declined to accept responsibility for the condition of the track. The arbitrator had now to be called in, but these arguments over blame were so common that there was a well-rehearsed routine. The arbitrator was a contractor, of course, Atomic Energy Authority (AEA) Technology, at Derby. A phone call elicited the fact that the gentleman concerned was attending to a derailment argument in Glasgow. Apparently, AEA, perhaps concerned for its costs, could not have two arbitrators, so the train would just have to stay derailed, blocking the station, until the sole arbitrator could get down there.

In 1985 empty carriages were drawn into the station by the Station Pilot and the train engine, a Class 47, then backed on at the front end, just like in steam days. Branch-line services to Yarmouth, Lowestoft, Cromer and Ely were provided by 1960s DMUs. *Adrian Vaughan*

Her Majesty's Railway Inspectorate arrived at 1.30pm. The on-call Control Centre Manager did not arrive until 1.45, together with a Scene of Crime policeman from British Transport Police. The re-railing gang, owned by EWS, arrived. The Foreman looked at the job and reckoned he could square it up in an hour, but had to join the rest – waiting. The arbitrator arrived in a helicopter at 7.00pm. After a brief examination of the sleepers showed him they could have been scraped up with a shovel, he laid the blame on Balfour Beatty. The re-railing gang set to work with jacks for the vehicles and tie bars for the track. The wheels were back on rails at 8.00pm.

In the Dark Ages, before we had the benefit of advice from Professors of Economics and Board Members of the Royal Automobile Club telling us how to run railways, the breakdown gang was a compact team stationed at all main depots – such as Yarmouth. They were all trained fitters and mechanics. To get onto the breakdown team was the ambition of many fitters – like joining the lifeboat crew. In the Dark Ages, when a breakdown team arrived at the scene, the Foreman of the gang took precedence over the General Manager of the railway and the police had – at most – the simple job of keeping onlookers at a safe distance. At some depots the breakdown gang organised an annual exercise with the local fire brigade and St John's Ambulance. Afterwards there was a party. All became a team.

In modern times the Foreman is a solitary individual who, when called upon to attend a derailment, has to get on his mobile phone and ask around, 'Do you want to come out on a job?'

'I don't know – is it a big one?'

One evening the 'detection' on the main-to-main facing crossover points at East Somerset Junction, Witham (Somerset), failed. The Up and Down line signals went to 'Danger' and an Up Weymouth-Bristol train was brought to a stand. There was no-one available to be sent from the relatively close Westbury signal control centre to Witham. Instead, the Bristol Area Operations Manager had to drive from Bristol Temple Meads to this remote location, miles away, deep in the Mendip lanes. The drive from Bristol took an hour. He parked in the sidings, walked to the points and applied a 'G'-clamp to pull the point blade tight to the stock rail so that trains could pass over the points safely. The Up Weymouth had stood at the signal for 80 minutes and following trains were delayed.

The following day the Operations Manager mentioned to the Profit Centre Manager that, before privatisation, Westbury panel would have sent a man out there and got the train on the move in around 30 minutes. Before Westbury panel came into use, the Witham signalman would have walked down the track and sorted the job out in 10 minutes. But that was, of course, before the change to a more enlightened 'culture'.

The Bristol Profit Centre Manager was unrepentantly callous. 'That's not our problem.' The Ops Manager protested that it was their problem. 'No it's not,' says the man in charge of profits. 'The train operator will claim the cost of the delay from Railtrack, who'll claim the cost of your attendance from the maintenance contractor. No-one will lose.'

'Only the passengers,' retorted the Operations Manager. Of course, a properly indoctrinated Operations Manager would have said 'customers'. Using the right word makes so much difference.

With BR's electrification of the Norwich-London expresses in 1986 the trains, powered by BR 1966 Class 86/2 locomotives, could be driven either from the locomotive cab or remotely from a driving compartment at the opposite end of the train, thus making the Pilot redundant. Shortly afterwards, the long-serving DMUs were superseded by BR's second-generation units, the diesel-hydraulic Class 158 'Sprinters'. Here we see a '158' and driving trailer No 82143 at the buffers at Norwich in June 2008. *Adrian Vaughan*

CHAPTER 13

Hatfield and after

In the aftermath of Ladbroke Grove the Railtrack Board saw that it was going to need a lot more money to repair the enormous damage caused and to pay compensation to the train operating companies. This extra capital would be unproductive, simply putting the railway back where it was before the crash, but increasing Railtrack's debt, reducing its share value and deterring the large investors from investing. Then there was the need to install the new Train Protection & Warning System (TPWS) throughout the railway. TPWS would have stopped Michael Hodder's train within a few yards after he had passed SN 109 at 'Danger'. Railtrack had kept its profits up – in order to attract investment – by holding back on maintenance costs, i.e. safety, and forcing its assets in the hope of good profits, as at Ladbroke Grove, where they forced a quart into a pint pot. Without strong profits Railtrack could not attract the amount of investment it required – or obtain that money at reasonable rates of interest. Profits must be less if more income is spent on maintenance and renewal. It is something the Adam Smith Institute overlooked when it was hatching its cunning plan for railways – the need to make enough profit to satisfy banks forces the railway to be inefficient.

Railtrack had divested itself of thousands of technical staff from 1994 onwards, most of them going to the infrastructure maintenance companies owned by the big contractors. There was only one engineer on the Board, Richard Middleton, and he was employed as Commercial Director. After Ladbroke Grove, it was decided to bring in an additional Director to take some of Corbett's work load. Middleton was not moved to the post of, say, 'Director of Engineering', but in March 2000 a Mr Jonson Cox was recruited from the water supply industry and made Director of Operations. 'Director of Operations' was an odd title, because Railtrack did not concern itself with operating the railway. It was, however, considered wise to take the safety responsibilities covered by whatever 'Operations' meant in the context of Railtrack and give them to Chris Leah, as 'Director of Safety'. Leah had started his railway career in 1967.

Between the Newton collision of July 1991 and the Cowden collision of October 1994 no passenger had been killed on the railway. In 1994 there were 656 incidents of broken rails. The number increased to a peak of 952 in 1999. In 2000 there were 919 and 706 in 2001. Responsibility for recording defects had been passed from Railtrack to its contractors. (Office of the Rail Regulator, Report 9, November 2000) Yet Railtrack was, in the eyes of the law, the guardian of the track and signalling. Railtrack did not know the condition of its track or the locations of defects. How could it honestly say that it would never jeopardise safety if it did not know what was safe and what was not safe?

The Railtrack Board saw a need to make a gesture towards the old ideal of public service as a good image-building strategy. Mr Corbett said, 'Our number one priority is to deliver our public service obligations. The increase is fundamental to the improvements in safety, train performance and track quality.' Early in February 2000 Railtrack promised the Rail Regulator that it would increase its promised expenditure for the year 2000-01 from £2 billion to £2.5 billion. But where would this extra investment come from? From extra public funds, of course. Gerald Corbett had extracted from the Rail Regulator, Tom Winsor, a promise of extra public money for the period 2000-05. The value of Railtrack shares rose at this point from £6.76p to £7.41½p, but this small rise and the prospect of a weak dividend because of the increased investment was not likely to attract the billions of investment from the global financiers that John MacGregor had so confidently predicted a few years earlier.

The fatal derailment at Hatfield took place on 17 October 2000. This was also the beginning of the end for Railtrack. Coming north from King's Cross, the East Coast Main Line approaches Hatfield through sweeping reverse curves. The cant, or superelevation, of the rails through these curves had to be a compromise between the greater amount required for a 115 mph passenger train and the lesser amount for a 75mph freight train. This compromise is called 'cant deficiency'. For the former, the track was insufficiently canted so that the express trains' wheels and flanges were pressing hard against the gauge corner of the outer rail; for the latter the track was canted too much, so the gauge corner of the inner rail of the curve was subjected to intense pressure. The track was therefore being subjected to severe lateral pressures and twisting motions, and the gauge corners of both rails were being rolled under great pressure. Small cracks were generated by the flexing, twisting, rolling and crushing and, left alone,

At Norwich Thorpe Junction in July 1985, the Cromer/Yarmouth/Lowestoft route diverges to the left, London and Ely to the right and the Crown Point maintenance depot in the centre. The signal box was erected in 1886 and worked the junction for 100 years until Colchester panel control area was extended to include Norwich in 1986.

Norwich Thorpe Junction in May 2008.

they would extend themselves through the metal.

The contractor for this area was Balfour Beatty, a contractor on a global scale, undertaking gigantic, governmental projects. The company had one of its Directors transferred to the Department of Trade & Industry in 1997. Balfour Beatty was the contractor for the Heathrow rail tunnel that collapsed on 20 October 1994. As in railway maintenance, the contractors were allowed to certify the correctness of their own work. In February 1999 Balfour Beatty was fined £1.2 million for breaches of the Health & Safety at Work Act during the construction of the tunnel. The Judge said, 'This is one of the worst civil engineering disasters in the United Kingdom in the last 25 years.' But that did not prevent Railtrack from giving Balfour Beatty the responsibility of maintaining parts of the national rail system.

On 23 September 1997 a gang of men employed by Balfour Beatty was working on the track at Rivenhall, between Witham and Kelvedon in Essex. They did not have the correct equipment to carry out their work and they were not properly monitored; as a result of their actions a Freightliner train was derailed, causing £1 million of damage but no casualties. Judge Watling QC, at Chelmsford Crown Court, fined Balfour Beatty £500,000 and said he would have been more severe 'but for the previous good record of Balfour Beatty'.

On 24 November 2000 BBC Radio 4 News stated that Railtrack had sent Balfour Beatty a letter two weeks before the Hatfield crash concerning the track re-laying work the contractors were carrying out at Leeds station. The Railtrack letter referred to their work as 'shoddy' and 'appalling'. 'Do not bother to apologise,' said the letter, 'just go and get the job right.' And yet Railtrack continued

to give Balfour Beatty contracts. It seems likely that Railtrack were so short of contractors that it had no choice. So much for competition.

In January 1999 (Statement by Mr Lissack QC, prosecuting counsel at the trial of Balfour Beatty and Network Rail) a length of rail in the Down Main line half a mile south of Hatfield station was seen by Balfour Beatty workmen to be severely afflicted with gauge corner cracking. In April 2000 Balfour Beatty got around to laying a length of new rail alongside the cracking-up rail, but the latter could not be replaced until November because that was the agreed time for doing the job and unscheduled delays to trains to change a rail would result in Railtrack paying compensation to the train operators. (They did not put a speed restriction on it for the same reason.) This might seem irresponsible to the old-fashioned observer, but it was a business-led decision and that is important. Unbusinesslike but solely responsible BR would definitely have put a speed restriction on that rail immediately and it would have been replaced ASAP.

Thousands of trains roared over the Hatfield reverse curves as the rail silently generated its cracks until, at 12.23pm on 17 October 2000, under the pressure of a Class 91 locomotive and its coaches running through at 115mph, it shattered into hundreds of pieces, just like the railway system itself. Four people were killed and 34 injured.

There was something resembling panic at Railtrack headquarters. They knew even at that stage that they were faced with a bill for repairs and compensation that was likely to reach £1 billion. They knew that they had a lot of dodgy rails but they could not be sure where they were. As a result, at 10pm on 17 October the Railtrack Board imposed 80 speed restrictions. Where the track was to be renewed in the current year's work plan or had been deferred from the previous year, the speed was reduced to one-third of the usual line speed. A 20mph temporary

Norwich Crown Point maintenance depot is seen in the new railway world of 'One' railway on 31 May 2005. No 90008 is in maroon livery and some Virgin-liveried coaches are stabled with others in the livery of the former franchisee. *Adrian Vaughan*

speed limit was placed at sites where (a) the rail head was spalling – small fragments were breaking off – or (b) where there was a known cant deficiency of more than 110mm on a line where the maximum permitted speed was more than 100mph, and at any sites carrying 25-tonne axle loads. Eventually there were 1,160 temporary speed restrictions.

On the evening of 24 October 2000 the Railtrack Board decided to close entirely the line from Carlisle north to Glasgow and Edinburgh 'with immediate effect', much to the astonishment of the entire kingdom and to the dismay of passengers on the Anglo-Scottish sleeper, which did not leave Euston. Gerald Corbett told the BBC, 'We are now going to blitz the system and *run it for safety*.' Which of course begs the question, what were you doing before that?

The RMT said that 'large parts of the network have been dangerous for some time.'

Jim Bellingham, Asset Manager for Railtrack, said, 'It would have extended the misery if we had "staggered" the closure. We have found some minor cracks but nothing to be concerned about.' Which makes one wonder what caused them to take such a sudden and radical decision on the 24th? To inconvenience an entire country without any pressing reason seems strange.

The dislocation of the railway brought vast congestion to the roads, while Railtrack was encumbered with yet another bill for repair and compensation. In the immediate aftermath, Railtrack estimated it would cost £500,000. It rose very quickly to £733 million and finally reached £3 billion! What could well-organised BR have done with that, on top of the costs of the Ladbroke Grove disaster?

On the evening of the Hatfield crash Gerald Corbett told the BBC's *Newsnight* that 'I am personally distraught that another tragedy has occurred on our railways. The families of the bereaved are foremost in my mind. As a matter of course I have tendered my resignation to the Board.' He also said that the railway had been 'ripped apart at privatisation and the whole complicated structure

should be slimmed down.' His resignation offer was rejected. On 19 October Corbett issued a statement for Railtrack taking the blame upon the company. 'The rail was due to be replaced in November. It should have been replaced sooner and that was Railtrack's responsibility.'

Gerald Corbett's apology was genuine. He was not only distraught, he was also angry at the crazy system that had brought about the tragedy. I have searched hard and unsuccessfully to find a similar statement of regret from his semi-detached Chairman, Sir Philip Beck. That is not to say he did not make one, but I have not found it after diligent search.

On 19 October Sir Philip gave a rare interview to the BBC in which he explained about the Hatfield crash. Beck was reported as saying that the rail network had been neglected for years – it had certainly been neglected by Railtrack since 1996 – and it would take time to carry out improvements. 'It is not a turn-around that can be achieved very quickly, it has to be achieved over a number of years, but we have to arrive at a situation where this sort of tragedy does not happen again.'

Before the Hatfield crash Railtrack had been criticised by Her Majesty's Chief Inspector of Railways, and by Tom Winsor, the Rail Regulator, for the annually increasing number of broken rails since privatisation. In August 2000 Mr Winsor commissioned Transportation Technology Centre Incorporated (TTCI), the consultancy arm of the Association of American Railroads, to carry out a special study. Two days after Hatfield TTCI's report was published. It stated that Railtrack did not have records of the types of defects in track or their locations and had passed responsibility for these defects to its contractors. Railtrack was not ensuring that its maintenance contractors removed broken rails promptly and,

Right: Rail maintenance took on a massive dimension as machinery took over the manual labour techniques of the 1970s and, indeed, any period before that. High-capacity, roller-bearing, air-braked wagons, fit to be hauled at relatively high speeds, are being loaded in minutes by a battery of large mechanical grabs in 2003. *Brian Garrett*

Right: 25-ton-capacity ballast wagons await unloading. *Brian Garrett*

judged on a criterion of broken rails removed 'per year per track mile', Railtrack performed 'significantly worse' than other passenger railways, and finally Railtrack used hand-held ultrasonic crack detection equipment where European railways 'used sophisticated ultrasonic test *vehicles*'.

Mr Corbett's evidence to the Parliamentary Transport Committee in early November 2000 showed that in June the site was tested by Balfour Beatty using ultrasound equipment that either 'did not work' or did not give a signal because of the state of the rail. When the scanner does not give a signal, it is a sure sign that the rail is very badly cracked. No speed restriction was put on. Mr Corbett said that he did not understand why a speed restriction was not imposed. The obvious answer – which might not be the right one – was that speed restrictions cost Railtrack money. The Transport Committee Report said:

'Whatever else is revealed during the investigation of the Hatfield accident, it is clear that Railtrack's management of Balfour Beatty on the East Coast Main Line prior to 17 October was totally inadequate.'

Mr Corbett also conceded that the maintenance contracts put in place at the time of privatisation included financial pressures that might affect 'the safety culture at the front line'. This was more modern business-led jargon meaning that the contractor had to agree to reduce his price to Railtrack year on year and that led inevitably to the contractor being obliged to reduce his own costs year on year. As a result there was sub-contracting, and contractors routinely employed unqualified and poorly trained staff to work on the railway.

The National Union of Rail, Maritime & Transport Workers (RMT) told the Committee that it was a fact that up to 84,000 people, working for more than 2,000 companies, held the Personal Track Safety Certificate. The number of permanently employed maintenance workers had fallen from 31,000 in 1994 to between 15,000 and 19,000 in 2000, which in the view of the RMT showed that there had been an enormous increase in the use of casual labour by contractors.

In November Mr Corbett offered his resignation again. Perhaps he was tired of being the front man for the Railtrack Board; certainly Sir Philip Beck was being referred to as 'the Invisible Man' by the newspapers and Corbett as 'the Man They Love to Hate'. On 17 November, the full Board of Railtrack assembled to 'decide Gerald Corbett's fate', as the newspapers put it. At the conclusion of this meeting Gerald Corbett resigned, his place as Chief Executive being taken by accountant Steve Marshall. Corbett and Marshall had worked together at Grand Metropolitan in the finance departments. Marshall was also a Director of Hungary's largest wine and spirit company. (BBC News 24, 17.11.00)

The railway had been so utterly smashed up by the free-market fundamentalists that it is doubtful if anyone could have been successful at Railtrack. Railtrack owned the rails but the contractors were supposed to change them when they were faulty. The extreme bitterness of Corbett's experience, drinking from the poisoned chalice of Railtrack, had of course been sweetened by an annual salary of £325,000. When he left Railtrack for the Chairmanship of Woolworth he left with £912,992, which was an enhanced pension entitlement paid as a lump sum, and, to make up for any disappointment he might have felt in not being able to drink any more from the Railtrack Cup of Sorrows, and for having to give up his company car, he received an additional £444,000. During his time as Chief Executive of Railtrack, the company had been discovered by the Crown Prosecution Service to have 'no controlling mind', while Lord Cullen, in his Report on the Ladbroke Grove crash, described the condition of Railtrack as 'institutional paralysis'.

Above: At the other end of the scale of construction – the 'Pacer'. These were introduced between 1985 and 1987 as one way of replacing the old cheap and cheerful DMUs dating from the 1950s. The opportunity was taken to make the cheapest possible people-movers – cheap but not cheerful. The 'Pacer' must be the most miserable passenger vehicle ever put on rails by British Railways. They are carried on two axles sufficiently far enough apart to make the rigid wheelbase too long for the curves of the rural branch lines they sometimes serve. It is – or used to be – a regular occurrence on the Middlesbrough-Whitby line to see one of these units wedged on the curve at Grosmont station. They had very poor engines originally but were refitted with 460hp power units driving a Voith hydraulic transmission. In 2002 a 'Pacer' engine fell off near Whitehaven and derailed the carriage. They had doors that frequently failed to open when asked, and in a collision their bodies were liable to be sheared from the underframes. They are capable of 75mph and are so much in demand for their cheapness that from 1990 they were refurbished and are still in use. This one, No 142016, is seen at the very remarkable Wrawby Junction on 10 November 2007. *Steve Thompson*

Below: No 56069 overtakes a canal barge on the Stainforth & Keadby Canal near Althorpe, Lincs. The engine is returning 'light' from working the 14.40 Goole Dock-Scunthorpe empty steel carriers on 17 April 2003. *Steve Thompson*

Top: The 'Freightliner' was a BR concept, introduced as an idea in 1965 and translated into trains of specialist wagons. Early examples included the permanently coupled, 21-ton-capacity, air-braked hopper wagons carrying coal to power stations at passenger train speeds. There were also air-braked, double-decker wagons for carrying new cars from the factories and flat-bed trolleys to carry containers to and from ships. As the years passed the capacity of the wagons increased: the 21-ton coal hoppers became 32-tonners, and 100-ton oil tanker wagons were introduced. Here, American General Motors Class 66 No 66578, of a class first imported into Britain by EWS in April 1998 and capable of hauling heavy freight at 75mph, comes through Oxford in May 2008 at a comfortable 50mph, with half a mile of Freightliner wagons.
Adrian Vaughan

Middle: English Welsh & Scottish Railway Class 66 No 66223, with a short train of returned empty petrol tanks, passes a rebuilt Totnes station on 5 August 2003. Its 3,000 horsepower will not be unduly taxed on the steep climb up to Dainton summit.
Steve Thompson

Right: Class 67 No 67012, a General Motors-designed 2,980hp 125mph diesel-electric, introduced to the UK in 2000, comes through the ghost of South Brent station with a mail train on 7 August 2003.
Steve Thompson

In July 2003 Network Rail, as inheritor of Railtrack's woes, including the ex-Chief Executive of Railtrack, Gerald Corbett, and employees of Balfour Beatty, were charged with four counts of manslaughter and of health and safety offences relating to the broken rail. Balfour Beatty 'saw no plausible basis' for the charge. The manslaughter charges were dropped in July 2004 at the direction of the judge because of a lack of evidence. Balfour Beatty then pleaded guilty to breaches of the Health & Safety at Work Act. At the trial on the health and safety charges, Mr Thwaites QC, for Balfour Beatty Rail Infrastructure Services (BBRIS), said:

'The accident arose as a result of a systematic failure of the industry as a whole. At no stage did BBRIS work outside industry standards on patrolling and inspection. No guidance was made available as to when rail affected by gauge corner cracking should be removed or subject to a speed restriction.'

How could BBRIS be in the railway maintenance business if it did not possess such basic knowledge as when a damaged rail needed to be changed? Of course it knew. BBRIS had decided in January 2000 to replace the rail and had laid a new one down on the ballast alongside the broken one. (Gerald Corbett's evidence to the House of Commons Transport Committee)

The judge at this trial, Mr Justice MacKay, a renowned judge of negligence cases, said that that the events leading up to the Hatfield derailment were 'the worst example of sustained industrial negligence I had ever seen' and fined Balfour Beatty £10 million plus £300,000 costs, and Network Rail £3.5 million plus £300,000 costs. The learned judge ordered that defendants' costs arising from charges on which they were found not guilty were to be paid from Central (public) Funds. Central Funds therefore paid £20.9 million of Balfour Beatty's costs. All the Network Rail people charged were found not guilty of any charge and all their costs were paid from public funds. In addition, the costs of Her Majesty's Courts Service were not less than £431,904.

Balfour Beatty appealed their fine on the ground that it was 'excessive', that their culpability was not three times that of Railtrack and that they ought to have been given a discount for pleading guilty. In July 2006 Balfour Beatty had its fine reduced to £7.5 million.

Mr Corbett gave evidence about Hatfield to the Parliamentary Transport Committee in October and November 2000. He said he did not understand why a speed restriction had not been imposed. Who was in charge? Did Balfour Beatty report to Railtrack for Railtrack to make a decision about a speed restriction? Certainly it is true that speed restrictions cost Railtrack money. In BR days any humble platelayer could see a fault, report it to the nearest signalman, and the trains would be stopped and held or stopped and cautioned. Under privatisation, reports had to pass through 'hoops' and then decisions were not taken. This was capitalist 'risk-taking' with a vengeance.

The Parliamentary Transport Committee observed that, while it welcomed Railtrack's decision to place a greater priority on engineering, it raised two questions.

'First, it suggests that the company had previously lost sight of the fact that its core responsibility is to run a safe and efficient railway, and that to do so requires Directors and managers with appropriate experience and knowledge. Second, the changes are hardly radical: the new Technical Director remains as before the only Executive Director with an engineering background, and also remains one of only two members of the Board with significant experience of operating a railway. Railtrack should look again at its senior management, and appoint to its Board and to other senior positions people with knowledge and experience appropriate for running the railway.'

Sir Philip Beck retired from Railtrack on 2 July 2001. His place as non-executive Chairman was taken by Mr John Robinson. Mr Robinson had been Chairman of the patent medicines and sticking plaster company Smith & Nephew and was Chairman of Wimpey, RJB Mining and Low & Bonar, but gave up two of these chairmanships to better concentrate on Railtrack. Jonson Cox left Railtrack, unlamented, in August. A Parliamentary statement announced that during 2001 Railtrack had spent £594 million on 'loss of office' payments to two, un-named, directors. (Hansard, col 557W, 10.12.01)

In April 2001 Railtrack was in very serious financial difficulty. There was a £3.6 billion debt, but it still paid out its highest dividend ever – £138 million, or 26.9p per share. How this was possible could only be explained by an accountant or by resurrecting George Hudson. Steve Marshall, Railtrack CEO, said that he felt 'humbled' by Hatfield and that he and his fellow Directors were even considering waiving their annual bonuses. The leaders of the train operating companies wondered how they could be thinking of bonuses at all. Railtrack's predicament was due – politicians and economists apart – to the costs of Hatfield, which Steve Marshall estimated had cost the company so far £2.6 billion in track repairs, compensation to train operating companies, and to incompetent Directors.

There were also the rapidly escalating costs of the WCML rebuild and the costs of rewiring the electric power supply for the new 'Desiro' electric trains from Kent and Sussex into London. Share values plummeted and the banks were reluctant to take a risk on Railtrack, so the company turned to the Government. The Railtrack Board also decided at this point to fragment the company into three Divisions:

Core Network Operations, which was supposed to spend the following three years developing strategies for network improvement.

Enhancement & Major Programmes, which was to ensure that before Railtrack committed to a new project it had the money and technical expertise to carry it out at a profit.

Property & New Business, which was to sell off the rest of the family silver to help pay for the railway.

While this demolition of the theories of the Adam Smith Institute was taking place, the French national railway opened a brand-new ultra-high-speed railway, 663 miles long, from Calais to Marseilles, and on 1 July 2001, to mark the event, ran a train over it at an average speed of 189mph, reaching a top speed of 229mph for 20 minutes, reaching Marseilles 3½ hours after leaving Calais.

On 20 March 2001, the Rail Regulator, Tom Winsor, changed the conditions of Railtrack's licence to oblige it to establish and maintain a comprehensive and reliable register of its assets. The Regulator said:

'If, after the Hatfield derailment, Railtrack had had the information which this licence condition requires it to possess, the disintegration of the integrity of the operation of the network – with over a thousand temporary speed restrictions imposed all over the country – could have been prevented.'

The legally responsible Railtrack did not have the information necessary for it to carry out its legal obligations. Is that not dysfunctional? In what way was Railtrack an advance on British Railways?

In April 2001 Railtrack persuaded the Rail Regulator to advance it £1.5 billion of public funds, which would not otherwise become available until after 2006. Having obtained this concession, the Board went back to the Regulator in May and asked for another £2 billion advance. All this was additional to the £498.6 million it would receive as its 'Network Grant' from the Government. Tom Winsor told them to 'forget humility and get on with delivery'. On Radio 4 Winsor was reported as saying:

'They must put away the begging bowl, stop hawking themselves unwanted around Whitehall and knuckle down to getting train services back to a sustainable level of reliability and quality of service. Railtrack was wrong if it thought it would be repeatedly bailed out by the Government.'

In June 2001 Railtrack issued its Network Management Statement, which was, in the estimation of the Rail Regulator, 'profoundly unsatisfactory', and in the opinion of the train operators full of generalised prophesies of what Railtrack hoped would happen. On the 26th the Regulator, having conferred with the train operators, said:

'The statement fails to contain the nitty-gritty infrastructure management information which shows that Railtrack is on top of the job. Railtrack has failed by a significant margin to achieve its track quality margins.'

In May, June and July Railtrack was losing money at an increasing rate as it struggled to improve the track condition as its top priority. From 1996 until 2000, when broken rails were increasing, leading up to Hatfield, it was making a profit. Immediately after the derailment, Railtrack had said it would require an additional £700 million a year to put the tracks into a proper condition. Can we fairly conclude, therefore, that the earlier profits had been gained at the expense of the track – of safety?

On 25 July John Robinson met the Secretary of State for Transport, Stephen Byers. The meeting was to discuss Railtrack's insatiable demand for money, but no written or taped record was made of the conversation. John Robinson said, according to Byers, that unless the Government was willing to make up all Railtrack's losses and provide enough funds to provide the shareholders with a profit, he, Mr Robinson, would not be able to report, on the November accounts, that Railtrack was 'a going concern'. Robinson denied using the words 'not a going concern', but in August Railtrack's advisers came back to Byers and told him that there were three options for Railtrack: more money, re-nationalisation or receivership. The use of the 'r' word first came from Railtrack.

Railtrack was asking for a blank cheque from the taxpayers.

On 1 October the Regulator gave Railtrack £337 million, the first instalment of the £1.5 billion advance of grant agreed in April. Further discussion took place with Railtrack. It was quite obvious that unless public funds were poured in, in quantities no-one could determine, the company would be insolvent. Byers took the view that public funds could not be poured into a bottomless pit and on 7 October obtained High Court permission to put the company into 'Railway Administration'.

Predictably the shareholders of this profoundly dysfunctional company were annoyed at not being supported by public funds and had the audacity to sue Byers. What was surprising was the 'fury' of the Regulator, Tom Winsor, who had been such a critic, and, one would have thought, knew better than anyone that Railtrack should be closed down.

The charge against Stephen Byers was 'targeted malice' and 'misfeasance in public office', and the trial opened on 27 June 2005. Happily he was found not guilty on 14 October 2005.

Epilogue

Lowly railwaymen, such as myself, up to the most senior people, although not all of them – some were willing to become collaborators – foresaw that the scheme of privatisation could only be a disaster. Early-19th-century railway managements did slowly come to the realisation that competitive capitalism was destructive. A series of amalgamations took place to create 'the great companies', which the modern privatiser affected so much to admire, together with a growing sense of public service, while a kind of a regimental loyalty developed among the staff. All this produced a great unity of purpose. In 1992 railwaymen could see that the new arrangements could not possibly work efficiently, but I do not think that any of us foresaw the incredible depths to which the railway would fall. The railway cannot work effectively without unity.

In 1999 the Rail Safety Regulations required that all 'slam-door' Mk 1 carriages be modified with central locking for the doors, withdrawn by 31 December 2002, and all modified Mk.1 carriages were to be withdrawn by 31 December 2004. These regulations were out of touch with reality – the work could not be done in the time given – but the regulations created a great rush to obtain new trains. The leasing companies saw their opportunity to supply a very large fleet to the Stagecoach Group and Connex, operating trains on the old Southern Region of BR. Angel ordered 'Desiro' electric trains worth £640 million from Siemens on 23 April 2001. The specification of the trains, including their power requirements, was jointly agreed between Siemens, Angel Trains, the Stagecoach Group and the SRA. But somehow the four organisations were unable to advise Siemens correctly, and it was discovered, when the first vehicles arrived in England, that the trains drew too much current relative to the supply capacity available. To avoid blowing up the transformers by the lineside, only 30 or 40 could be run on the Southern network and the rest, 500 new carriages, had to be stored; the cost, anything from £30 to £50 million, was paid for out of public funds.

Angel Trains' Managing Director, Haydn Abbott, said, 'The rolling stock side of privatisation has worked very well. To have ordered the trains and had them manufactured and then find out the trains can't run is, of course, disappointing.'

It was also disappointing that the new trains in the South East had, for at least two years after they were introduced, a failure rate almost twice that of the 1957-built trains they replaced.

Railtrack, the 1990s flagship of the private enterprise culture, sank, top heavy with bonuses, contractors, consultants, lawyers and complexity, quite unable to steer itself. This was the system put in place by people who slandered British Railways management as being 'unable to manage, like a ship where the tiller was not connected to the rudder'. The fragmentation of British Railways was an act of overbearing pride and overconfident ignorance. It was the ancient crime of hubris and it led, inevitably, to the downfall of the arrangements. The crime of hubris was believed by the ancients to open the way to the downfall and suitable punishment of the perpetrators. Unfortunately the fragmenters of the railway only benefited from their crime, given honours and Directorships of banks. It was the victims of their hubris who paid. It would be justice see the economic fundamentalists who destabilised the railway system, Lord MacGregor, Sir Steve Robson, Sir Christopher Foster, to name but three 'key players', up before a judge on a charge of 'gross economic dogmatism leading to a fourfold increase in costs'.

Index